# Building
# the Learning
# Organization

**3rd edition**

**Achieving Strategic Advantage
through a Commitment to Learning**

## Michael J. Marquardt

*Author of Leading with Questions*

NICHOLAS BREALEY
PUBLISHING

BOSTON • LONDON

This edition first published by Nicholas Brealey Publishing, in 2011.

20 Park Plaza                                    3-5 Spafield Street, Clerkenwell
Suite 610                                           London, EC1R4QB, UK
Boston, MA 02116                            Tel: +44-(0)-207-239-0360
Tel: 617-523-3801                            Fax: +44-(0)-207-239-0370
Fax: 617-523-3708

www.nicholasbrealey.com

© 2011 Michael J. Marquardt

Printed in the United States of America

17 16 15 14 13     2 3 4 5 6 7 8 9 10

ISBN: 978-1-90483-832-6

Library of Congress Cataloging-in-Publication Data
Marquardt, Michael J.
  Building the learning organization : achieving strategic advantage through a commitment to learning / Michael J. Marquardt. — 3rd ed.
    p. cm.
  Includes bibliographical references and index.
  ISBN-13: 978-1-904838-32-6 (pbk.)
  ISBN-10: 1-904838-32-4 (pbk.)
  1. Organizational learning.  I. Title.
  HG5162.C67 2011
  658.3'124—dc22

                                                                    2011004237

### Praise for *Building the Learning Organization*

Dr. Marquardt's strategies to becoming a learning organization are easily applicable in the corporate setting. His examples elucidate past applications, which aid the reader in creating a local plan. If your aim is to develop a learning organization that gains insights into ever-growing customer expectations, *Building the Learning Organization* will facilitate your journey.

**—Simon Reese, Global Revenue Management Advisor,**
**ExxonMobil Lubricants & Specialties**

*Building the Learning Organization* has something significant to offer both the researching scholar and practicing CEO. Michael has done an excellent job of highlighting the five subsystems required to create and sustain a learning organization. Most importantly, he has described the complex set of interactions between these subsystems, which should assist organizational leaders with the challenge of how to create a learning organization.

**—J. Mike Stice, CEO, Chesapeake Midstream Partners**

Organizations have enjoyed unprecedented success in driving sustainable employee engagement through action learning.

**—Florence Ho, Senior Lecturer, School of Professional Education &**
**Executive Development, Hong Kong Polytechnic University, Hong Kong**

Once again, Michael Marquardt provides us with wonderfully rich ideas and examples of what it means to be a true learning organization. In this third edition, he reminds us that organizational learning is no longer a "nice to have;" rather, embedding learning practices, processes, policies, and structures is absolutely essential for an organization's success and competitive advantage. Once thought a fad twenty years ago, Marquardt makes a compelling case that organizational learning is here to stay.

**—Hallie Preskill, Executive Director, Strategic Learning and**
**Evaluation Center, FSG**

Professor Marquardt has re-inspired us to engage creatively in fast paced quantum leaps. By continuously transforming our organizations so that fast learning know-how truly becomes the centerpiece, we gain a competitive advantage and guarantee future success. This edition is like a new book on the five core subsystems required to grow learning organizations, and is intricately enhanced in each chapter by new case studies of best practices from organizations around the world, including Europe and Asia.

**—Professor Francesco Sofo, PhD, University of Canberra, Australia**

*Building the Learning Organization* is a must-read for researchers, consultants, business practitioners, and anyone who wants to see their organization run faster than their competitors. The book contains both theoretical and practical insights, providing a balanced perspective of what it takes for an organization to learn.

—**Roland K. Yeo, Associate Professor of Organizational Behavior & International Business, Kuwait Maastricht Business School, and Adjunct Senior Researcher of Management, University of South Australia**

Considering the recent changes in global economic, technological, and socio-political environments affecting today's workplace, Dr. Michael Marquardt has done a wonderful job in updating this best-selling book on the learning organization—an area which is gaining importance from corporate leaders, policy makers, and academicians. This book has provided clear and significant guidelines for developing an effective learning organization through presenting detailed analyses of the five subsystems of the "total systems learning organization model." As an author of several impactful books like this, Mike is also a popular scholar practitioner in the dynamic Asia-Pacific region. I am sure this publication will make him more famous for his scholarly and professional contributions to the field.

—**AAhad M. Osman-Gani, MBA, PhD, Professor of HRD & International Management, IIUM University, Kuala Lumpur, Malaysia, and Chair of the Academy of Human Resource Development, Asia**

# Contents

CHAPTER 6

CHAPTER 7

CHAPTER 8

CHAPTER 9

# Foreword

Despite some of the most challenging economic times in recent history, business leaders continue to dedicate substantial resources to building their learning organizations. Since the second edition of this book was published in 2002, organizations have undergone tremendous change and transformation. Globalization, technology, leadership, sustainability, and many other trends are influencing organizations in all industries, especially the development of the workforce.

ASTD was pleased to have co-published the first edition of this book in 1996 and the second edition in 2002. Over the intervening years, thousands of organizations worldwide have learned about and applied the learning organizational model and strategies in the book. In this updated edition of *Building the Learning Organization*, Dr. Marquardt provides additional strategies for developing each of the five subsystems of his model: learning dynamics, organizational transformation, people empowerment, knowledge management, and technology application.

Current research shows that senior executives understand that investing in learning is critical to survival and future growth. As the economy continues to recover, organizations in all sectors must train and reskill their workforce to position themselves for growth. Findings from ASTD's 2010 *State of the Industry Report* show that there is executive support and an understanding that learning matters:

- Learning expenditures per employee increased 1.2 percent.
- As a percent of revenue and a percent of profit, learning expenditures increased, demonstrating organizations' steady financial commitment to learning even while profits and revenue decreased in the recession.
- Technology-enabled learning has reached its highest level yet with 36.5 percent of training delivered using some form of technology.

This research supports data from the ASTD 2010 Learning Executives Confidence Index: While many learning functions saw budget and resource cuts during the global recession, learning executives also saw a commitment from business leaders to the value of learning as a strategic driver. This is indeed good news for our profession.

With case studies from several global corporations, and a review of the key organizational and leadership theories, Dr. Marquardt helps all of us understand how to leverage existing resources and support to build a truly successful learning organization. I encourage you to apply the principles from this book to support a culture of learning, and to build a highly skilled and competitive workforce that helps your organization grow and achieve success.

—Tony Bingham, President and CEO, ASTD

# Preface

When we entered the twenty-first century, we began a new era in the evolution of organizational life and structure. Immense changes in the economic environment caused by globalization and technology have forced companies to transform themselves significantly in order to survive in a new world and its new economy. Organizations with smart brains and the ability to learn quickly have become the global leaders.

Organizations with the adaptability of dinosaurs cannot survive in the faster, information-rich environment of the new millennium. Becoming bigger, heavier, and thicker skinned will be no substitute for developing increasingly agile and more creative brainpower. Or, to cite another biological metaphor, even a caterpillar with speedier legs will never be able to equal the range and flexibility it achieves after it transforms into a butterfly.

As we enter the second decade of the twenty-first century, organizations must learn even faster and adapt more seamlessly to changes in the environment or they simply will not survive. As in any transitional period, the dominant but dying species (i.e., non-learning or slow-learning organizations) and the emerging, more adaptive species (learning organizations) presently exist side by side. I predict that within the next ten years, only learning organizations will be left. Companies that do not become learning organizations will soon go the way of the dinosaur; they will die out because they were unable to adjust to the changing environment.

## Demanding New Learning

Manville (2001) writes how we now "demand of the new learning a more nimble, more customized and more immediately relevant way of working, yet one that also allows us to perform better and to do so in a way that more quickly and effectively reaches the threshold of making a difference" (p. 45).

Learning thus becomes a critical process, but only if it is both pursued strategically and embedded operationally in real work. To attract and retain talent, the successful global organization will use learning as a tangible offering to new employees, saying, in effect, "Join us, and you'll learn better, more, and faster than you would with our competitors."

This evolution is not happening accidentally. It is developing through daily experiments and the "learning about learning" of frontline managers and executives who know its importance and push the envelope of its applications. And we are not talking about simply changing the external elements of the organization—its products, activities, or structures—but, rather, about altering its intrinsic way of operating: its values, mindset, and even its primary purpose.

## Why Are Learning Organizations So Important?

The demands placed on organizations worldwide now require that learning be delivered with greater speed, at less cost, and more effectively to workplaces and mobile workforces that are affected more dramatically than ever by daily changes in the marketplace. And what are some of the crucial issues facing today's corporations?

- Reorganization, restructuring, and reengineering for success, not just survival
- Increased skills shortages caused by schools that have not adequately prepared people for work in the twenty-first century
- Doubling of knowledge every two to three years
- Global competition from the world's most powerful companies
- Overwhelming breakthroughs in new and advanced technologies
- Spiraling need for organizations to adapt to change

Learning that occurs throughout the corporation and across systems offers organizations the best opportunity of not only surviving but also succeeding. The prospect that organizational learning offers is one of managing change by allowing for quantum leaps. Continuous improvement means that every quantum leap becomes an opportunity to learn and therefore prepare for the next quantum leap. If we learn faster than our competitors, the time span between leaps reduces and progress accelerates.

To obtain and sustain competitive advantage in this new environment, companies will have to learn better and faster from both successes and failures. They will need to continuously transform themselves into learning organizations, to become places in which groups and individuals at all levels continuously engage in new learning processes.

Shoshana Zuboff, in her classic book *In the Age of the Smart Machine* (1988), noted organizations have little choice but to become a "learning institution, since one of its principal purposes will have to be the expansion of knowledge—not knowledge for its own sake (as in academic pursuit), but knowledge that comes to reside at the core of what it means to be productive. Learning is no longer a separate activity that occurs either before one enters the workplace or in remote classroom settings. Nor is it an activity reserved for a managerial group. The behaviors that define learning and the behaviors that define being productive are one and the same. Learning is the heart of productive activity. To put it simply, learning is the new form of labor" (p. 395).

## What Is the New Learning in Organizations?

There must be a whole new mindset regarding the concepts of work and learning. Learning must take place almost as a byproduct of working, in contrast to acquiring knowledge before performing a particular task or job. In today's environment, organizational learning represents a new form of learning in the following ways:

- It is performance based and tied to business objectives.
- It emphasizes the importance of learning processes, or learning how to learn.
- The ability to define learning is as important as finding answers to specific questions.
- Organization-wide opportunities exist to develop knowledge, skills, and attitudes.
- Learning is part of everybody's job.

The need for individuals and organizations to acquire more and more knowledge will continue unabated. But the knowledge itself is secondary to how, and how quickly, they can learn. Learning skills will be more important than data. Penetrating questions will be more important than good answers.

## Emergence of Learning Organizations

The concept of organization-wide learning, and recognition of its importance, can be traced in the research literature back to the 1940s, but not until the 1980s did a few companies began to realize its potential for increasing organizational performance, competitiveness, and success.

In the 1980s, Shell Oil began to consider organizational learning in relation to strategic planning. Teamwork and more extensive communications were seen as crucial factors in creating a more responsive, successful corporation. Shell spent twelve months experimenting with work groups and researching the implications of the organizational learning concept. The company concluded that learning as an organization did indeed prove valuable for both strategic planning and corporate success and had enabled Shell to gain an advantage of a year or two over its competitors.

During the 1990s, the number of firms committing themselves to becoming learning organizations increased dramatically. Companies such as General Electric, Johnsonville Foods, Quad Graphics, and Pacific Bell in the United States; Sheerness Steel, Nokia, Sun Alliance, and ABB in Europe; and Honda and Samsung in Asia were among the early pioneers.

Peter Senge's *The Fifth Discipline* (2006) and feature articles on learning organizations in the *Harvard Business Review, The Economist, BusinessWeek, Fortune,* and *Asiaweek* have led many other companies to begin considering the process of transforming themselves into learning organizations. The ever-increasing changes brought forth in the first decade of the twenty-first century have made learning organizations ever more important.

## A Comprehensive Systems Approach to Learning Organizations

Most organizations are still struggling with becoming learning organizations, while many others still don't grasp the importance of the process or how it can actually work. Books that describe the learning organization refer only to parts of the entity, depicting it in a piecemeal manner similar to that of the five blind men in the Indian folktale, each of whom described an elephant by whatever portion he touched—the trunk, a foot, the tail, and so on. Likewise, learning organizations have been described by a single attribute—the learning dynamics of teams, organizational structure, knowledge, or better application of new technology. Other perspectives totally misconstrue even their limited focal points and confuse total quality management (TQM), or reengineering, or better training as the totality of organizational learning.

My experience over the past 20 years with more than 300 of the top learning organizations worldwide and my analysis of the myriad articles and books on learning organizations have led me to conclude that before individuals or companies can adequately comprehend the richness of the learning organization, they must incorporate five subsystems of a true learning organization: learning, organization, people, knowledge, and technology. Without all five subsystems, they will have only a partial appreciation of the processes and principles necessary to move an organization from a state of non-learning to learning.

This book presents each subsystem and explores how all five interface with and complement one another. The core subsystem of the learning organization, of course, is learning—at the individual, group, and organization levels—including the skills of systems thinking, mental models, personal mastery, self-directed learning, and dialogue. Each of the other subsystems—organization, people, knowledge, and technology—are required to enhance and augment the quality and effectiveness of learning across the corporation.

## Overview of the Book

Chapter 1 assesses rising social, political, and economic forces as well as the new expectations of workers, customers, and even communities that have necessitated the emergence of learning organizations. The eight key forces causing this shift from institutions based on manufacturing (manual labor) to those based on mentofacturing (mental labor) are discussed.

Chapter 2 introduces the total systems learning organization model with an overview and brief synopsis of the five subsystems: learning, organization, people, knowledge, and technology. The interactional and complementary nature of the subsystems is also discussed.

The dimensions, principles, practices, and ideals of the five subsystems are explored in chapters 3 through 7. Each chapter contains examples of best practices from learning organizations around the world. More and more organizations from Asia and Europe have been included in this third edition of *Building the Learning Organization*. At the end of these chapters, I list ten top implementation strategies for building the subsystem under discussion.

Chapter 8 describes how action learning can serve as a cornerstone in building a learning organization, while chapter 9 provides a general framework and guidelines, as well as the critical steps, for becoming a learning organization.

## Getting Started in Your Organization

Learning quickly and systematically is critical for surviving in the twenty-first century. The organization that makes learning its core business can rapidly leverage its new knowledge into new products, new marketing strategies, and new ways of doing business. Learning organizations will become the only place where global success is possible, where quality is more assured, and where energetic and talented people want to be.

Whether or not to become a learning organization is no longer the question; becoming a learning company is required to remain competitive. And, anyone who asks "when?" should be told "quickly" because becoming this new species will soon be essential to survival in the increasingly global environment. Answering the question "how?" is the essence of this book. I hope these pages will provide valuable guidance for you and your organization.

# Acknowledgments

This book owes much to the encouragement and assistance of many people. First, to the people at Nicholas Brealey Publishing, especially Erika Heilman, who strongly supported a third edition of this bestselling book, and to Jennifer Delaney, who has carefully reviewed, edited, and improved the content of the manuscript.

I want to thank the people at ASTD for their support and guidance in copublishing this edition of *Building the Learning Organization*, in particular, Tony Bingham, ASTD's president and CEO, who kindly authored the foreword to this third edition.

I am especially grateful for the many superb insights and ideas I received from people in organizations that practice organizational learning, who inspired much of this book: Karen Scott and Mary Tomasello of Alcoa; Jim Eckels, Bethany Greene, and Nancy Stebbins of Boeing; Pierre Gheysons of Caterpillar; Garry Luxmoore of World Institute of Action Learning-Australia, Eric Charoux of DCDM; Jim O'Hern of Marriott; Pentti Sydanmaanlakka of Nokia; Verieux Mourillion at National Bank of Dominica; Shannon Banks at Microsoft; Jasmine Liew of Panasonic; and Joerg Puma of Krones.

Also, special thanks to the many individuals who have energized me with their thinking and experiences in organizational learning, including David Schwandt, Andrea Casey, Jerry Gilley, Bea Carson, Skip Leonard, Arthur Freedman, Chuck Appleby, Victoria Marsick, Joel Montgomery, Barrie Octoby, Peter Senge, Karen Watkins, and Kevin Wheeler, among others.

Over the years, many professors and students from around the world have supported my research and writing in the field of learning organizations, especially Nancy Berger, Neal Chalofsky, Wong Wee Chee, Lex Dilworth, Mary Futrell, Carol Hanson, Antony Hii, Effendy Mohamed-Rajab, Viwe Mtshontshi, Ken Murrell, Linda Raudenbush, Somsri Siriwaiprapan, Frank Sofo, Richard Swanson, and Marissa Wettasinghe.

Finally, I am indebted to my family and dedicate this book to them: my wife, Eveline, for her love and patience as I spent many a weekend and evening researching and writing; to my children—Chris, Stephanie, Catherine, and Emily—who are proud of their father, though I am even prouder of each of them; and to my grandchildren—Patricia, Hannah, Milagros, Maia, Finn, and Milo—whose presence has caused me to realize that the greatest joy in the world is that of being a grandfather.

# About the Author

Dr. Michael Marquardt is Professor of Human Resource Development and International Affairs as well as Program Director of Overseas Programs at George Washington University. Mike also serves as President of the World Institute for Action Learning.

He has held a number of senior management, training, and marketing positions with organizations such as Grolier, American Society for Training and Development, Association Management Inc., Overseas Education Fund, TradeTec, and U.S. Office of Personnel Management. Dr. Marquardt has trained more than 95,000 managers in nearly 100 countries since beginning his international experience in Spain in 1969. Consulting assignments have included Marriott, Microsoft, Motorola, Nortel, Alcoa, Boeing, Caterpillar, United Nations Development Program, Xerox, Nokia, Constellation, Samsung, Organization of American States, and Singapore Airlines as well as the governments of Indonesia, Laos, Ethiopia, Zambia, Egypt, Kuwait, Saudi Arabia, Turkey, Russia, Jamaica, Honduras, and Swaziland.

Mike is the author of twenty-two books and more than one hundred professional articles in the fields of leadership, learning, globalization, and organizational change, including *Action Learning for Developing Leaders and Organizations, Optimizing the Power of Action Learning, Leading with Questions, Building the Learning Organization* (selected as Book of the Year by the Academy of HRD), *The Global Advantage, Action Learning in Action, Global Leaders for the 21st Century, Global Human Resource Development, Technology-Based Learning,* and *Global Teams.* Over one million copies of his publications have been sold in nearly a dozen languages worldwide. Dr. Marquardt also served as the Editor of the UNESCO Encyclopedia volume on Human Resources. He has been a keynote speaker at international conferences in Australia, Japan, Philippines, Malaysia, South Africa, Singapore, and India as well as throughout North America.

Dr. Marquardt's achievements and leadership have been recognized through numerous awards, including the International Practitioner of the Year Award from the American Society for Training and Development. He presently serves as a Senior Advisor for the United Nations Staff College in the areas of policy, technology, and learning systems. Mike is a Fellow of the National Academy for Human Resource Development and a cofounder of the Asian Learning Organization Network. His writings and accomplishments in action learning have earned him honorary doctoral degrees from universities in Asia, Europe, and North America.

He received his doctorate in Human Resource Development from George Washington University and his Masters and Bachelor Degrees from Maryknoll College. Dr. Marquardt has also done graduate work at Harvard, Columbia, and the University of Virginia. He enjoys skiing, music, and traveling with his Swiss wife, four children, and six grandchildren.

# CHAPTER 1

# The Emerging Need for Learning Organizations

Over the past ten years, numerous economic, social, and technological forces have intensified significantly, dramatically altering the work environment. These changes have occurred so rapidly and competition has increased so intensely that the large organizational dinosaurs with small pea-size brains that flourished in the twentieth century cannot survive in this new world of the twenty-first century. The survival of the fittest is quickly becoming the survival of the fittest to learn (Kline & Saunders, 2010; Frappaolo, 2006).

In his book *Riding the Tiger: Doing Business in a Transforming World* (1998), Harrison Owen writes, "There was a time when the prime business of business was to make a profit and a product. There is now a prior, prime business, which is to become an effective learning organization. Not that profit and product are no longer important, but without continual learning, profits and products will no longer be possible" (p. 1). Unless an organization continuously adapts to the environment via speedy, effective learning, it will die.

In short, external change and forces demand either organizational adaptation or organizational extinction. Only companies that can transform themselves into more intelligent, proficient engines of change will succeed in the new millennium. As Reginald Revans (1983), a pioneer of action learning, notes, "Learning inside must be equal to or greater than change occurring outside the organization or the organization dies" (p. 11). The new organization that emerges will need to possess greater knowledge, flexibility, speed, power, and learning ability so as to better confront the shifting needs of a new environment, more demanding customers, and smarter knowledge workers.

The successes are obvious. Organizations that learn faster will be able to adapt more quickly and thereby achieve significant strategic advantages in the global world of business. The new learning organization is able to harness the collective genius of its people at the individual, group, and system levels. This capability, combined with improved organizational status, technology, knowledge management, and people empowerment, will enable organizations to leave the competition in the dust.

Let us now examine the major winds of change that have compelled organizations to either learn or face extinction, forces that have altered the economic environment and the workplace as well as workers and customers. The eight most significant forces that have changed the business world and necessitate company-wide learning in the twenty-first century are:

1. Globalization and the global economy
2. Technology and the Internet
3. Radical transformation of the work world
4. Increased customer power
5. Emergence of knowledge and learning as major organizational assets
6. Changing roles and expectations of workers
7. Workplace diversity and mobility
8. Rapidly escalating change and chaos

Each of these forces must be understood and harnessed before the transformation to a learning organization is possible. Let's briefly explore the influence of each one.

## Force 1: Globalization and the Global Economy

We have entered the Global Age. We are an increasingly more global people with many common values and practices, and we are working increasingly for organizations with an international presence. Globalization has caused a convergence of economic and social forces, of interests and commitments, of values and tastes, of challenges and opportunities. We can easily communicate with people around the world because we share a global language (English) and a global medium for communications (computers and the Internet). The signs of the global marketplace are all around us. Consider the following statistics.

In 2010, U.S. corporations invested over $4 trillion abroad and employed more than 20 million overseas workers (Jackson, 2010); more than 100,000 U.S. firms are engaged in global ventures valued in excess of $2 trillion. For instance, McDonald's operates more than 30,000 restaurants serving 58 million people a day in 120 countries, and Coca-Cola earns more money in Japan than in the United States. In addition, more than 70 percent of the profits for the $30 billion U.S. music industry is generated outside our country, and most big-bucks movies depend on global viewers for big profits.

At the same time, 10 percent of U.S. manufacturing is foreign owned and employs 4 million Americans. Mitsubishi USA is the United States' fourth-largest exporter, and Toyota sells more cars than any U.S. auto manufacturer. Foreign investment in the United States has now surpassed $5 trillion. In fact, more than one-third of U.S. economic growth has been due to exports, which have provided jobs for more than 11 million Americans. In 2010, more than half the Ph.D.s in engineering, mathematics, and economics awarded by American universities went to citizens of other countries.

Worldwide, increasing numbers of companies, including Nokia, Xerox, Motorola, Honda, Samsung, and Microsoft, are manufacturing and selling chiefly outside their country of origin; for example, more than 70 percent of Canon's employees work outside Japan. We hardly know anymore if a company is French, Japanese, Swedish, or American. The populations of many Gulf countries are made up of more foreign-born workers than native residents.

Financial markets are open twenty-four hours a day around the world, and global standards and regulations for trade and commerce, finance, products, and services have emerged.

Four main forces have brought us quickly to this global age: technology, television, trade, and travel. These four Ts have laid the groundwork for a more collective experience for people everywhere. People are watching the same movies, reading the same magazines, and dancing the same dances from Boston to Bangkok to Buenos Aires. We share tastes in food (hamburgers, pizza, tacos), fashion (jeans), and fun (Disneyland, rock music, television). Growing numbers of us speak a common language, English, which is now spoken by nearly 2 billion people in more than 150 countries, where it is either the first or the second language. Like all languages, English transmits culture and social values, and it is the global language of media, computers, and business. In addition, nearly 1 billion passengers fly the world's airlines each year.

The global economy has in turn forced the creation of global organizations, companies that operate as if the entire world is their marketplace. They are fully integrated so that all their activities link, leverage, and compete on a worldwide scale. Global firms emphasize global operations above national or multinational ones. They use global sourcing for human resources, capital, technology, facilities, and raw materials. They deem cultural sensitivity to employees, customers, and patterns as critical to organizational success. A company is globalized when it develops a global corporate culture, strategy, and structure as well as global operations and people.

Although certain industries globalized earlier than others (especially telecommunications, electronics and computers, finance and banking, transportation, automotives, pharmaceuticals, petroleum, and biotechnology), every industry now has global players. The growing similarity in what customers want to purchase, including quality and price, has spurred tremendous opportunities, as well as tremendous pressures, to globalize. Even the largest firms in the biggest markets can no longer compete in domestic markets alone. Thinking and operating globally will be critical to organizational survival and growth in the twenty-first century.

## Force 2: Technology and the Internet

Welcome to the new technological workplace, with teletraining, infostructures, and ubiquitous computers. In 1990, Alvin Toffler wrote that the advanced global economy and workplace cannot run for thirty seconds without computers; now it may be only for ten seconds. Yet today's best computers and CAD/CAM systems will be Stone Age primitives within two years. The workplace will demand and require ever more technological advancements and innovations.

We already have technologies such as smart phones, mobile phones, cloud computing, optoelectronics, DVDs, information highways, local area networks (LANs) and wide area networks (WANs), groupware, virtual reality, and electronic classrooms. Workplace computer technology has progressed from mainframe to desktop to laptop to handheld. A significant proportion of a company's operations requires computer-generated automation and customization. These technologies have become necessary for managing the data deluge so that we can learn faster in rapid-change, turbo-charged organizations. In a global economy—in which being informed, being in touch, and being there first can make all the difference between achieving success and failing—technology provides a big advantage indeed.

## ORGANIZATIONAL IMPACT OF TECHNOLOGY

The impact of technology on organizations, management, and learning is mind-boggling. And it has only begun. The emerging power and applicability of technology will turn the world of work on its head. Because of technology, organizations will move toward being virtual rather than physical. People will be more closely linked to customers in Kuala Lumpur than to coworkers across the hall because of technology. Technology has made learning, not work itself, the prime purpose of business, and learning, as Zuboff (1988) proclaims, has become "the new form of labor."

Technology increasingly requires that managers manage knowledge instead of people. Technology alters what, how, and why workers learn. Employees now need to train themselves through self-directed learning. And workplace learning no longer takes place in groups, at fixed times, and in certain locations for just-in-case purposes; instead, it is being implemented on the basis of exactly what's needed, just in time, and only where it's needed. The technology that has already restructured work will force those who are responsible for employee development to create ever more flexible and responsive learning and performance solutions (Waddill & Marquardt, 2011).

We inhabit a world in which virtual reality and interactive multimedia technologies will become commonplace. Cloud computing, smart phones, and worldwide access to Wi-Fi are a part of everyday life. Artificial intelligence technologies (expert- and knowledge-based systems, user interfaces that understand speech and natural language, sensory perception, and knowledge-based simulation) will be generally available. Intelligent tutoring systems will allow learner-based, self-paced instruction. Personalized digitized assistants, telecommunications and network advances, groupware, desktop videoconferencing, and collaborative software/group systems technology are now omnipresent in the workplace.

And the speed and impact of technology continue to accelerate. Trying to figure out the capabilities and future directions of this rapidly changing technology is a mind-boggling challenge. Let's look at just a few of the already existing powers of technology.

Highly reliable, easily utilized, and affordable connectivity is rapidly becoming available anywhere, anytime. Superconducting transmission lines convey data up to one hundred times faster than fiber-optic networks: One line carries 1 trillion bits of information a second, enough to send the complete contents of the Library of Congress in two minutes.

Neural networks advance computer intelligence by utilizing associative "reasoning" to store information in patterned connections, thereby sequentially processing complex questions and commands using their own logic. Expert systems, a subset of artificial intelligence, are beginning to solve problems in ways that resemble the thinking processes of human experts.

The Internet is one of the most amazing and transforming technological additions to our lives. Its use is one of the fastest-growing phenomena the business world has ever seen, built from a base of less than 1,000 connected computers in the early 1980s to more than 2 billion today, and more and more of the searches are being performed by smart phones.

Intranets (for in-company connections) are rapidly catching up. Implementation of intranets is growing three times faster than electronic commercial applications, and almost all companies have intranet applications. As intranet sites continue to evolve, additional features will emerge. For example, it is already possible to engage in real-time training that combines a live mediator, online information, and remote attendees. Today, every business recognizes the critical value of developing comprehensive strategies for using both intranets and the Internet.

Some of the new high-tech learning programs have been called "the most powerful learning tools since the invention of the book." With virtual reality, our minds are cut off from outside distractions and our attention is focused on powerful sensory stimulation (from a light-sound matrix) that bombards the imagination.

Technology is increasingly a part of all products and the total GNP, including aerospace, advanced industrial systems, and automotive. Already, nearly 30 percent of an automobile's value is in its electronics. The computer service and computer software market has surpassed $900 billion, an increase of 50 percent in the past four years. Information technology is expected to form the basis of many of the most important products, services, and processes of the future.

The latest advance in technology is *cloud computing*, whereby shared servers provide resources, software, and data to computers and other devices on demand, as with the electricity grid. Cloud computing is a natural evolution of the widespread adoption of virtualization, service-oriented architecture, and utility computing. Details are abstracted from consumers, who no longer have need for expertise in, or control over, the technology infrastructure "in the cloud" that supports them.

Finally, an array of technological developments has now emerged for use in the home as well as in the office. These developments include the following:

- Integration of television, telecommunications, and computers through digitization and compression techniques
- Reduced costs and more flexible use and application of telecommunications through developments such as integrated services digital network (ISDN) lines, fiber optics, and cellular radio
- Increased portability through use of radio communications and miniaturization (cell phones, cameras, microphones, and high-resolution display screens)
- Expanded processing power resulting from new microchips and advanced software
- More powerful and user-friendly command and software tools that make it much easier for individuals to create and communicate their own materials

## THE PROMISE OF NEW TECHNOLOGIES

The commodification of ultra-high technology offers spellbinding opportunities for creating new knowledge-exchange products. British Telecom, for example, thinks that future generations of portable phones could be installed in the user's ear. A person could talk and simultaneously glimpse images or data pulled off the Internet and projected onto a magnifying mirror positioned beside one eye.

The technology of the future will respond to our voices and extend our senses. It will simulate complex phenomena—weather patterns, stock market crashes, environmental hazards—solving problems and predicting outcomes at a price anyone can afford. Computers, or networks of them, will become even more widespread as they are embedded in other objects or fixtures. These machines will reconfigure themselves as new applications are required. A whole new metaphor for computing is taking shape, patterned on the natural resilience and elegance of biological organisms. Patients may soon be able to have a detailed genetic analysis that will give them and their doctors an idea of what health risks they might face in the future (Venter, 2007).

To better prepare ourselves for the effects of technology on work, workers, and the workplace, it is important to grasp and understand the many emerging ideas and applications of technology. This understanding can help us direct that technology to increase the speed of learning and of managing knowledge in the workplace. In chapter 7, we will discuss how technology can augment the speed and quality of learning as well as help us better manage knowledge.

## Force 3: Radical Transformation of the Work World

The world of work and the workplace has been dramatically transformed. Workers no longer occupy offices. Corporations collaborate and compete with one another at the same time. Customers provide supervision as well as dictate services. Fellow employees work closely without ever meeting. Companies employ temporary part-time CEOs and permanent full-time janitors. Corporate headquarters staff may consist of less than 1 percent of the company's workforce, if there even is a headquarters.

Organizations have gone from the quality efforts of the 1980s through the reengineering processes of the 1990s to the radical transformation of the workplace itself as we entered the twenty-first century. They have moved from focusing on reducing defects and streamlining business processes to pursuing totally new forms that will enable them to manage continuous, whitewater change. In this way, they have created work organizations in which routines are reorganized, redesigned, or reengineered to improve performance. The practice of breaking work into smaller and smaller tasks is coming to an end. Instead, teams of employees will take charge of key business processes from beginning to end. Impatience with the rate of change will cause many organizations to revamp their key processes by starting from scratch.

### STRUCTURES BASED ON CORE COMPETENCIES

Companies will focus on and organize around what they do best. Therefore, they will be built on core competencies instead of products or markets, with peripheral tasks assigned to temporary and contract workers. The organizational architecture of companies will evolve around autonomous work teams and strategic alliances. These firms will be virtual organizations, temporary networks of independent companies, suppliers, customers, and even rivals linked by information technology to share skills, costs, and access to one another's markets. For example, a manufacturer will produce an item and rely on a product-design outfit to sell its output.

The advances in information technology described earlier are providing faster transmission of data and expanded storage capacity as well as greater computer power and clearer, more complex links among users. Such innovations will permit greater control of more decentralized organizations while enabling the information flow needed to give local managers substantive decision-making authority. Because of this technology, corporations will become cluster organizations or adhocracies, groups of geographically dispersed people—typically working at home—who come together electronically for a particular project and then disband. More organizations will be composed of a minimal core of permanent employees supported by independently contracted professionals.

As more companies realize that the key resource of business is not capital, personnel, or facilities, but rather knowledge, information, and ideas, many new views of the organization are beginning to emerge. Firms everywhere are restructuring, creating integrated organizations, global networks, and leaner corporate centers. Organizations are becoming more fluid, constantly shifting in size, shape, and arrangement.

## COEVOLUTION AND THE VIRTUAL MODEL

An emerging view rests on the concept of coevolution: the idea that by working with direct competitors, customers, and suppliers, a company can create new businesses, markets, and industries. Companies are urged to view themselves as part of a wider environment, a sort of business ecosystem, so that they can evaluate business opportunities not simply as a solo player but as one player among many, each coevolving with the others. Coevolution differs from the conventional idea of competition, in which companies work only with their own resources and do not extend themselves through the capabilities of others. In the global market, companies must make use of the other players—for capacity, innovation, and capital. Such a "best of everything" organization could be a world-class competitor, with the speed, muscle, and leading-edge technology to pounce on the most fleeting of opportunities.

The virtual model could become the most important organizational innovation since the 1920s, which is when Pierre DuPont and Alfred Sloan developed the principle of decentralization by which to organize giant complex corporations. The virtual corporation will have neither central office

---

## TABLE 1
### Organizational Transformation

| Dimension | Old | New |
|---|---|---|
| Critical tasks | Physical | Mental |
| Relationships | Hierarchical | Peer-to-peer |
| Levels | Many | Few |
| Structures | Functional | Multidisciplinary teams |
| Boundaries | Fixed | Permeable |
| Competitive thrust | Vertical integration | Outsourcing and alliances |
| Management style | Autocratic | Participative |
| Culture | Compliance | Commitment and results |
| People | Homogeneous | Diverse |
| Strategic focus | Efficiency | Innovation |

---

nor organizational chart; it will have no hierarchy or vertical integration. Teams of people in different companies will routinely work together. After the business is done, the virtual organization disbands.

The emergence of these network-type organizations as replacements for more traditional bureaucratic structures can be summarized by the transformative organizational shifts shown in Table 1.

## Force 4: Increased Customer Power

Customers will become more influential in determining how organizations set strategies and carry out operations. They, rather than workers, will be the focus of leadership attention and organizational priorities. On a worldwide scale, customers will continue to push for new performance standards in quality, variety, customization, convenience, time, and innovation. They will quicken the pace at which companies are compelled to move beyond domestic markets. Organizations will have no choice but to shop the world for customers, employees, resources, technology, markets, and business partners.

New demands for quality, constant changes in taste, global fads, and short product life cycles are forcing new global partnerships and alliances. Challenges raised by new niche markets, new and emerging industries, deregulation, fights over market share, and aggressive national competitors have created the need to merge global forces in order to survive.

Global communications and marketing has increased consumers' awareness of possible products and services, and global competition has offered customers a more varied and higher quality of choices. Together, these two forces created a convergence of consumer needs and preferences. Consumers are now able to choose those products and services that meet their standards of the following criteria:

- Cost: What is the least expensive, most economical
- Quality: Meets and exceeds expectations
- Time: Available as quickly as possible
- Service: Pleasant, courteous, and available, with products that can be easily repaired or replaced
- Innovation: New, something not yet envisioned by the customer
- Customization: Tailored to specific needs

Customers are much more competent in acquiring and using information; they are becoming more and more connected, culturally conscious, and proud of their backgrounds.

In a world where consumers have choices and power, organizations must adapt to a startling new reality—the cost of poor service will soon be borne by the companies that serve it, not the customers that receive it (Fornell, 2007).

## Force 5: Emergence of Knowledge and Learning as Major Organizational Assets

Technology and globalization have led to an economy based on knowledge. Knowledge workers now outnumber industrial workers by 4 to 1. The workforce has moved from manufacturing to mentofacturing. Continuous learning and knowledge provide the key raw materials for wealth creation and have become the fountainhead of organizational and personal power.

The wealth of nations will depend increasingly on knowledge-based, high-tech industries, such as biotechnology, health, environmental products and services, tourism and hospitality, telecommunications, computer software and its applications, financial services, and entertainment. These are all highly competitive global industries. Keeping even a few months ahead of the competition, in terms of innovation and knowledge, is critical to survival. Information—processed by human brainwork into knowledge, and then integrated and intuited into wisdom—has quite suddenly become the world's most important resource. Knowledge will play the primary role in the world's future, a position claimed in the past by physical labor, minerals, and energy.

## IMPORTANCE OF KNOWLEDGE

Knowledge has become more important for organizations than financial resources, market position, technology, or any other company asset. Knowledge is seen as the main resource used in performing an organization's work. The company's traditions, culture, technology, operations, systems, and procedures are all based on knowledge and expertise. Knowledge is necessary to increase employees' abilities to develop and implement improvements, thereby providing quality service to clients and consumers. Knowledge is required for updating products and services, changing systems and structures, and communicating solutions to problems. In the new knowledge economy, individuals at every level and in all kinds of companies will be challenged to develop knowledge, take responsibility for their new ideas, and pursue them as far as they can go. The job of the leader will be to create an environment that allows workers to increase knowledge and act on it.

Knowledge is created continuously in every corner of the globe and doubles every two to three years. One reflection of the growth of scientific knowledge is the rate at which scientific journals are developed. The first two scientific journals appeared in the mid-1600s. By 1750, this number had grown to 10, and by 1800, to approximately 100. Today, there are more than 100,000 such journals.

Brainpower is becoming a company's most valuable asset, which creates a competitive edge in the marketplace. We are challenged to find and use it. As Thomas Stewart (1991) asserted more than twenty years ago, brainpower is becoming ever more important for business. Every company depends increasingly on knowledge—patents, process, management skills, technologies, information about customers and suppliers, and old-fashioned experience. This knowledge that exists in an organization can be used to create differential advantage. In other words, it's the sum of everything everybody in your company knows that gives you a competitive edge in the marketplace" (p. 44).

The location of the new economy is not in technology, be it a microchip or a global communications network, but in the human mind. Junkunc (2009) points out that specialized knowledge is the essence of success in entrepreneurial activity.

## WORK EQUALS LEARNING

Increasingly, work and learning are becoming the same thing. Zuboff, in her 1988 classic, *In the Age of the Smart Machine*, wrote, "The behaviors that define learning and the behaviors that define being productive are one and the same. Learning is at the heart of the productive activity. To put it simply, learning is the new form of labor" (p. 395). Because the new global economy is based on knowledge work and innovation, there is a convergence between work and learning. While you perform knowledge work, you learn. And you must learn minute by minute if you are to perform knowledge work effectively. Learning is becoming a lifelong challenge as well as a lifelong process.

In the new economy, the learning component of work is huge. It includes everything from a software developer creating a new multimedia application, to the manager responsible for corporate planning at a bank, to the consultant assessing a client's markets, to the entrepreneur starting up a new business, to a teaching assistant in a community college setting up lab projects. We are now in the era of knowledge workers. At the beginning of the new century, three-quarters of the jobs in the U.S. economy involved creating and processing knowledge. Knowledge workers have already discovered that continual learning is not only a prerequisite of employment but a major form of work. Learning has indeed become the new form of labor in the twenty-first century.

## Force 6: Changing Roles and Expectations of Workers

As society moves from the industrial era to the knowledge era, job requirements are changing. We have entered an era in which production involves the mind more than the hands. Employees are moving from needing repetitive skills to knowing how to deal with surprises and exceptions, from depending on memory and facts to being spontaneous and creative, from avoiding risk to taking risk, from focusing on policies and procedures to building collaboration with people.

As a result, the workforce is changing rapidly. In 2010, more than 85 percent of all jobs in the United States were in knowledge and service industries. Many of these jobs require a much higher level of skill than in the past, especially in manufacturing and resource-based fields. People in this century will retain existing jobs only if they are retrained to higher standards.

The organization of the future will be composed more and more of knowledge workers, not only senior executives but also workers at all levels. In the new postindustrial society, knowledge is not just another resource alongside the traditional factors of production, land, labor, and capital; it is the only meaningful resource. Given an economy based on knowledge, the knowledge worker is the greatest asset. In the successful organizations of the future (those offering high value), only one asset becomes more valuable as it is used—the knowledge skills of people. Unlike machinery that gradually wears out, materials that become depleted, patents and copyrights that expire, and trademarks that lose their ability to attract, the knowledge and insights that come from the learning of employees actually increase in value with use and practice.

The key assets of high-value enterprises are not tangible. They are the skills involved in linking solutions to particular needs and the reputations that come from being successful in the past. The distinction between manufacturing and services is becoming less real. The real impact of the information economy is to create increasing similarity in the world of work (Castro, Atkinson & Ezell, 2010).

A fascinating aspect of knowledge workers is that they do, in fact, own the means of production, and they can take it out the door with them at any moment. Therefore, managers have to attract and motivate; reward, recognize, and retain; train, educate, and improve; and, in the most remarkable reversal of all, serve and satisfy knowledge workers. Organizations must provide a structure within which knowledge workers can apply their knowledge. Specifically, organizations must provide contact with other knowledge workers, since it is through dialogue and interaction with their peers that they refine and improve their ideas.

## TEMPORARY WORKERS

The amount and rate of hiring of temporary workers has jumped significantly in the past two years as companies remain hesitant to increase permanent employment in light of shaky economic trends. Temporary employment grew 23.4 percent between September 2009 and 2010, the largest yearly gain since the U.S. Bureau of Labor Statistics began tracking temporary employment data in 1991, according to the American Staffing Association (ASA). Currently, there are 2.2 million people working on a temporary basis, but just 2 percent retain full-time employment at the same company. Richard Wahlquist, president and CEO of the ASA, noted that 404,000 temporary jobs were added in 2010 alone, including a 19 percent increase in temporary payrolls in November. That figure coincides with the 39,000 jobs added nationwide in the latest report by the Bureau of Labor Statistics.

The Bureau of Labor Statistics estimates that employment in personnel-supply services will continue to grow by up to 5 percent every year. Organizations in the telecommunications, computer, heavy manufacturing, and banking fields are the greatest users of temp help. Businesses have made acquiring temporary help an integral part of the hiring process as well as overall human resources policy. Temporary workers allow organizations greater flexibility—although at the expense of worker loyalty and knowledge retention.

## TELECOMMUTING WORKERS

A 2009 survey by Citrix Online found that 23 percent of American workers regularly do their jobs from someplace besides the office, and that number is expected to jump to 43 percent of the workforce by 2016. Telecommuting enables corporations to decrease office space and hire key talent that might not otherwise be available, as well as reduce air pollution caused by automobile use. Local phone companies offer ISDN lines that transmit voice, data, and video simultaneously, making it easier to telecommute. The entire 240-member core sales staff at American Express Travel-Related Services Company is made up of telecommuters. Ernst & Young has implemented "hoteling," in which up to ten people share a single desk in a fully equipped office on an as-needed basis; employees must reserve time in advance. Over the past three years, the accounting firm has slashed its office space requirements by about 2 million square feet, saving roughly $25 million a year.

## IDEAL WORKPLACE OF THE TWENTY-FIRST CENTURY

What would be the ideal workplace of the twenty-first century? According to a recent Development Dimensions International (DDI) survey, people consider the following characteristics desirable:

- Leaders build an environment of trust by listening to and communicating with employees. They champion continuous improvement, facilitate learning, and reinforce effective performance. Leaders and associates work together to establish goals, expectations, and accountabilities. Clearly defined and communicated vision and values help guide decision making, which occurs at the lowest level.
- Employees control resources, systems, methods, working conditions, and work schedules. Individuals have the ability and data to measure their own performance and progress, while performance feedback comes from peers, customers, and direct reports. Jobs are designed to promote employee ownership and responsibility. Effective training builds skills at the appropriate, just-in-time moment.
- The ideal workplace encourages risk taking and treats mistakes as learning opportunities. Systems—such as selection and promotion, rewards and recognition, compensation, and information management—are aligned to reinforce and drive desired behaviors.

## Force 7: Workplace Diversity and Mobility

The global workforce is becoming ever more diverse and mobile. Physicists at corporate R&D centers are as likely to come from universities in England or India as from Princeton or MIT. At research centers around the world, the first language of a biochemist could be German, Hindi, or Japanese. U.S. hospitals routinely advertise for nurses in Dublin and Manila.

Corporations increasingly reach across borders to find the skills they need. This movement of workers is driven by the growing gap between the world's supply of labor and demands for it. Much of the planet's skilled and unskilled human resources are in the developing world. Yet most of the well-paid, high-skill jobs are generated in the cities of the industrialized world.

Friedman (2005) and Reich (2010), among others, have written on how globalization and technology have transformed the world of work and affected work patterns, resulting in a number of workplace changes:

- *Relocation:* A massive relocation is occurring as people, especially the young and better educated, flock from rural to urban areas around the world. For example, hundreds of millions of Chinese peasants have moved to cities, turning small villages such as Shenzhen into cities of millions in less than twenty years.

- *Competition for labor:* More industrialized nations will come to rely on, and even compete for, foreign-born workers. An interesting recent phenomenon is that many U.S. and European employees from developing countries are returning to their countries of origin to work, especially back to China and India.
- *Improved productivity:* Labor-short, immigrant-poor countries like Japan and Sweden are being compelled to dramatically improve labor productivity in order to avoid slow economic growth. The need for increased outsourcing of jobs to other countries is escalating.
- *Standardization:* There is a gradual standardization of labor practices around the world in the areas of vacation time, workplace safety, and employee rights.
- *Caught between rising aspirations and stagnant wages:* Reich (2010) notes how middle-class workers have gone through a series of coping mechanisms. First, women joined the workforce, giving families a second income. Then husbands and wives put in longer shifts, creating a species of family called DINS: "double income, no sex." Finally, families went into debt. In this sense, inequality helped to stoke the credit bubble.

Nations with slow-growing workforces but growth in service sector jobs (such as Canada, Germany, and the United States) have become magnets for immigrants. Nations whose educational systems produce prospective workers faster than their economies can absorb them (such as Argentina, Egypt, and the Philippines) will continue to export people.

The combination of a globalized workforce and massive mobility forces organizations to develop the ability to work with growing numbers of people of differing cultures, customs, values, beliefs, and practices.

## Force 8: Rapidly Escalating Change and Chaos

For nearly three centuries, the world and the workplace have been built on Newtonian physics: the physics of cause and effect, predictability and certainty, distinct wholes and parts, and reality as visible phenomena. Newtonian physics is a science of quantifiable determinism, linear thinking, and controllable futures—in sum, a world that does not change too quickly or in unexpected ways.

In the Newtonian mind-set, people engage in complex planning for a world that they believe is predictable. They continually search for better methods of objectively perceiving the world. This mechanistic and reduction-ist way of thinking and acting dominates life even though it was disproved nearly one hundred years ago by Albert Einstein and others who introduced the scientific community to quantum physics in the 1920s. Margaret Wheat-ley (2001) rightly notes, however, that this old, disproved mind-set is, in today's world, "unempowering and disabling for all of us."

Quantum physics deals with the world at the subatomic level, examining the intricate patterns that give rise to seemingly discrete events. Quantum physics recognizes that the universe and every object in it are, in reality, vast empty spaces filled with fields and movements that represent the basic substance of the universe. Thus, relationships between objects and between observers and objects determine reality. The quantum universe is composed of an environment rich in relationships; it is a world of chaos and process, not just of objects and things. Quantum physics deals with waves and holograms, with surprises rather than predictions

In understanding quantum physics, organizations realize that they can-not predict anything with certainty, that chaos is part and parcel of reality. It forces us to change the way we think, the way we attempt to solve problems, and the way we deal with order versus change, autonomy versus control, structure versus flexibility, and planning versus flowing.

## Emergence of Learning Organizations

Albert Einstein once wrote that "No problem can be solved from the same consciousness that created it; we must learn to see the world anew." The eight forces described here have altered the world of work so dramatically that old dinosaur-like organizations can no longer respond to or handle the new challenges. As Einstein warned, we won't be able to effectively attend to these new problems using the same structures, mind-sets, or knowledge that worked for organizations in the past.

Today, a growing number of organizational people are becoming aware that the knowledge, strategies, leadership, and technology of yesterday will not lead to success in tomorrow's world. It has become obvious to them that companies must increase their corporate capacities to learn if they are to function successfully in an environment that includes continual merg-ers, rapid technological advances, massive societal change, and increasing competition (Garvin, 2003). With all these challenges and potential benefits to the organization, it was just a matter of time before the new species of learning organization arrived (Kline & Saunders, 2010).

To obtain and sustain a competitive advantage in this new world, companies realized that they would have to evolve a higher form of learning capability that would enable them to learn better and faster from their successes and failures. They would have to continuously transform themselves into organizations in which everyone, groups and individuals, could increase their adaptive and productive capabilities by quantum leaps. Only by enhancing their capacity to learn would they avoid the fate of the dinosaur, which was unable to adapt to its changing environment.

In the early 1990s, a number of organizations began the process of becoming learning organizations. Companies such as Corning, Federal Express, Ford, General Electric, and, Motorola in the United States; ABB, Nokia, and Sheerness Steel in Europe; and Samsung and Singapore Airlines in Asia were among the early and successful pioneers. These companies saw corporation-wide, systems-wide learning, with its resulting product and service improvements, as the best route toward not only surviving but succeeding.

As is the case with many evolutionary processes, some of the organizations that began the process of adaptation and learning did not accomplish enough to sustain long-lasting change. They were not fully prepared to give up the security of their existing size and successes, to fully and systematically metamorphose into that new species, the learning organization. They chose to take on more modest, safer changes, such as quality circles or reengineering, thus realizing only a portion of the full benefits of organizational learning.

## Forces That Enable Learning Organizations

Fortunately, some of the same forces that created changes in the business environment may also serve as the foundation for building the learning organization. For example, the competitive and technological forces that mandated a flatter, seamless organization enable that company to move knowledge more quickly with less internal filtering. Know-how workers with greater mobility and choices force an organization to empower them so that they can be more productive. Customer expectations and options require companies to continually learn new ways to create customer delight.

The power of the computer and telecommunications erases distance and time as it facilitates information flow. Rapid and ongoing changes in the skills required of workers compel them to be continuous learners who do not have the luxury of waiting to be trained. The organization that is able to capture all these forces and systematically synergize them will be the one to advance up the evolutionary ladder to the next stage of organizational life—the learning organization.

Learning speeds workers' readiness to do their new jobs and fit the roles needed, thus supporting better deployment of human capital. We now have a new metric, "time to competence." Learning is the foundation of professional development, the ongoing growth of human capital with which companies drive more innovation, higher levels of service, and greater margins. Learning is the key to adapting and surviving massive discontinuities in markets and competitive environments (Manville, 2001).

Experience and research have shown that when companies incorporate five distinct subsystems (learning, organization, people, knowledge, and technology) into the process of becoming a learning organization, they are quicker and much more successful at attaining their goal. Attempts to become learning companies without all five dimensions will be insufficient and frustrating.

# CHAPTER 2

# The Systems Learning Organization Model

Most organizations now recognize the critical importance of becoming learning organizations: They must learn better and faster or they will die. The challenge for them is, how? Many seek quick and easy approaches. Others focus on only one or two aspects of organizational change and learning, such as acquiring new skills or technology. As a result of these shortcut attempts, most companies have failed dismally. They neglected to take into account the challenging complexity of creating and maintaining company-wide learning. They did not examine and implement the various inherent components that make up the learning organization.

Based on the author's experience with hundreds of learning organizations over the past twenty-five years, it is clear that this kind of learning is not possible nor can it be sustained without understanding and developing five related subsystems. These subsystems are learning, organization, people, knowledge, and technology (see Figure 1). All five are necessary to sustain viable, ongoing organizational learning and ensuing corporate success.

The organization, people, knowledge, and technology subsystems are necessary to enhance and augment learning, which, in turn, permeates the other four subsystems. They are indispensable partners in building and maintaining organizational learning and productivity. The five subsystems are dynamically interrelated and complement one another. If any one subsystem is weak or absent, the others will be significantly compromised.

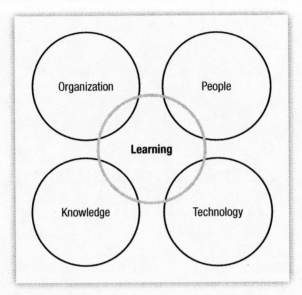

**FIGURE 1**   Systems Learning Organization Model

## Learning Subsystem

Learning is the core subsystem of the learning organization. It takes place at the individual, group, and organizational levels. The skills of systems thinking, mental models, personal mastery, self-directed learning, and dialogue are necessary to maximize organizational learning. The learning subsystem refers to levels and types of learning that are crucial for organizational learning and the relevant organizational skills (see Figure 2).

### LEVELS OF LEARNING

Three distinct but interrelated levels of learning are present in learning organizations:

*Individual learning* refers to changes in skills, insights, knowledge, attitudes, and values acquired through self-study, technology-based instruction, and observation.

*Group or team learning* covers the increase in knowledge, skills, and competencies accomplished by and within groups.

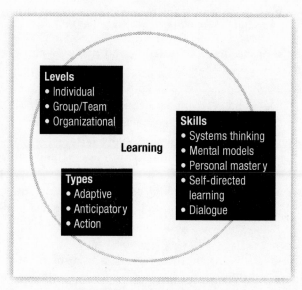

**FIGURE 2**   Learning Subsystem

*Organizational learning* represents the enhanced intellectual and productive capability gained through commitment to and opportunities for continuous improvement across the organization.

## TYPES OF LEARNING

Three methods or approaches to learning are of significance and value to the learning organization. Although each is distinctive, there is often overlap and complementarity among them.

*Adaptive learning* occurs when we reflect on past experience and then modify future actions.

*Anticipatory learning* is the process of acquiring knowledge from envisioning various futures (an approach that moves from vision to action to reflection). This approach to learning seeks to avoid negative results and experiences by identifying the best future opportunity and determining ways to achieve that future.

*Action learning* is the ability to learn while engaged in action, be it by oneself, with another person, or in a group. It is built around a problem and relies on reflective inquiry.

## SKILLS FOR ORGANIZATIONAL LEARNING

Five key skills are needed for initiating and maximizing organizational learning.

*Systems thinking* represents a conceptual framework with which to make full patterns clearer and determine how to change them effectively.

*Mental models* are the deeply ingrained assumptions that influence our views of and actions in the world. For example, our mental model or image of learning, work, or patriotism influences our interactions and behavior in specific situations that pertain to those concepts.

*Personal mastery* indicates a high level of proficiency in a subject or skill area. It requires a commitment to lifelong learning that leads to expertise or exceptional, enjoyable proficiency in our organizational tasks or responsibilities.

*Self-directed learning* means that everyone is aware of and enthusiastically accepts responsibility for being a learner. Elements of self-directed learning include knowing our own learning style, being able to assess our needs and competence, and connecting business objectives to learning needs.

*Dialogue* denotes a high level of listening and communication between people. It requires the free and creative exploration of subtle issues and the ability to listen deeply to another person while suspending our own views. The discipline of dialogue involves learning to recognize the patterns of team interaction that may promote or undermine learning. For example, patterns of defensiveness are often deeply ingrained in group or organizational dynamics. If such patterns are unrecognized or ignored, they undermine learning, but when recognized and surfaced creatively, they can actually accelerate learning. Dialogue is the critical medium for connecting, inventing, and coordinating learning and action in the workplace.

## Organization Subsystem

The organization itself, the setting and body in which the process occurs, is a subsystem of a learning organization. The four key dimensions or components of this subsystem are vision, culture, strategy, and structure (see Figure 3).

*Vision* encompasses a company's hopes, goals, and direction for the future. It is the image of the organization that is cultivated within the company itself and then transmitted to those outside the organization. The

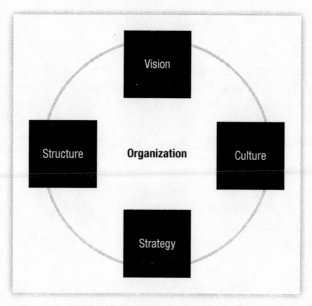

**FIGURE 3**  Organization Subsystem

culture of a learning organization supports an evolving vision of the company, within which learning and learners are able to create the company's continuously new and improved products and services.

*Culture* refers to an organization's values, beliefs, practices, rituals, and customs. It helps shape behavior and fashion perceptions. In a learning organization, the corporate culture is one in which learning is recognized as absolutely critical for business success; in such an organization, learning has become a habitual and integrated part of all organizational functions. This rich, adaptable culture creates relationships and enhances learning by encouraging values such as teamwork, self-management, empowerment, and sharing. It is the opposite of a closed, rigid, bureaucratic architecture.

*Strategy* relates to the action plans, methodologies, tactics, and steps employed to achieve a company's vision and goals. In a learning organization, strategies optimize the learning acquired, transferred, and utilized in all company actions and operations.

*Structure* includes the company's departments, levels, and configurations. A learning organization is a streamlined, unbounded, flat structure that maximizes contact, information flow, local responsibility, and collaboration within and outside the organization.

## People Subsystem

The people subsystem of the learning organization includes managers and leaders, employees, customers, business partners and alliances, suppliers, vendors, and the surrounding community (see Figure 4). Each group is valuable to the learning organization, and all must be empowered and enabled to learn.

As learners, *managers and leaders* carry out coaching, mentoring, and modeling roles with the primary responsibility of generating and enhancing learning opportunities for the people around them.

*Employees* are empowered and expected to learn, plan for their future competencies, take action and risks, and solve problems.

*Customers* participate by identifying needs, receiving training, and establishing a connection to the learning of the organization.

*Business partners* and alliances benefit by sharing competencies and knowledge.

Suppliers and vendors receive and contribute to instructional programs.

*Community groups* such as social, educational, and economic agencies share in providing and receiving learning.

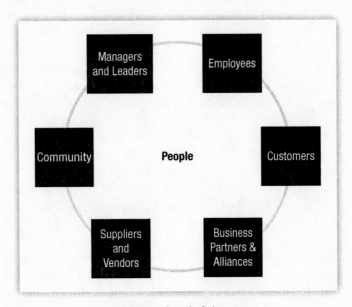

**FIGURE 4**   People Subsystem

## Knowledge Subsystem

The knowledge subsystem of a learning organization manages the acquired and generated knowledge of the organization. It includes the acquisition, creation, storage, analysis and data mining, transfer and dissemination, and application and validation of knowledge (see Figure 5).

The six knowledge elements of organizational learning are ongoing and interactive instead of sequential and independent. Distribution of information occurs through multiple channels, each with different time frames. Knowledge management is continually subjected to perceptual filters as well as to proactive and reactive activities. The management of knowledge is at the heart of building a learning organization. Successful learning organizations systematically and technologically guide knowledge through each and all of these six stages.

*Acquisition* is the collection of existing data and information from within and outside the organization.

In *creation*, new knowledge is generated through a number of different processes ranging from innovation to painstaking and elaborate research. It can also come through the ability to see new connections and combine previously known knowledge elements through complex inductive reasoning.

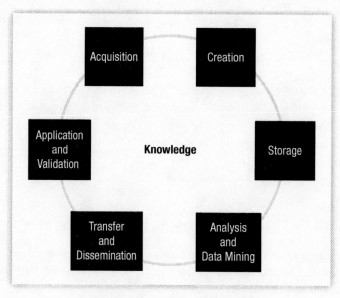

**FIGURE 5**   Knowledge Subsystem

*Storage* refers to the coding and preservation of the organization's valued knowledge for easy access by any staff member, at any time, and from any place.

*Analysis and data mining* involves techniques for analyzing data as well as for reconstructing, validating, and inventorying this critical resource. Mining enables organizations to find meaning in their data.

*Transfer and dissemination* is the mechanical, electronic, and interpersonal movement of information and knowledge, both intentionally and unintentionally, throughout the organization

*Application and validation* covers the use and assessment of knowledge by members of the organization. This is accomplished through continuous recycling and creative utilization of the organization's rich knowledge and experience.

## Technology Subsystem

The technology subsystem is composed of supporting, integrated technological networks and information tools that allow access to and exchange of information and learning. It includes technical processes, systems, and structures for collaboration, coaching, coordination, and other knowledge skills. It encompasses electronic tools and advanced methods for learning, such as simulation, computer conferencing, and collaboration. All these tools work to create knowledge freeways.

The two major components of the technology subsystem apply to managing knowledge and enhancing learning (see Figure 6).

*Technology for managing knowledge* refers to the computer-based technology that gathers, codes, stores, and transfers information across organizations and worldwide.

*Technology for enhancing learning* involves the utilization of video, audio, and computer-based multimedia training for the purpose of delivering and developing knowledge and skills.

## Characteristics of the Systems Learning Organization

The systems learning organization has tremendous power to engender corporate success. What are some of the dimensions and characteristics of such an organization?

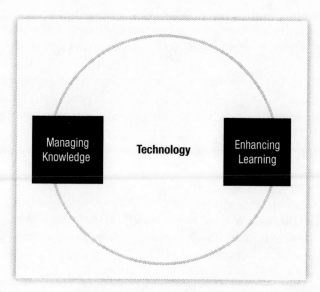

**FIGURE 6** Technology Subsystem

First, learning is accomplished by the organizational system as a whole, almost as if it were a single brain. Members recognize the critical importance to current and future success of ongoing learning that occurs throughout the organization. Learning is a continuous, strategically used process that is integrated with and runs parallel to work. In such a learning organization, there is a focus on creativity and generative learning. Well-developed core competencies serve as a launching point for new products and services. Systems thinking is fundamental. Agility and flexibility are valued. An organization of this type possesses the ability to continuously adapt, renew, and revitalize itself in response to the changing environment.

As we will see in chapter 5, there is a corporate climate that encourages, rewards, and accelerates individual and group learning. Employees network in an innovative manner that resembles a community both inside and outside the organization. Change is embraced, and unexpected surprises and even failures are viewed as opportunities to learn. Everyone is driven by a desire for quality and continuous improvement. Aspiration, reflection, and conceptualization characterize day-to-day activities. People have uninterrupted access to information and data resources that are vital to the company's success.

The organization that incorporates and integrates all five subsystems of this model will have tremendous capabilities to do the following:

- Anticipate and adapt more readily to environmental influences
- Accelerate the development of new products, processes, and services
- Become more proficient at learning from competitors and collaborators
- Expedite the transfer of knowledge from one part of the organization to another
- Learn more effectively from its mistakes
- Make greater use of employees at all levels of the organization
- Shorten the time required to implement strategic changes
- Stimulate continuous improvement in all areas of the organization
- Attract the best workers
- Increase worker commitment and creativity

Learning must be linked to fundamental business needs and the results demanded by managers, customers, partners, and shareholders. They will be measuring effectiveness not by counting training courses or classroom attendance but by evaluating business performance. In these companies, learning underpins business outcomes such as talent acquisition, channel management, leadership capacity, decreased cycle time, new-product rollout speed, merger and acquisition integration, risk management and legal compliance, and employee and customer retention and satisfaction (Manville, 2001). Only organizations that have embraced all five subsystems will be able to meet these challenges.

Explanations, principles, applications, and best practices of the five subsystems that form the Systems Learning Organization model will be presented and applied in the remainder of this book. Together, the subsystems build a sturdy structure that ensures organizational learning and success. Let's now explore each of these subsystems so that we can begin to design and build our learning organization.

# CHAPTER 3

# Building Learning Dynamics

The core subsystem of the learning organization is learning itself. The speed, quality, and leverage of the learning processes and their content form the medium that supports, nourishes, and extends into the other subsystems of the learning organization.

## Learning in Organizational Settings

The learning subsystem is composed of three complementary dimensions: levels of learning (individual, group, and organizational), types of learning (adaptive, anticipatory, and action), and skills (systems thinking, mental models, personal mastery, self-directed learning, and dialogue). The subsystem is illustrated in Figure 7.

Before examining these three dimensions of the learning subsystem, it is important to understand and appreciate some basic principles, especially those that relate to organizational context. Learning has traditionally been defined as a process by which individuals gain new knowledge and insights that result in a change of behavior and actions. It comprises cognitive (intellectual), affective (emotional), and psychomotor (physical) domains.

### PRINCIPLES OF LEARNING

Throughout the past century, learning theorists have identified a number of principles that encourage and enhance the learning process. They have found

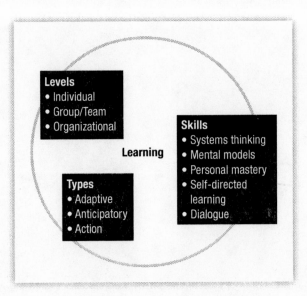

**FIGURE 7**    Learning Subsystem

that we learn best when we are motivated to achieve something as opposed to being motivated to learn. Thus, performance-based learning that is tied to business objectives will be more successful than abstract learning. Learning is also most thorough when it involves the whole person—mind, values, and emotions. And because learning is a cyclical, iterative process of planning, implementing, and reflecting on action, we usually learn best when we have the opportunity to reflect on our immediate actions.

The ability to know what we must know and then to learn it on our own is a critical survival skill. People tend to be more receptive to learning that they have helped to create, and they will know the information they acquire in this way better than anyone else. However, learning about ourselves can be threatening and is often resisted if it might lead to changes in self-image.

Learning is, in part, a product of the activity, context, and culture in which it is developed and used, yet the process can accommodate and challenge different learning-style preferences. For example, to better prepare its sales force for a new technology platform, Royal Bank of Canada developed a five-part learning program entitled Enhancing Sales Performance, designed to meet the wide range of learning styles and needs among an audience of disparate experiences and abilities. Each component fulfilled a specific learning need via the most appropriate medium: print, computer, video, or audio. Sessions were text based and facilitator led in order to achieve maximum comprehension and retention. These components allowed staff to practice skills on an ongoing basis, as often and in as many variations as needed. The success of this tailored learning program earned Royal Bank the ASTD Citation for Excellence in Practice.

## Learning at Canadian Imperial Bank of Commerce

Canadian Imperial Bank of Commerce (CIBC) is a highly diversified financial services company operating on a global basis with more than 6.5 million individual customers and 10,000 commercial customers. The bank has more than 42,000 employees and invests in excess of $40 million in employee development each year. In February, 2010, CIBC became the first chartered bank in Canada to launch a Mobile Banking iPhone application. It surpassed 100,000 downloads in just over one month following launch, with more than one million client logins to CIBC Mobile Banking within the first ten months of its introduction.

CIBC recently launched a major effort to develop the necessary tools and techniques for capturing the intellectual capital that will ensure its success. Its criterion for success was that the rate of learning by individuals, teams, and the corporation as a whole must equal or exceed the pace of change in the external environment. The purpose of all knowledge management is improving output for the customer. It is not knowledge for knowledge's sake. At CIBC, knowledge gathering proceeded on each of the three levels of learning—individual, team or group, and organizational.

At the individual level, responsibility for continuous learning rests with the worker. To assist, CIBC mapped the knowledge requirements of each position in the organization— the theoretical understanding, skill sets, and experience required for each job—and electronically posted the requirements of all vacant positions. The company provided a variety of methods for acquiring the necessary knowledge, which included classes, correspondence courses, seminars, video and audio aids, reference material, and external courses. Employees chose the method most suited to their needs.

At the team level, task-focused employee groups also take responsibility for their learning. This demands a change in structures: Management responsibilities and styles shifted from authoritarian to coaching and mentoring, brokering team knowledge, and assessing knowledge needs across the organization. Compensation systems were redesigned to reflect team as well as individual success. Teams were expected to find ways of ensuring that the knowledge and ideas of all members were recognized and shared.

At the level of the organization, particularly across such a large, multinational firm, "silos" of knowledge develop, which are useful to those on the inside but are unavailable and therefore of little help to others. At CIBC, team successes and achievements are viewed as one team's potential contribution to another and are shared through learning networks.

## Levels of Learning

Learning in organizations can occur at three levels: individual, team or group, and organizational. Learning organizations have developed the capacity to encourage and maximize all three levels.

### INDIVIDUAL LEARNING

Individuals are the basic units of groups and organizations. Peter Senge (2006) asserts that "organizations learn only through individuals who learn. Individual learning does not guarantee organizational learning, but without it no organizational learning occurs" (p. 236). Argyris and Schön (1995) concur, noting that "individual learning is a necessary but insufficient condition for organizational learning" (p. 20). Individual learning is essential for the continual transformation of an organization because it expands the capability of the organization and prepares it for the future.

Therefore, each person's commitment and ability to learn is essential. Individual learning opportunities include self-managed learning, learning from coworkers, computer-assisted learning, daily work experiences, special assignments on projects, and personal insights. There are a number of important factors and techniques that contribute to increasing the power and impact of individual learning in the organization.

#### Locus and Focus of Individual Learning

Learning should be a constant in the work environment, whether through on-the-job coaching, electronic performance support systems (EPSS), action learning, or reflective planning. Classroom training, whenever possible, should be designed for small "just in time" formats that provide immediate application to the job.

#### Web-based Learning and Individual Learning

Web learning represents an exciting and powerful resource. It provides a way to find information for course assignments and projects without the need to physically visit a library or buy books. It also allows individual workers to post their own ideas in a public location that can be accessed by others inside and outside the workplace. The web provides access to thousands of online magazines (ejournals), newsletters, discussion groups and entertainment sites that can broaden their intellectual horizons. It goes a long way to breaking down geographical, socioeconomic, cultural, gender, and age-related barriers to accessing information and interacting with others (Waddill & Marquardt, 2011).

*Accelerated Learning*

The many, varied techniques of accelerated learning augment the ability to learn more information in less time and increase retention. Accelerated learning techniques engage all parts of the brain and do so in conjunction with both conscious and subconscious mental functions. This ensures that every means of learning and retention is utilized as simultaneously and fully as possible. Accelerated learning has also proved effective at building innovation, imagination, and creativity into the learning process.

The following learning accelerators are among the most powerful:

- Mnemonics for greater recall and retention
- Music to engage the whole brain
- Metaphors and stories to engage the whole learner for concept development and transfer of learning
- Peripherals to create a richer and more integrated learning environment
- Lighting, color, and room arrangements that create receptive learning states
- Mind mapping or information graphs to aid learning, recall, concept formation, idea generation, and planning

Of course, different accelerators are more effective for different people. Learning organizations should therefore provide a variety of choices. There are a number of basic principles for enriching the learning environment:

- Provide an environment that is comfortable, colorful, and supportive.
- Utilize technologies and resources that can accommodate different learning styles, speeds, and needs.
- Present material in a variety of ways: pictures, text, and sound.
- Treat the learner as an adult and in a collaborative manner.

Verizon is one learning organization that recently established accelerated learning techniques for its customer service programs. The results were overwhelming. Training time was cut by more than half, trainers and learners were much more satisfied, job performance was higher, and costs were reduced by nearly 60 percent.

*Personal Development Plan*

Individuals in learning organizations see learning as a way of life rather than an occasional event. They recognize that employers cannot guarantee them lifelong employment but will assist them in becoming lifelong employable. The organization and the individual work together toward the employee's long-term career development. Organizations should be as upfront and open as possible about future corporate directions and plans, and then employees can create programs for self-development that will make them valued assets to their companies. And if a firm moves in a direction that no longer matches the skills or interests of an employee, that individual will possess competencies and know-how that are in demand at other organizations.

A number of learning organizations have developed excellent personal development packages for their employees. Royal Bank of Canada guides employees through Planning Your Career while PPG Industries offers the Professional Development Sourcebook.

Learning organizations constantly encourage, support, accelerate, and reward individual learning through an organizational system that promotes continuous self-development and employability. Professional development opportunities are available to everyone in the organization. Resources include courses, workshops, seminars, self-learning materials, development groups, coaching, mentoring, and data banks. Employees are expected to learn not only the skills related to their own jobs but also the skills of others in their units.

Learning is performance based—that is, closely tied to business needs—and is also an integral part of all organizational operations. Individual learning, whether creative or adaptive, is transferred to the organization database for future application.

## Individual Development Plans at Yap ve Kredi Bankasi

Yap ve Kredi is the first nationwide private bank in Turkey, established in 1944, and positioned as the fourth largest privately owned bank in Turkey, with interest in credit cards, assets under management, non-cash loans, leasing, factoring, private pension funds, and non-life insurance. The combined KFS Group's financial services network now consists of more than 13 million customers and 835 branches across the country. All Yap ve Kredi employees have individual development plans, participate in performance goal setting, and are evaluated annually on their performance. The bank's competency model includes eight major competencies that cascade down to key performance indicators. A position-based job training catalog is customized based on role and shows employee paths to promotion as well as necessary development activities. The employee and his or her manager meet to select training programs from the catalog based on the individual key performance indicator goals and competency gaps. Choices include both technical and soft-skill training programs (Salopek, 2010a).

## GROUP OR TEAM LEARNING

Teams have become more and more important in organizations—whether they are running cross-functional projects, working on manufacturing lines, or reengineering business processes. In order to equip these teams with the knowledge and skills they need, learning organizations have taught them quality processes, problem-solving techniques, and team interaction skills.

As organizations must deal with increasingly more complex problems, they are discovering that they must become skilled in group and team learning. Work teams must be able to think, create, and learn effectively as an entity. Team learning can and should occur every time a group of people is brought together, whether for short-term specific purposes or to address long-term organizational issues.

It is important to recognize that team learning differs radically from team training because it involves more than the acquisition of group skills. Team learning emphasizes self-managed learning, creativity, and the free flow of ideas. A successful team learning system ensures that teams share their experiences, both negative and positive, with other groups in the organization and thereby promote vigorous corporate intellectual growth.

Teams learn to generate knowledge by analyzing complex issues, taking innovative action, and solving problems collectively. They become able to better learn from their own experiences and past histories, to experiment with new approaches, and to quickly and efficiently transfer knowledge among themselves and throughout the organization. As teams learn, they may become microcosms for learning throughout the organization. The team's insights can be put into action, while its newly developed skills are passed along to other individuals and groups. A team's accomplishments can set the tone and establish a standard of mutual learning for an entire organization.

Learning organizations seek to create a full range of teams, including continuous improvement, cross-functional, quality management, and organizational learning teams. These groups take time to reflect, to practice action learning. They serve as vehicles for fundamental organizational change and renewal. Teams not only are encouraged to solve problems, but also should help to create a greater understanding of the business through their collective learning. Teams, particularly action learning teams, can serve as a mini-model of a learning organization (Marquardt, 2011a).

Team learning focuses on the process of aligning and developing the group's capacity to create the desired learning and results for its members. Most groups do not learn. Frustration and wasted energy are fundamental characteristics of relatively unaligned groups: Individuals may work extraordinarily hard, but their efforts do not translate into a team effort. By contrast, an aligned team develops a commonality of direction, and the energies of individual members harmonize. There is less wasted energy. In fact, as Senge (2006) notes, "a resonance or synergy develops, like the coherent light of a laser rather than the incoherent and scattered light of a light bulb."

Team learning meets the need to think insightfully about complex issues. Through innovative, coordinated action, teams learn how to tap the potential of many minds. Outstanding teams develop operational trust, in that each team member remains conscious of the others and acts in ways that complement their actions. This is how outstanding sports teams and orchestras work and learn together.

Team learning requires these three elements:

- The need to address complex issues through collective insight
- The need for innovative, coordinated action
- The ability to encourage and stimulate learning in other teams

Team learning occurs more quickly and fully if teams are rewarded for their contributions to the organization. Learning at the team level requires practice and reflection. High-level team learning enables high-level collective thinking and communication as well as the ability to work creatively and constructively as a single entity. As will be discussed later in this chapter, action learning has proved to be the most effective way of creating team learning.

## Groupware for Group or Team Learning

*Groupware* is a term for collaborative software (also referred to as *workgroup support systems* or simply *group support systems*) designed to help people involved in a common task achieve their goals. Often the groupware incorporates video, chat, Instant Messaging, polling capabilities, emoticons for feedback, hotlinks for virtual tours, whiteboards, and presentation software. It may rely upon both telecommunications and Internet or strictly Internet.

At both ends of the groupware spectrum, the goal is for the product to enable interaction between individuals or groups that are not co-located. Figure 8 offers a picture of the range of sophistication in groupware. At one end of the spectrum, there is the teleconference. We are all familiar with that form of collaboration. For these simpler versions of groupware, typical peripherals include a telephone and phone connection. When the phone transmission takes place over the Internet, the voice message may travel over the phone lines or over the Internet. *Voice over Internet Protocol (VoIP)* is a technology that allows you to make voice calls using a broadband Internet connection

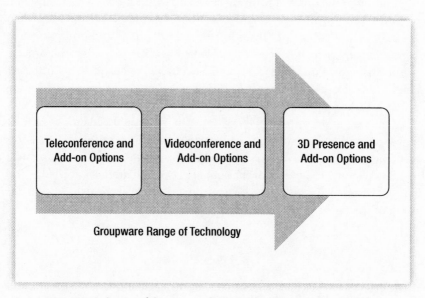

Teleconference and Add-on Options

Videoconference and Add-on Options

3D Presence and Add-on Options

Groupware Range of Technology

**FIGURE 8** Range of Groupware Options (Waddill & Marquardt, 2011)

instead of using a regular (or analog) phone line. Some VoIP services may only allow you to call other people using the same service, but others may allow you to call anyone who has a telephone number—including local, long distance, mobile, and international numbers. Also, while some VoIP services only work over your computer or a special VoIP phone, other services allow you to use a traditional phone connected to a VoIP adapter.

As the technology becomes more sophisticated, groupware systems may require peripherals such as a webcam and/or microphone attached to the computer with software to enable the interaction online. And at the most sophisticated level, the technology requires accommodations or rooms that provide high-end video uplink/downlink equipment.

## ORGANIZATIONAL LEARNING

Organizational learning can be distinguished from individual and team learning in two basic respects. First, organizational learning occurs through the shared insights, knowledge, and mental models of members of the company. Second, organizational learning builds on past knowledge and experience—that is, on organizational memory, which depends on mechanisms such as policies, strategies, and explicit models with which to store knowledge.

Although the types of learning associated with individuals, teams, and organizations are interrelated, organizational learning is seen as more than the sum of individual and team learning. Individuals and groups are the agents through which organizational learning takes place, but the process is influenced by a much broader set of social, political, and structural variables. It involves the sharing of knowledge, beliefs, or assumptions among individuals and groups (Schein, 2010).

One way to show the difference between individual and group learning and organizational learning is to consider a performing organization, such as an orchestra or a sports team. A musical performance or game win cannot be attributed to any individual or the sum of every individual's knowledge and skills, or even to any group, such as the horn section or the defense. It is the result of the know-how of the whole organization working in unison.

## Types of Learning

There are three types of organizational learning: adaptive, anticipatory, and action. They are not exclusive of one another in that an individual, team, or organization may employ more than one type at the same time.

## ADAPTIVE LEARNING

Adaptive learning occurs when an individual, team, or organization learns from experience and reflection. Organizationally, adaptive learning proceeds as follows: The company takes an action intended to further an identified goal, the action results in some internal or external outcome, the resultant change is analyzed for congruence with the goal, and the company initiates a new action or modifies the previous action based on the outcome. Adaptive learning moves from action, to outcome, to results assessment, and then to reflection.

Adaptive learning may be either single loop or double loop. Single-loop learning is focused on gaining information to stabilize and maintain existing systems. It emphasizes error detection and correction. Single-loop learning is concerned with obtaining direct solutions to immediate conflicts or obstacles, which are often symptoms of underlying problems. This type of learning is by far the only kind of loop learning used in most organizations today. Double-loop learning involves in-depth questioning of the system itself to ascertain why errors or successes occur in the first place. It looks at organizational norms and structures and raises questions about their validity in terms of organization, action, and results. Argyris (1999) notes that most organizations and individuals are unwilling to engage in double-loop learning because it involves disclosure of errors and mistakes as well as the (often uncomfortable) process of questioning existing assumptions, norms, structures, and practices.

## ANTICIPATORY LEARNING

Anticipatory learning arises when an organization learns from anticipating various futures. This approach seeks to avoid negative results and experiences by identifying the best future opportunities while discovering ways to achieve them. Royal Dutch Shell credits its global learning and success to the "planning as learning" approach. Anticipatory learning enabled the company to prepare for a sharp drop in the price of oil. When the expected drop occurred, Shell was the only oil company equipped with the appropriate organizational skills and resources. Anticipatory learning thus moves from vision, to reflection, and then to action.

In comparing adaptive and anticipatory learning, we can note that adaptive learning is more a coping form of learning. Anticipatory learning is a more generative or creative type of organizational learning. Anticipatory learning greatly empowers the organization because staff members are more proactive, reflective, and creative in their learning. Organizational learning may start as reactions to events, but the proactive organization soon takes charge of its learning to shape events.

## Anticipatory Learning and Scenario Planning at Royal Dutch Shell

Royal Dutch Shell is one of the world's largest and most successful companies, with more than 100,000 employees in 90 countries around the globe. One perceived reason for the company's superior performance is its use of strategic organizational learning tools such as scenarios forecasting, a form of anticipatory learning. Through the use of anticipatory learning, Royal Dutch Shell has become known as a premier learning organization in its scanning for information and its understanding of trends in the global economic environment.

Scenarios constantly rephrase possible pathways into the future. Planning, when based on forecasts from history, can be accurate when times are stable. But since the global economic environment is turbulent and volatile, scenario planning has proved to be a more valuable way to look toward the future.

For example, in the 1970s Shell undertook a study of the year 2000, analyzing the question, "Is there life after oil?" One scenario developed was the possibility of $15 for a barrel of oil, a seeming disastrous scenario in a world of $30 a barrel. When oil actually dropped to the $15 level, Shell weathered the storm better than their competitors because they had anticipated the possibility and had made tentative plans for the downturn. Through scenario forecasting, Shell developed a team of highly diverse experts that brought varying knowledge to planning efforts.

## ACTION LEARNING

Action learning involves working on real problems, focusing on the acquired knowledge, and actually implementing solutions. It provides a well-tested method of accelerating learning that enables people to learn better and handle difficult situations more effectively. Used as a systematic process, it increases organizational learning so that a company can respond to change more effectively.

Action learning is both a dynamic process and a powerful program. As a process, it involves a small group of people focusing on what they are learning and how their new knowledge can benefit each individual and the organization as a whole. Action learning is built on a well-tested framework that enables people to learn effectively and efficiently as they assess and solve difficult, real-life problems. It combines the generation and application of new questions to existing knowledge with reflection on actions taken during and after problem-solving sessions (Marquardt, 2011a).

## SCHEIN'S TYPES OF LEARNING

Edgar Schein (1993) points out that before individuals or organizations can learn competently, they must understand that there are distinct types of learning, each operating within different time frames and possibly applicable to different stages of a learning or change process. He cites three types.

The first is *habit and skill learning*. This form of learning is slow because it calls for practice, and learners must be willing to put up with their own temporary incompetence. Learning of this type takes hold when we are given opportunities to practice and make errors and are consistently rewarded for correct responses.

The second, *emotional conditioning and learned anxiety*, has become familiar through the work of Pavlov on the conditioning of dogs. Once this type of learning has occurred, it will continue even after the original stimuli are discontinued.

*Knowledge acquisition* is the third type of learning. Most learning theories imply that the essence of learning is acquiring information and knowledge through various kinds of cognitive activities. This point of view, according to Schein, ignores the following factors:

- Learning happens only if the learner recognizes a problem and is motivated to learn.
- Even with insight, the learner often cannot produce the right type of behavior or skill with enough consistency to solve the problem.
- Insight does not automatically change behavior, and until behavior changes and new results are observed, we do not know whether or not our cognitive learning is valid.

Peter Senge (2006) agrees that "learning has very little to do with taking in information. Learning, instead, is a process that is about enhancing capacity. Learning is about building the capability to create that which you previously couldn't create. It's ultimately related to action, which information is not" (p. 191).

Learning is essentially a social phenomenon—our ability to learn and the nature of our knowledge are determined by the quality and openness of our relationships. Our mental models of the world and of ourselves grow out of our relationships with others. Dialogue, which includes continuous critical reappraisal of our views, increases the possibilities for learning. Learning and dialogue are incompatible with self-sufficiency.

It is important to recognize that all learning is not equally valuable or applicable; some knowledge is impracticable, and some insights or skills that might lead to useful new actions are often hard to come by in a given organization.

## DEUTERO LEARNING

Deutero learning occurs when the organization learns from critically reflecting on its assumptions. Chris Argyris and Donald Schön (1995) call this "learning about learning." When a company engages in deutero learning, its members become cognizant of previous organizational contexts for learning. They discover what they did that facilitated or inhibited learning, they invent new strategies for learning, and they evaluate and generalize on what they have produced. The results become encoded and reflected in organizational learning practice.

## Learning Skills

Several organizational learning skills are necessary to maximize learning company wide and attain ultimate business success: systems thinking, mental models, personal mastery, self-directed learning, and dialogue. We will explore these skills next.

## SYSTEMS THINKING

At an early age, we are taught to break down problems, to fragment the world. This initially appears to make complex tasks and subjects more manageable, but we end up paying an enormous hidden price. We lose our concept of, and intrinsic sense of connection to, the whole; we also lose our ability to correlate actions and consequences. When we then try to see the big picture, we attempt to reassemble the fragments in our minds, to list and organize all the pieces. The task is futile, much like trying to reassemble the fragments of a broken mirror.

Systems thinking is a conceptual framework that helps us see the overall patterns more clearly and thus improves our ability to change them. It is a "discipline for seeing wholes," says Senge (2006), "a framework for seeing interrelationships rather than linear cause-effect chains, for seeing underlying structures rather than events, for seeing patterns of change rather than snapshots" (p. 68).

High-leverage changes usually are not obvious to most participants in the system, who lack proximity to overt symptoms of problems. Systems thinking, however, shows that small, well-focused actions can sometimes produce significant, enduring improvements, if they are applied in strategic places. Solving a difficult problem is often a matter of seeing which change will produce the maximum effect while expending comparatively minimal effort.

Systems thinking—in particular, systems dynamics—can be a powerful tool for facilitating organizational learning. Systems dynamics recognizes that organizations are like networks of interconnected nodes. Changes, planned or unplanned, in one part of the organization can affect other areas, with surprising, often negative, consequences.

## MENTAL MODELS

A mental model is our image of or perspective on an event, situation, activity, or concept. It is a deeply ingrained assumption that influences how we understand the world and take action in it. For example, each of us may have a different mental model of *school* or *parent* or *government*, based on our experiences, previous perceptions, or upbringing.

Mental models of what can or cannot be done in different situations vary tremendously from person to person and are often entrenched and difficult to change. Senge (2006) stresses that the discipline of working with mental models starts with turning the mirror inward, learning how to unearth internal pictures or images of the world and then bring them to the surface and hold them up to rigorous scrutiny. It includes the ability "to carry on learningful conversations that balance inquiry and advocacy, where people expose their own thinking effectively and make that thinking open to the influences of others" (p. 9).

## PERSONAL MASTERY

Personal mastery refers to a special level of proficiency, similar to that of the master craftsman who is committed to lifelong learning and continually improves and perfects his or her skills. It is a discipline of constantly clarifying and deepening our personal vision, energies, and patience. Senge (2006) sees personal mastery as a cornerstone of the learning organization because a company's commitment to and capacity for learning can be no greater than the sum of those of each individual member.

Personal mastery entails a commitment to continuous learning at all levels of the organization. This includes pervasive support for any kind of development experience for all members of the organization. Traditional training and development activities are not sufficient; they must be accompanied by a conviction that no member is ever finished with learning or practice.

Few organizations encourage personal mastery among all employees. The result is a vast pool of untapped resources, people who may have lost the commitment, sense of mission, and excitement with which they began their careers. Yet this energy and spirit are exactly what is needed to rigorously develop personal and organizational mastery.

## SELF-DIRECTED LEARNING

All members of a learning organization should be aware of and enthusiastically accept the responsibility both to be learners and to encourage and support the learning of those around them. Our purpose is not only to perform our present jobs as well as we can but to continuously learn how we can function even more effectively.

In learning organizations, it is no longer possible for expert supervisors to know everything that subordinates must know. We must learn how to learn on our own, partly through knowing our preferences regarding learning style in order to optimize our learning opportunities.

## DIALOGUE

Dialogue is intense, high-level, high-quality communication based on the free, creative, and mutual exploration of subtle issues; on listening deeply to one another; and on suspending our own views. By applying the discipline of dialogue, we learn how to recognize the patterns of team interaction that either promote or undermine learning.

Dialogue is the critical medium for creating and coordinating learning and action in the workplace because it promotes collective thinking and communication. Dialogue improves the organization's ability to tap the collective intelligence of groups, equips us to see the world as a whole rather than as fragmented parts, and encourages us to focus on understanding

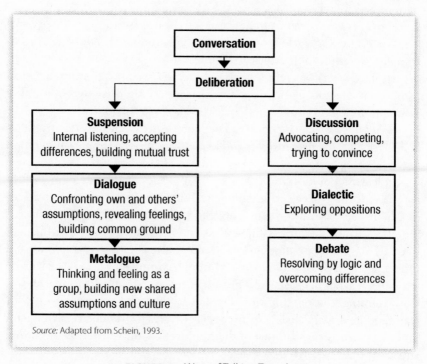

*Source:* Adapted from Schein, 1993.

**FIGURE 9**  Ways of Talking Together

how and why our internal perceptions influence our views of reality. Schein (1993) discusses the difference between dialogue and other communication processes (see Figure 9).

Successful dialogue enables us to recognize leaps of abstraction, or jump from an observation to a generalization; uncover what we are not saying while engaged in conversation; balance inquiry and advocacy; and recognize distinctions between espoused theories (what we claim) and theories in use (the implied theory behind our actions).

## Learning Capacity of Organizations

John Redding (1994) has identified three dimensions to consider while building the learning capacity of the organization:

- Speed of learning
- Depth of learning
- Breadth of learning

*Speed of learning* refers to how quickly the organization is able to complete each learning cycle (planning, implementing, and reflecting) and to complete iterations of the cycle.

*Depth of learning* refers to the degree of learning the organization achieves at the end of each cycle, which it accomplishes by questioning assumptions and improving its capacity to learn in the future.

*Breadth of learning* is concerned with how extensively the organization is able to transfer the new insights and knowledge derived from each iteration of the learning cycle to other issues and parts of the organization.

In learning organizations, we are now witnessing a paradigm shift in emphasis from training to learning. Training signifies a one-way transfer of established wisdom or skill from the expert instructor, whereas learning varies from this process in several important ways. Learning involves not only absorbing existing information but also creating new solutions to problems that are not yet fully understood. Learning may take place with or without a teacher because it is a personal, group, and organizational ability. With training, the organization supplies information to employees; with learning, the organization encourages employees to wonder, question, and find their own answers. Some of the significant contrasts between training and learning are shown in Table 2.

## TABLE 2
### Contrasts Between Training and Learning

| Training | Learning |
|---|---|
| From the outside in, done by others | From the inside out, learner motivated |
| Assumes relative stability | Assumes continuous change |
| Focuses on knowledge, skills, ability, and job performance | Focuses on values, attitudes, innovation, and outcomes |
| Appropriate for developing basic competencies | Helps organizations and individuals learn how to learn and create novel solutions |
| Emphasizes improvement | Emphasizes breakthrough (metanoia) |
| Not necessarily linked to organization's mission and strategies | Directly aligned with organization's vision and requirements for success |
| Structured learning experiences with short-term focus | Formal and informal, long-term future oriented, learner initiated |

## The Learning Organization and Organizational Learning

It is important to note the difference between the terms *learning organization* and *organizational learning*. In discussing learning organizations, we are focusing on the what—the systems, principles, and characteristics of organizations that learn and produce as a collective entity. In discussing organizational learning we are concerned with how organizational learning occurs—the skills and processes of building and utilizing knowledge (Schwandt & Marquardt, 2000). As discussed next, organizational learning is just one aspect of a learning organization.

## Organizational Learning at Accenture

Accenture is the largest consulting firm in the world, as well as a global player within the technology consulting industry. As of 2010, the company had more than 200,000 employees in more than 200 locations in over 120 countries. Accenture's clients include 96 of the *Fortune* Global 100 and more than three quarters of the *Fortune* Global 500.

From its earliest days, Accenture has striven consistently to hire the best people it could find and then provide them with the best training available. A high standard of service to customers has always been a company trademark. In addition, Accenture has been an innovator among the major consulting firms. Having a clearly defined vision, Accenture believes, is critical to organizational learning and achieving business success. To further ensure and expand the learning quality of its staff, Accenture delivers cutting-edge training programs at its learning centers in St. Charles, Illinois; London, England; and Kuala Lumpur, Malaysia.

### TABLE 3
#### Mental Model Shifts at Accenture

| Old | New |
| --- | --- |
| Supervisors | Coaches |
| Workers | Continuous learners |
| Activities | Learning opportunities |
| Workplace | Continuous learning environment |

Becoming a learning organization and a leader in learning dynamics was therefore a natural evolution for Accenture. Let's review the many exciting steps the company has taken on its ongoing journey toward learning as an organization.

## SHIFTS FROM BUSINESS TO LEARNING

The first major change Accenture made was requesting that staff make a shift in their perceptions of their roles, environment, and everyday activities. Everyone was encouraged to transform his or her old mental model of supervisors, workers, activities, and the workplace to a new learning-oriented mental model (see Table 3, which was printed on a 3-by-5 card and distributed to staff).

## FOCUS SHIFTS FROM TRAINING TO LEARNING

Until recently, Accenture's focus, like that of most companies, was on more efficient instruction. Training concentrated on content and instructor, pace, and getting the right answer. This "transmittal training" is based on the following assumptions: All learners have the same basic knowledge and skills; people learn in the same way; listening is the same as learning; and focusing on observable behaviors, not on ways of thinking, is more effective at producing change. This model is not really concerned with what is happening to the learner internally, whether he or she is bored or overwhelmed with the pace of instruction or understands the content well enough to apply it.

Several years ago, Accenture decided that it needed a new approach to professional education. Only with a radical change in training methodology and strategy could the company meet five newly identified training and educational requirements: to develop broader and deeper skills, to build specialists capable of delivering seamless service to clients, to focus on business process change and integration, to balance common and unique skills development, and to adapt to complexity and continual change.

The new learning model at Accenture recognizes that learning the process of getting the right answer is most important. The company's critical task is to make that learning more efficient and effective. The new model of staff development at Accenture centers on learners who choose from among various available tools and resources to acquire the skills and knowledge they need for success. Those who formerly served as instructors have become coaches, mentors, and facilitators.

According to Joel Montgomery, a former education specialist at Accenture's Center for Professional Education, learners are now "much more active in the learning process, and are jointly responsible for their learning. Learners are asked to use what they have learned rather than repeating or identifying what they have been exposed to" (Marquardt, 2002, p. 58).

Accenture now designs its learning programs to stimulate learners to engage in activities that focus on the needs they have identified for themselves. In the process, they are given the tools to reflect on their actions, evaluate them according to specified standards, and give and receive feedback on what they are doing and learning. After they have gone through the process once, Montgomery notes, "we again stimulate them to reengage in learning, bringing with them what they learned the first time, again reflecting on, evaluating, and giving and receiving feedback on what they are doing and learning. This ensures a greater depth of learning."

This view focuses on the learner's internal processes and encourages increased sensitivity to the learner while instruction takes place. Instructional approaches are adjusted to meet the individual learner's needs. This represents a shift from a supply-push instructional approach to what we might call a demand-pull approach.

## SELF-STUDY, POINT-OF-NEED LEARNING

To promote and enable continuous self-development, Accenture focuses on delivering self-study, point-of-need training that provides staff with opportunities to learn by doing as they develop individual skills. Because individual needs typically derive from current job assignments, skills training that is accessible on demand has become increasingly important.

Accenture's training features built-in flexibility for developing critical job skills at the individual level. It emphasizes the increasing need for and benefits of individualized learner-paced instruction, which is increasingly provided on a just-in-time basis because most learning is most effective when it occurs immediately before it is to be applied.

By coupling technology with new learning strategies, Accenture has successfully developed interactive, multimedia self-study training that is significantly more effective than traditional instructor-led training. The firm has demonstrated that effective skills building can be developed within a self-study format.

A key pathway to personal mastery is the development of metacognitive skills, which augments each learner's ability to learn how to learn. Accenture anticipates that such skills will be a key component in future success. The more metacognitive skills an individual gains, the stronger are his or her chances of keeping current with change.

## CONTINUOUS LEARNING

Accenture has placed a major emphasis on learning from experience (including reflection) at all levels of the organization; the company even considers this type of learning the vehicle for building executive skills at the partner level. Throughout the organization, there are efforts to move action learning from the training environment to the overall work environment.

Accenture's coaching and continuous learning framework is one example of the ongoing action learning built into the organization's process. The framework, which is structured around the coach and the learner, is as learner driven as possible.

## COLLABORATIVE LEARNING

Accenture has implemented the practice of collaborative learning, in which the members of small groups learn from one another by working together. This approach creates a rich learning environment by allowing participants to take on various roles, including that of instructor. Collaborative learning promotes the sharing of ideas and knowledge and gives learners the opportunity to review one another's work. It also allows them to coach, model, teach, and learn by using the abilities of individual team members as well as the team's overall synergy as part of the learning process.

## LEARNING FROM OTHERS: GLOBAL BEST PRACTICES

Accenture has placed a high priority on developing and utilizing a global best practices knowledge base. The knowledge base identifies and describes best practices, best companies, engagement experiences, studies and articles, performance measures, diagnostics, process definitions, and Accenture process experts. Workshops on global best practices have been conducted for Accenture staff in offices around the globe. This base represents a powerful tool for learning for Accenture staff and is a valuable service for clients.

## PARTICIPATION IN CONFERENCES AND ASSOCIATIONS

Accenture has a deliberate strategy for gaining and sharing knowledge through training, research, and participation in professional and trade associations. To these ends, it produces publications for internal and external use, such as "Retail Customer Satisfaction and Merchandising,""Physician Health Integration," and "Vital Signs: Using Quality Time and Cost Performance Measures to Chart Your Company's Future."

In order to maximize widespread conference participation throughout the company, Accenture strives to have at least three staff members attend seminars or conferences that are identified as valuable for the firm. The firm encourages employees to serve as presenters at conferences because doing so not only enhances an individual's reputation but directs that person toward quality preparation, research, and learning.

## EXCEL THROUGH LEARNING STRATEGY

Accenture developed the *Excel Through Learning* strategy as another means of achieving its corporate mission. The company has incorporated advanced technologies that enable diverse training development and delivery, powerful and effective education theories, best-practices standards, and a performance support approach, all of which ensure the timeliness and relevance of its learning processes.

## GOAL-BASED SCENARIOS

Accenture recently introduced Goal-Based Scenario (GBS) learning, originated by Roger Schank, director of the Institute for Learning Sciences at Northwestern University. This specialized program is based on task simulations that help participants pinpoint the skills they need and why, the problems they are likely to encounter and when, and the most effective approaches to dealing with those problems and why. Teaching and learning always take place within the context of a clearly perceived need or as part of a larger task. GBS provides a motivational framework that facilitates the acquisition of individual skills and knowledge and enables learners to understand how they can be applied to solve business problems.

GBS contains the following components:

- Learners are presented with an end goal that is motivating and challenging.
- The goal is structured so that learners must build a predetermined core set of skills and knowledge in order to successfully meet it.
- The environment is holistic, with skills and knowledge taught as part of an integrated whole.
- The learning environment is designed to take advantage of the different sets of experiences, cultural backgrounds, interests, and motivations of the learners.
- Learners are able to explore and develop skills other than those of the predetermined set.
- Learners are free to select their own strategies for meeting the end goal.
- Stress levels are managed by appropriate use of reflection, a genuine focus on the learning, and easy-to-use resources that support learners in their pursuit of their end goals.
- Learners use resources as needed, on a just-in-time basis.
- The environment often includes real-world tasks, learners working in teams, and coaches who are experts in both content and process.

---

## Top 10 Strategies for Building Learning Subsystems

### 1. DEVELOP MODULAR, EXCITING, PORTABLE LEARNING CONTENT

The shift to just-in-time learning and greater business ownership is paralleled by another evolution that supports nimbler learning processes. Content—expertise, knowledge, substance, or ideas that enhance the knowledge worker's performance—must itself become nimbler. Leading-edge companies, such as Cisco Systems, AutoDesk, and iPlanet, are developing learning content around the concept of *reusable learning objects*, that is, chunks of content or modularized training programs with pieces that may be used on a stand-alone basis or combined with other chunks to produce a tailored program.

Chunkable learning is one of the great promises of e-learning; in this approach, instructions may be divided into segments and then viewed as needed. When combined with skill-specific assessments, learning objects allow learners to address gaps in a timely, accurate fashion instead of wading through quantities of material they already know. For example, GE Power Systems allows for precise targeting of knowledge about business policies, which follows a detailed architecture describing the knowledge needs of different categories of workers. Cisco chunks its product knowledge to allow faster identification of specific skill gaps and rapid acquisition of necessary knowledge.

Chunkable content is manifested in learning approaches that are shorter, more concise, and segmentable according to need. In addition, these approaches incorporate the understanding that every piece of content can be considered for potential reuse. For example, training for employees can also be used for training customers, administrative communications can also be frontline tools, executive presentations can be divided into critical analyses for audience-specific applications, and FAQs can become knowledge diagnostics for new employees (Manville, 2001).

## 2. INCREASE ORGANIZATION'S ABILITY TO LEARN HOW TO LEARN

Even though most of us attended school for ten, fifteen, or even twenty years, we never learned how to learn. We struggled with remembering facts and relationships, we forgot quickly, and we did not understand the learning process. And yet, according to many leading learning organizations and researchers, a key pathway to personal mastery and more powerful and quicker learning is the development of metacognitive skills, learning how to learn. Only by increasing individual metacognitive skills will each learner be able to stay abreast or ahead of change.

Several years ago, the American Society for Training & Development (ASTD) developed a program to help individuals with the following key skills aimed at learning to learn:

- How to question new information
- How to break up complex ideas and large tasks into smaller parts
- How to test ourselves to see how much we are learning
- How to direct our learning to meet specific goals
- How to accelerate learning

Metacognitive skills enable people to think through, understand, and use new information quickly and confidently; find patterns in information; and focus on the most important information.

## 3. DEVELOP THE DISCIPLINE OF ORGANIZATIONAL DIALOGUE

The discipline of dialogue is central to organizational learning insofar as it enhances and augments team learning. Dialogue forces new ways of viewing the organization's assumptions and creates a cool communications field within which to deal with the hot issues of change and chaos.

Members of the organization can develop an environment that favors dialogue by taking the following actions:

- Regard one another as colleagues
- Adopt a spirit of inquiry
- Suspend assumptions and certainties
- Observe the observer
- Slow down the inquiry

Employees should also have opportunities to practice dialogue with a skilled facilitator who uses the following kind of format. To begin, organize the physical space around a circle to promote a sense of equality among participants. Introduce the concept of dialogue and ask participants to think about effective communications they have experienced. Then ask them to share these instances and identify the qualities that made them effective. Finally, ask the group to reflect on these qualities, always allowing the conversation to flow naturally and giving everyone the opportunity to explore and share.

A number of key points relative to initiating dialogue in your organization will probably emerge. These might include the following:

- How to avoid factors that prevent dialogue (defensiveness, smoothing over, competitiveness)
- How to draw on diversity as a resource rather than a source of conflict
- How to build shared visions and reflect on ways of looking at the world
- How to improve observation, listening, and communication skills
- How to utilize listening and feedback to minimize distortion of information and blocked communication channels
- How to balance advocacy with inquiry as a means to overcoming impasses

## 4. DESIGN CAREER DEVELOPMENT PLANS FOR EMPLOYABILITY

The pace of change requires each employee to take a proactive stance toward learning. Every person should have a clearly articulated career development plan that outlines a combination of formal and informal learning activities to be completed and a timetable for completing them.

Many learning organizations (notably, Royal Bank of Canada, Nokia, and PPG Industries) work closely with staff to develop an individual development plan (IDP) that serves a number of purposes, such as the following:

- Allows individualized self-development of employees, using methods such as courses, self-learning, and mentoring, among others
- Provides sequenced learning that permits employees to learn what they need to know just before they need to apply it
- Instills a commitment to self-management in each employee
- Holds each employee accountable for achieving his or her learning goals
- Helps develop lifetime employability

The human resources department should be available to assist in identifying available learning resources, such as courses, mentors, conferences, or agencies. Supervisors should encourage ongoing learning, provide time and support for outside learning opportunities, and assist in long-range planning.

## 5. ESTABLISH SELF-DEVELOPMENT PROGRAMS

Learning organizations should encourage and expect all employees to continuously learn, and to learn what will enable them to develop skills that will be of benefit to them and to their organizations. Performance reviews should include planning for and assessment of the individual's self-development program. Organizations should provide time, resources, and opportunities that will generate ongoing learning for their workers. Giving employees small cash allowances for their own self-development perhaps best demonstrates a company's commitment to continuous learning. Encouraging employees to develop personal interests to their fullest potential creates people who enjoy learning and are better prepared to adapt to future personal and organizational change.

## 6. BUILD TEAM LEARNING SKILLS

Teams are to learning organizations as families are to the community. Teams form the connections between individual and organizational learning and enable the organization to recognize and capitalize on latent resources within its workforce. Therefore, organizations must be committed to team learning, growth, and development; they should seek to build teams that are able to create and capture learning.

Team learning can occur every time a group of people is brought together. It emphasizes self-managed learning and the free flow of ideas and creativity among members. There are a variety of ways in which teams learn, such as by generating knowledge through analysis of complex issues, innovative action, and collective problem solving.

The following specific steps will enhance team learning:

- Establish team responsibility for learning
- Reward teams for the learning they contribute to the organization
- Develop and practice team learning activities
- Build capability to achieve metalogue, a state in which the team thinks and feels as a group, creates shared assumptions and culture, and works as an organic whole

## 7. ENCOURAGE AND PRACTICE SYSTEMS THINKING

An absolutely critical skill for learning organizations is that of systems thinking, the capacity to "see and work with the flow of life as a system rather than dissecting and trying to fix the problematic parts" (Senge, 2006). The ability to think about the big picture while seeing the underlying, unexpected influences is rare and difficult to develop, but it is an essential skill for "smart" learning.

The following elements of systems thinking will be most valuable when practiced throughout the organization:

- Focus on areas of high leverage
- Avoid symptomatic solutions and concentrate on underlying causes
- Distinguish detail complexity (when there are many variables) from dynamic complexity (when the connection between cause and effect is not obvious or consequences are subtle over time)
- See interrelationships, not things
- See process, not snapshots
- See that people and problems are part of a single system
- Recognize the difference between systems and fragmentation thinking

## 8. UTILIZE SCANNING AND SCENARIO PLANNING

A primary purpose of ongoing scanning of the environment is to prepare for future changes that are most likely to affect the organization. Organizations that are best at anticipating the future and using planning as a learning opportunity are the ones that will be most able and prepared to adapt. Developing scenarios about possible futures is an excellent method for anticipatory learning. By monitoring key trends, accessing strategic research, and analyzing the data, an organization has a better chance of determining what is important to learn.

## 9. EXPAND MULTICULTURAL AND GLOBAL MIND-SETS AND LEARNING

Learning organizations realize that different views and ways of doing things are a source of richness, not a conflict. The more open we are to the values, ideas, and perspectives of others, the greater the possibilities for individual and corporate learning.

Diversity initiatives work best when they are integrated into a larger system of business practices, such as total quality management, team-building reengineering, and employee empowerment. All share a commitment to continuous learning.

## 10. CHANGE THE MENTAL MODEL OF LEARNING

Most people still retain a negative picture of learning, the one they acquired in their school days—hard work, impossible tests, tough teachers, irrelevant facts, control, memorization, drills, long hours at desks, and so on. These mental models cause many to resist a lifelong commitment to learning and belonging to a learning organization. Jim Gannon, former senior vice president of human resource planning and development at Royal Bank of Canada, states that the bank is reluctant to use the term *learning* because of employees' negative associations with their school experiences (Schwandt & Marquardt, 2000).

Unless the mental model of learning changes, efforts on the part of senior management to build learning organizations will be doomed to failure because workers will not practice new ideas. The internal images held by employees will confine them to past perceptions of learning institutions. Since mental models have a powerful effect on our actions, it is important to change the mind-set that equates *learning* with *schoolroom* and replace it with one that envisions learning as an exciting, collaborative, highly rewarding enterprise. The mental model for learning organizations must be revitalized with feelings of energy, excitement, business success, personal responsibility, fun, integration, sharing, and personal and organizational growth. Once this image is established, individuals and organizations will want to jump quickly onto the bandwagon.

Through training, management communications, and continual practice, organizations can help employees become more aware of their mental models and acquire the means to better reflect on, surface, and examine them. In doing so, these individuals will be able to participate enthusiastically in the learning efforts of their organizations.

# CHAPTER 4

# Transforming the Organization for Learning Excellence

The organization is the structure and body in which and for which individual, group, and overall learning occurs. To go from a non-learning to a learning organization requires a significant transformation, similar to the metamorphosis from caterpillar to butterfly. The caterpillar undergoes some messy transitions on its way to becoming a butterfly. The raw protoplasm in the cocoon re-forms (reengineering, restructuring, refocusing) to become a butterfly, a beautiful creature with the power to fly in all directions, to flow with the wind or find safety from it.

A company's structure and strategies must change in comparably dramatic ways before it can become a learning organization. To flourish as this new kind of entity, the company must reconfigure itself by focusing on the four dimensions of the organization subsystem: vision, culture, strategy, and structure (see Figure 10). Each of the four dimensions must change in purpose and design from one focused solely on work and productivity to one that is equally focused on learning and development.

## Vision

Shared vision gives individuals and the organization "stars to steer by." It is hard to think of any organization that has achieved and sustained some measure of greatness without a deeply shared vision. Taco Bell's vision is to

**FIGURE 10**   Organization Subsystem

become "number one in the stomach"; Federal Express delivers packages "absolutely, positively overnight"; Panasonic aims to be the "No.1 Green Innovation Company in the Electronics Industry in 2018," the one hundredth anniversary of its founding. Each of these organizations are able to bind people together around a common identity and sense of destiny.

The first and probably most important step in becoming a learning organization is building a solid foundation based on a shared vision of learning. Along with this, the company must understand that unless it becomes a learning organization, it cannot achieve its vision. There are many reasons why the shared vision of being a learning organization is so important.

First, shared vision provides the focus and energy for learning. Powerful, generative learning occurs only when people are truly committed to accomplishments that matter deeply to them.

Second, vision impels people toward action. It represents their hopes and dreams and provides meaning for them. Shared vision and values enable people to examine their established ways of thinking and give them reason to surrender deeply held views and accept new ways of thinking and acting. The loftiness of the target acts as a rudder that keeps learning processes on course should stresses or other distractions develop.

Third, the pull toward a highly desired goal counteracts the overwhelming force of the status quo. Vision establishes an over-arching goal, and shared vision encourages risk taking and innovation. Jim Gannon, former senior vice president of human resource planning and development for Royal Bank of Canada, underscores the decisive importance of vision for learning as an organization when he says that "visions are what energize the organization"; they are "the dreams that pull us forward" (Marquardt, 2002).

Fourth, shared values and meaning are important in determining the kind of knowledge an organization stores and transfers. This point will be examined in detail when we explore the knowledge subsystem in chapter 6.

Vision can and should guide strategic thinking and planning as well as lead to multiple strategies and procedures for becoming a learning organization. This occurs when all stakeholders—managers, employees at all levels, customers, partners, shareholders—are urged to become involved in developing the vision.

Learning organizations are living organisms, not machines. Much like human beings, they need a collective sense of identity and a fundamental purpose. Visions should be exhilarating. They should create the spark and excitement that empower the organization to develop renowned, visionary products. Learning must be a part of that vision.

## A Mission and Vision of Growth at Shangri-La Hotels and Resorts

In 2010, Shangri-La Hotels and Resorts had more than seventy hotels and 40,000 employees, with a vision to double within five years, all while maintaining their unique culture of high-quality caring and hospitality. In recent years, the hotel chain has won almost every global award, including Asia's Best Hotel Brand for Business and Vacation, Best Luxury Hotel Chain (*Asiamoney*), Best Business Hotel Brand in Asia Pacific (*Business Traveler*), and Top Five Best Overseas Hotel (*Observer and Guardian*).

Shangri-La has a powerful vision for its employees as well as its guests. Employee learning and development is an integral role in Shangri-La and is part of the company's mission, which states that its aim includes "enabling all employees to achieve their personal and professional growth." Eng Leong Tan, Director for HR, notes, "We seek to be the first-choice employer among hospitality workers. We are committed to providing an environment in which employees can learn and grow. It is not enough just to pay well and offer good benefits. Growth opportunities are equally important, especially to younger employees" (ASTD, 2009, p. 58).

Shangri-La backs this mission with a financial commitment: to spend 4 percent of payroll on training and development. Recently, training has been transformed from instructor-led delivery to experiential learning environments that include interactive group exercises and role play. For instance, a series of animated videos illustrated customer interaction scenarios and demonstrated cultural challenges. Training cascades down: the hotel general manager trains his or her subordinates, and this process continues downward until all are skilled via train the trainer.

Employees who exhibit desired skills are designated as "angels" and serve as exemplars for their counterparts. To ensure sustainability and maintain strong succession-planning practices, Shangri-La has developed the PASS (Prepare, Accountability, Support, celebrate Success) process, the ultimate result of which will be a database of individual skills that can be compared to organizational needs. Over 60 percent of employees have documentation of individual competencies, most of these in the key areas of leadership, management, supervision, and technical skills. Training and development activities are linked to business needs and defined objectives (ASTD, 2009, p. 59).

# Culture

Just as nations have distinct cultures, organizations have distinct ways of believing, thinking, and acting that are manifested by symbols, heroes, rituals, ideology, and values. The nature of learning and the manner in which it occurs are determined in large measure by organizational culture.

The culture of most organizations is one of non-learning, if not actually anti-learning. Taking risks, trying new approaches, and sharing information may be discouraged, whereas "not making waves" may be rewarded. Before such a company can become a learning organization, it must transform these cultural values.

Values complement the pulling force of an organization's vision by pushing the company to reach that vision. A corporate learning culture is characterized by a number of values that push that organization up the learning ladder.

## VALUING AND REWARDING LEARNING

Learning organizations provide a facilitative climate that encourages and prizes learning. Learners are the heroes. Learning is recognized when performances are appraised, at award ceremonies, and in paychecks and incentive plans that compensate employees for acquiring new knowledge.

In learning organizations, learning processes (learning how to learn) are considered as important as, if not more important than, the learning content. The ability to define learning needs is as important as finding answers. Opportunities are created across the organization to develop knowledge, skills, and attitudes. Continuous learning is essential for survival and success in today's world.

3M Corporation provides an excellent example of a climate that encourages and rewards learning. Employees are allowed to devote up to 15 percent of their workday to their own projects. 3M has also created the Pathfinder Award, which recognizes those who "develop new products or a new application of a product for a particular country or culture." Over the past decade, hundreds of different awards were conferred on different work teams; those creative ideas resulted in billions of dollars in sales.

## SHARED RESPONSIBILITY FOR LEARNING

Employees are responsible for their own learning as well as the learning of others. They must also understand the relationship between their responsibilities and the goals of the organization as a whole. Employees are expected to teach and learn from their coworkers. The entire workplace culture is geared to organizational learning.

## Linking Learning and Culture at Shell Oil Company

Royal Dutch Shell, commonly known as Shell, is a global oil and gas company headquartered in The Hague, Netherlands. In 2010, it was the largest energy company and the second-largest company in the world measured by revenues, with more than 100,000 employees working in nearly 100 countries. Shell Oil Company (SOC) is the United States-based subsidiary of Royal Dutch Shell, with approximately 22,000 Shell employees based in the U.S. The head office in the U.S. is in Houston, Texas.

Several years ago, SOC undertook a transformation based on learning, planning, and leadership changes. Internally, the organization's focus was the human system, and, externally, it was concerned with the immediate customer and business environment. The dominant culture at Shell was difficult to change because the company, like most organizations, tended to perpetuate its thinking by selecting new members in its own image.

While Shell globally had begun to hire systems thinkers and people who see an organization's current reality as only one of many long-term possibilities, SOC was heavily populated with event thinkers, people who view current developments as inevitable and corporate life as a series of unrelated events. While the changing environment of the petroleum industry cried out for a reexamination of mental models, little reexamination occurred at SOC. Instead, the U.S. company was characterized by a parochial, short-term orientation that was typical of American corporations of the 1990s (Brenneman, Keys, and Fulmer, 1998).

Shell Oil Company clung tenaciously to its mental models, including confidence in a continued price of $30 for a barrel of oil and a success model based on cash generation through performance improvement achieved by short-term cost reduction. In the 1980s, SOC was not a model of organizational learning, and little changed until the early 1990s, when a new CEO, Phil Carroll, arrived on the heels of the worst business results in years. Carroll wasted no time in seeking alternative paths for the company.

In the years that followed, Phil Carroll led SOC toward a significant transformation of its corporate culture. The new culture comprises a new vision, a new business model, a new system of governance, a new concept of leadership, and the use of learning both as the foundation of SOC's transformation and as a permanent part of its culture. The transformation, initially known as the Learning and Development Initiative, began with a process designed to create a mission, with a vision and values powerful enough to engage the minds and hearts of the company's people.

The dialogue that emerged from this process also invited people to look within themselves and discover their personal visions. The new business model allows the company's leaders to build winning strategies by recognizing the points at which they can exert the greatest leverage and add the most value. Through the model, employees gain a better understanding of their individual contributions to the company.

To unleash the potential of SOC's people, the company has moved toward systems of governance that disperse authority and responsibility throughout the organization and create a greater sense of ownership and enlarged opportunities for personal growth. Shell Oil Company believes that leadership skills can be broadened and deepened in everyone. Through leadership development workshops, the company is helping managers understand their own potential and discover new ways of thinking and acting. These transformational activities are taking place under the Learning and Performance (LEAP) program. This corporate initiative provides the framework within which both individual and collective learning take place. The company believes that the most powerful learning experiences, the ones that produce the fastest and most lasting results, are those in which real people are engaged in finding real solutions to real problems—in other words, an action learning process.

Throughout Shell Oil Company, conditions for learning must be created by new or transformed power holders who articulate, model, and reinforce learning attributes. Training or experiential workshops cannot replace these conditions. Top management develops such workplace attributes as clearly defined goals, roles, and expectations; openness; curiosity about alternatives; respect; and attentive listening. Honesty about current cultural reality frees the organization from unacknowledged factors that constrain learning and performance. Management is expected to model accountability and insist on rigorous, fact-based, systemic reasoning instead of event thinking. These attributes make up the company's new corporate culture.

Shell Oil Company defines organizational learning competencies for leaders as the ability to build shared vision, an in-depth knowledge of the business, the skill to think systemically, and the ability to communicate through open and honest dialogue. Although these competencies are established at the corporate level, they are not viewed as edicts from on high. LEAP actually works with the operating units to convince them of the expediency of these competencies and of the need for leaders to find opportunities to teach their subordinates.

## TRUST AND AUTONOMY

In learning organizations, people trust and care for one another. Inadequacies can be disclosed without fear of consequences. The culture encourages feedback and disclosure. There are daily opportunities to learn from experience. Managers see their prime task as facilitating members' experimentation and learning from experience, and they make time to seek feedback on their success with facilitating learning.

Despite the high degree of interdependence, people are able to make decisions on their own and are expected to do so because many occasions will require autonomous action.

## INCENTIVES FOR INNOVATION, EXPERIMENTATION, AND RISK TAKING

Learning organizations take brave, bold steps to encourage as many people as possible to experiment, innovate, and get out of the habit of asking for permission and waiting for instructions. They realize that risks are a necessary part of achieving quantum leaps in product and service quality.

To attain and sustain competitive advantages in this new environment, organizations will have to learn better and faster from their successes and failures. They must be able to continuously transform themselves into learning organizations, to become places where groups and individuals are constantly involved in new learning processes. The organization promotes responsible risk taking and being open to new approaches and processes. Mistakes are not only allowed but valued because they can be the source of new ideas and new ways of doing things.

In companies such as Ford and Harley-Davidson, core values include intellectual curiosity, which means challenging the status quo, looking for ways to improve learning, and pursuing new approaches to meeting and exceeding customer expectations.

## Financial Commitment to Training and Development

Learning companies make strong commitments to providing the financial and human resources necessary to improve the learning quality of their staffs. J. Y. Pillay, former chairman of Singapore Airlines, went so far as to state that "our company's self-respect will be eroded, if we do not pay attention to the training needs of all our employees" (Marquardt, 2002, p. 80). The airline commits more than 12 percent of total payroll costs to learning. Learning organizations such as Federal Express, General Electric, and Motorola are not far behind. Over the past ten years, ASTD has conducted studies that consistently demonstrate the correlation between investments in training and overall business success, which are reported in its Annual States of the Industry reports.

### COLLABORATIVE CREATIVITY, VARIETY, AND DIVERSITY

A learning culture is one in which there is collaborative creativity in all contexts, relationships, and experiences, and the measure of success is the combined wisdom and the synergy of the organization. The whole culture learns in a self-aware, self-reflective, and creative way.

Operational variety is also encouraged so as to generate more ways of accomplishing organizational goals. An organization that supports variations in strategy, policy, process, structure, and personnel will be more adaptable when unforeseen challenges arise.

In learning organizations, different learning styles are recognized and appreciated. No single style is necessarily deemed best because an adaptive, innovative organization needs many styles, each of which can mitigate any deficiencies of the others.

### COMMITMENT TO CONTINUOUS PRODUCT AND SERVICE IMPROVEMENTS

Organizations committed to quality take continuous improvement seriously because one question is always uppermost in everyone's mind: "How can we do this better?" Quality management requires a comprehensive learning approach with all members of the organization engaged in continuous learning. A learning culture seeks world-class standards in quality and service. Its pride and high self-esteem are linked to the high quality of its service, products, and operations.

## RESPONSIVENESS TO CHANGE AND CHAOS

A learning culture does not fear constant change and chaos; instead, it evidences an excitement and determination to vigorously and creatively respond to new challenges. Chaos provides the opportunity for higher levels of learning, innovation, and breakthrough technology. As Harrison Owen (1998) notes, "Chaos creates the differences that make a difference, through which we can learn" (p. 29).

## QUALITY OF WORK LIFE

Learning organizations are committed to the development of the full range of human potential in an environment that invites participation and enjoyment. Work is exciting and challenging because both mental and physical talents are being tapped. The social and physical surroundings encourage respect for each person. People care about one another.

## Organizational Learning at Canadian Imperial Bank of Commerce

Canadian Imperial Bank of Commerce (CIBC), a financial services company with more than 42,000 employees worldwide, is a global leader in credit card products and PC banking. CIBC also operates in the United States, the Caribbean, Asia, and the United Kingdom, and it serves more than eleven million clients. CIBC invests heavily in employee development each year, with emphases on skills enhancement, relationship building, and leadership training.

Michele Darling, executive vice president of human resources, describes the former barriers to creating a culture of organizational learning at CIBC: "The formal decision to become a learning organization can yield some very practical benefits, but it imposes additional demands." For example, a direct focus on knowledge can "unchannel conventional thinking, but it also questions conventional organization" (Marquardt, 2002, p. 82). It may also increase responsibilities for some individuals and change those of management. Inevitably, it focuses attention on recognizing barriers. Darling adds,

We all have heard the adage that "knowledge is power." In most organizations, what this really means is that knowledge is saved and put on display at the most opportune moment—likely when the boss is in the room. Rarely is knowledge shared with others at an equivalent level in other parts of the organization. Knowledge hoarding has the added advantage of never having to expose the fact that your knowledge may be partial or stale! People generally use their unique knowledge to reaffirm their position in the organization; if others knew what you knew, then how valuable would you be to your organization? What happens to your indispensability if you dump your knowledge into a pool, where others can take it and make it theirs? There is also the all-too-familiar phenomenon of "not invented here." This is the inevitable urge to disparage the really insightful idea or insight that comes from outside our organization or group simply because we did not think of it ourselves.

These reactions are understandable. The challenge is to break free of such traditional approaches to learning and managing knowledge in the organization. The first step is to create a knowledge culture. An organization's culture is not decreed by management memo and does not happen by accident. It is the collection of shared values and beliefs that accumulates over time, the unstated consensus of common understandings and conventions, or "the way things work around here."

So, what is a knowledge culture? Darling notes:

We do not yet have a neat, tight definition, but we have developed some insights into its essential characteristics. A knowledge culture:

1. Values knowledge and puts that knowledge where needed. Knowledge is placed directly at the customer's service and into the hands of the people who deal with the customer.
2. Democratizes knowledge. It is delinked from the individual holder, transferred to others and valued according to its effectiveness in dealing with problems and meeting customer needs.
3. Values diversity. It recognizes that new ideas and insights are not the preserve of age, experience, race, or gender.
4. Has a subversive effect on traditional management hierarchies. Instead of operating in command-and-control mode, managers must become coaches, advisers and cheerleaders for their teams, and facilitators, brokers and networkers to link their teams with others in the organization.
5. Always has its eye on what academics call the "knowledge grid." Succinctly, the knowledge grid examines what we know we know, what we know we don't know, what we don't know we know, and what we don't know we don't know. (Marquardt, 2002, 82–83)

# Strategy

A number of powerful, leveraged strategies can quickly and successfully enable an organization to transform itself into a learning organization. In this section, we will explore a number of key, powerful strategies.

## ALIGN ORGANIZATIONAL LEARNING WITH BUSINESS AND PERSONAL SUCCESS

Probably the most important strategy for inspiring and motivating an entire organization to move quickly and emphatically toward becoming a learning organization is to link increased learning with increased organizational success. This shows that learning is the only source of sustainable strategic advantage for the company.

Businesses know that, in the long run, strategic and competitive advantages accrue to organizations with core competencies that enable them to create new products or services swiftly and thus adapt to rapidly changing conditions. These core competencies represent the collective learning of the organization.

Human resource development professionals explicitly link learning events and outcomes to business needs and strategic goals by undertaking the following actions:

- Map out the relationship between strategic goals and areas such as job behaviors, job skills, job success indicators, and business objectives.
- Design pre-learning activities, learning-event activities, and post-learning activities that are integrated into key business processes.
- Create an iterative process of delivery, feedback, and redesign for achieving effective and timely learning that keeps pace with shifting business goals.

## BUILD LEARNING INTO ALL OPERATIONS

Learning organizations quickly and deliberately plan and structure learning into all organizational processes, such as design, manufacturing, marketing, and accounting. After firms begin to incorporate learning processes into practical work settings, they will see dramatic results.

For example, at Ford Motor Company, a car-development learning laboratory uses a computer simulator and related tools to aid systems thinking and methods of enhancing reflection and conversation. The laboratory helped a development team assemble a manufacturing prototype at full line speed—a first at Ford—which allowed advanced testing of assembly processes. The prototype was voted the highest quality ever by Ford's manufacturing organization; with the exception of minor adjustments, the vehicle was completed a record ten months early.

The value chain of any organization should include a domain of integrated learning. This means thinking of the value chain as an integrated learning system. When considering each major step of the work process, beginning with strategic planning and continuing through to customer service, think of how to constantly engage in learning experiments. Thus, structures and processes for achieving outcomes may be viewed simultaneously as operational tasks and learning exercises.

Organizations must fundamentally redesign work so that producing and learning are inextricably intertwined. In such settings, organizational work becomes a practice field that allows for the kind of continual movement between performance and practice that characterizes learning in sports and the performing arts.

If learning occurs through planning and experience, it follows that guided experiences will lead to more learning. Until companies understand that organizing for production at any stage of the value chain is a learning experiment as well as a production activity, learning will happen slowly. Managers must act like applied research scientists even as they are delivering goods and services. When an organization systematically and deliberately builds learning capacity by integrating learning and production, it is also building performance capability.

## Connecting Business and Learning at Deloitte

Deloitte Touche Tohmatsu Limited (Deloitte), which employs more than 170,000 people in 150 countries, is the largest professional services company in the world, delivering audit, tax, consulting, enterprise risk, and financial advisory services through its member firms. Deloitte generated a global consulting revenue of $6.5 billion in 2010. Recently, Deloitte reevaluated and retooled its people strategy, building on its corporate philosophy that holds lifelong employee learning as one of its four tenets.

The coaching initiative is one way in which the strategy is put into practice. Jennifer Gardner, former director of national education and development at Deloitte, noted that

Deloitte's "people strategy is a living, breathing part of [the] organization, and coaching gives employees a real way to experience it." Kathryn Hallenstein, national e-learning director, added, "Our employee learning is now more aligned with business objectives and thereby more relevant. We are focusing on application-based training" (ASTD, 2007a, p. 44).

At Deloitte, every employee has an individual learning plan. Deloitte's Global Excellence model maps competencies to professional development and links them to performance expectations that include explicit behavior measures. Employees are accountable for mandated training. Performance rating and compensation can be negatively affected by noncompliance. In addition, managers and partners are compelled to allow their staff to participate in developmental opportunities.

Gardner noted that Deloitte wants "to be a thought leader in learning. As learning becomes more important, we are proud to say that Deloitte takes a broad view of learning as a strategic initiative and makes smart investments" (ASTD, 2007a, p. 44).

To determine those investments and to set priorities, Deloitte arranges for learning and development leaders to consult with business function leaders annually to set a direction for learning that will help the company meet its business goals. Learning directors confer with practice leaders to determine key initiatives and strategies for each function, and then develop plans and budgets based on the needs indentified. The resulting prioritized initiatives for the year are thus closely connected between learnings and actions.

## DEVELOP PERSONNEL POLICIES THAT BUILD LEARNING ORGANIZATIONS

Personnel policies that reward learning are among the most efficient ways to introduce learning and learners into an organization. Learning organizations recruit and hire people who continually learn, who enjoy expanding and exploring their potential. Under these policies, dedicated learners who enhance learning in others are promoted to supervisory positions. Non-learners are encouraged to learn or seek employment elsewhere.

## RECOGNIZE AND REWARD LEARNING

"That which gets rewarded gets done" is a valid and well-respected maxim in learning organizations. Learners, especially learning teams, are promoted and receive bonuses, recognition, and praise. New ideas that lead to better services or products result in "royalties" for their originators. People who collect and transfer knowledge from internal or external sources are commended. Performance appraisals evaluate learning acquired and distributed on an equal basis with other factors. Teamwork is encouraged, and the ability to build and motivate teams and team learning is generously rewarded.

### MEASURE AND BROADCAST THE IMPACT AND BENEFITS OF LEARNING

Companies that hope to become learning organizations should develop a variety of ways to measure learning. Focusing only on the typical measures of output (cost or price) ignores learning that affects other competitive values, such as quality, delivery, or new product introductions.

One of the most innovative and valuable tools for measuring learning is the half-life curve, developed by Analog Devices, a leading learning organization. A half-life curve measures the time it takes to achieve a 50 percent improvement in a specified performance measure. By logic, companies that take less time to improve must be learning faster than their peers, and, in the long run, their short learning cycles will translate into superior performance.

South African Breweries (SAB) sought to demonstrate the economic value added (defined as net operating profit less operating costs) between learning and such areas as cost savings and profit levels. SAB discovered that if its learning is focused and based on high-performance systems, and if sound instructional design principles are augmented by performance support factors such as leadership, learning culture, standards of operation, and feedback mechanisms, then greater profits and success occur (ASTD, 2001).

## Measuring Learning at Whirlpool

Whirlpool is another example of a learning organization that carefully measures nonfinancial factors as well as financial ones. During his tenure as Whirlpool CEO, David Whitwam announced that the four value-creating objectives of the organization (cost, quality, productivity, and customer satisfaction) would be measured publicly on an annual basis. Continuously tracking these objectives, Whitwam stated, "would become a powerful tool" in maintaining Whirlpool's learning power.

Whirlpool began building its measurement system by benchmarking companies such as Fiat, Hitachi, Mitsubishi, and Nestlé so as to obtain appropriate standards for world-class performance. "Unless you put visible measures in place that you can quantify, it is very hard for people to manage them," according to Ralph Hake, then corporate controller for Whirlpool.

Nonfinancial measures are now analyzed at bimonthly board meetings, not only to examine results, but also to identify correlations between financial and nonfinancial factors. Identifying areas for improvement and constantly developing the measurement tools are areas of intense focus. Hake proclaimed that "Whirlpool ... significantly improved its learning and its performance" by using nonfinancial measures. Board member Robert Burnett, retired chairman and CEO of Meredith Corporation and a member of several other boards, said that, relative to measurement, Whirlpool is "doing a better job than anyone else in the industry."

## CREATE A LARGE NUMBER OF LEARNING OPPORTUNITIES

Generally, an environment that contains greater opportunities for learning produces more and better learning. Learning organizations build in both the desire and the opportunity to learn. Action and reflective learning is a regular part of day-to-day corporate activity.

Companies that favor learning call on renowned specialists from inside and outside the organization, either in person or using media such as video, audio, e-mail, and teleconferences. They design learning forums with explicit learning goals in mind. Strategic reviews and planning are seen as golden learning opportunities for the whole corporation. Learning also takes place as people examine the changing competitive environment and the company's product portfolio, technology, and market position. Systems audits offer yet another opportunity for learning.

In addition, internal benchmarking reports, which identify and compare best-in-class activities within the organization, may also serve as learning opportunities. Outside activities include study missions, to analyze and understand the performance and distinctive skills of leading organizations around the world, and jamborees or symposiums that bring together customers, suppliers, outside experts, or internal groups to share ideas and learn from one another.

## SET ASIDE TIME FOR LEARNING

Making time for learning is one of the most important steps in building a learning organization. Learners need time to reflect and analyze, think about strategic plans, dissect customer needs, assess current work systems, and develop new products. Learning is difficult when employees are harried or rushed and can easily be diminished by the pressures of the moment. Frequent learning occurs only when top management explicitly frees up employees' time for it.

## CREATE A PHYSICAL ENVIRONMENT FAVORABLE TO LEARNING

We all know that the physical environment has an effect on the quality and quantity of learning. We simply don't learn well in noisy, crowded, dreary surroundings. Companies can create environments that serve learning in a number of ways, including removing dividing walls; constructing colorful and open central courtyards, atriums, and balconies; and installing many large windows. Changes such as these create physical settings that encourage sharing and demonstrate corporate commitment to continuous experimentation as a means of institutionalized learning. Nokia's new headquarters in Finland was built to encourage creativity, learning, and excitement.

## MAXIMIZE ON-THE-JOB LEARNING

Most organizations now recognize that up to 90 percent of learning occurs at work. It is therefore highly productive for managers and other employees to not only appreciate the learning that occurs but also create ongoing learning opportunities and strive to build a learning-reflecting mentality.

## MAKE LEARNING "JUST IN TIME," NOT "JUST IN CASE"

As business speeds up and the demands of customers, partners, and other value contributors change with greater speed, workers need the relevant knowledge more quickly. One-week training courses and off-site programs become harder to justify due to their decreasing ability to provide immediately usable learning. As mentioned earlier, promptly applied learning is usually retained for maximum benefit.

The answer is to tilt toward just-in-time learning. Increase investment in flexible learning tools and support for frontline staff who need knowledge for customer-related value on demand. Make content modularized and reusable.

Manville (2001) notes that just-in-time learning is "tricky for any organization to implement. It requires a foundational technical infrastructure that is multifaceted, flexible, and scalable, one that is able to deliver documents, learning programs, virtual product samples, and personalized expertise over broad domains and often beyond the boundaries of the traditional organization" (p. 40). In addition, just-in-time learning requires sophisticated knowledge inventory and content-owner management to ensure smooth and responsive delivery and output. Fundamentally, it requires a deep, overall organizational capability to "develop content quickly and adapt it to frontline needs rapidly through a process of ongoing experimentation, feedback, and refinement" (p. 40).

Just-in-time learning must be balanced by the understanding that classroom and formal instruction may also have their uses: For example, at Ford, employees still participate in instructional labs on repairing engines. Organizations should also determine the best methods of leveraging just-in-time learning with the use of other, supporting processes.

For example, take the case of the Dow Chemical Company. Realizing that it needed a clear strategy to help employees at all levels understand the reasons behind a recent corporate reengineering effort and to promote alignment among staff, Dow created the Leadership Development Network (LDN), a "revolutionary approach to training based upon adult learning strategies that stimulate thought processes and discussion."

Dow's goals include increased knowledge of business fundamentals, company strategy, and critical business issues, as well as recognition of each employee's contributions to company success. Outcomes are measured by employee surveys, which show that the LDN program is a positive learning experience: Employees are retaining information acquired in LDN sessions well after the seminars are over; and employee morale, satisfaction, and business knowledge have increased. Although it is difficult to link organizational learning directly to financial outputs, Dow Chemical's financial results have outperformed historic levels and analysts' predictions.

## Organization Structure

Structure imposes a powerful directive on a company's life and people. It determines the work organization, performance monitoring, lines of communication, decision-making processes, and degree of internal control that will exist in the firm.

Although form should follow function, the opposite is often the case; as a result, the form or structure of many organizations prevents them from ever beginning the journey toward corporate-wide learning. Rigid boundaries, bulky size, disjointed projects and tasks, and bureaucratic restrictions all help kill rather than nourish learning.

The structural characteristics of learning organizations, however, exhibit flexibility, openness, freedom, and opportunity. Boundaries are highly permeable, thus maximizing the flow of information and exposing the organization to its experiences. The firm's structure is based on the need to learn, and the driving organizing principle is to put the necessary freedom, support, and resources in the hands of the people who need them. As tasks, needs, and people change, the structure changes so that employees and customers alike can respond and grow. Ultimately, what best allows and supports learning establishes the guidelines for building corporate structure.

## FLAT, STREAMLINED HIERARCHY

Tall, rigid hierarchies with impregnable department silos are a bane to learning because they block the fast and unimpeded flow of knowledge that is essential to being competitive. Power and authority cannot extend to the point of greatest impact, further diminishing the organization's interest in and ability to learn. A flat, streamlined structure that incorporates team collaboration and few modes of control maximizes the flow of knowledge and learning.

## SEAMLESS, OPEN-ENDED, AND HOLISTIC

A learning organization should feature fluid, unbounded structures with no divisional barriers. Boundaries inhibit the flow of knowledge; they keep individuals and groups isolated and tend to reinforce preconceptions, distrust, and bias.

A culture that focuses on maximizing organizational learning capability builds learning that crosses all boundaries. Employees possess a holistic, systemic view of organizational life and all its systems, processes, and relationships. There is integration and intimacy between management, employees, customers, competitors, and community. These factors make it possible for learning organizations to better understand and appreciate the changing needs and successes of people within and outside the organization.

## PROJECT-BASED ORGANIZATION AND IMPLEMENTATION

In the future, an increasing majority of work will be done by project teams, which are more capable of responding to and serving the needs and interests of customers. The life of a project team may be indefinite or only a few hours. Dynamic, short-lived project configurations will be commonplace, and employees may work with four to five project teams a year, with the same or different colleagues forming the teams. The smaller size, quickness, and accountability of project teams encourage greater efficiency in learning processes and more applicable knowledge.

## NETWORKING

Effective learning organizations understand the critical need to collaborate, share, and synergize with resources both inside and outside the company. The network structure—which may include global alliances, informal ties among teams that work across functions, and new means of sharing information—uses a variety of connecting tools such as management information systems and videoconferences. These methods provide a form and style that is fluid and adaptable.

A traditional corporate structure, no matter how much it reorganizes or downsizes, cannot muster the speed, flexibility, and focus needed in today's highly competitive marketplace. Networks are faster, smarter, and more flexible, functioning as small companies within large companies, which is indispensable for organizational learning and global success. Networks differ from teams or task forces in three ways: They are not temporary, they solve problems that have been assigned to them as well as act on their own initiative, and they are able to make substantive operating decisions for themselves.

## SMALL UNITS THAT THINK ENTREPRENEURIALLY

Learning organizations, no matter what their size, are structured to operate with the dynamism and entrepreneurial spirit of new, small companies. Why? Because when a working unit becomes too large, and communications and commitment are lessened, knowledge and empowerment are lost.

Asea Brown Boveri (ABB) is an excellent example of a large learning organization that has achieved the advantages of a small company, or many small companies. With more than $30 billion in sales per year and about 100,000 employees working in 100 countries worldwide, ABB is streamlined into 5,000 autonomous profit centers, each containing no more than 50 people.

## ELIMINATE BUREAUCRACIES

General Electric, a successful learning organization, has stated that "a passion for excellence requires hatred of bureaucracy and all that goes with it." Royal Bank of Canada believes that an organization should centralize paper but decentralize people. Staff should clear out meaningless forms and policies that create gridlock and strangle learning. Fewer boundaries and bureaucracies allow the lifeblood of knowledge to flow quickly and freely throughout the organization.

Hewlett-Packard, an innovative company that had in recent years become something of a lumbering dinosaur, decided to dismantle its growing bureaucracy—which had become so cumbersome that three dozen committees oversaw every decision, delaying new products and crushing learning, speed, and innovation. Employees were urged to rethink every process from product development to distribution. The new sleek learning organization is now called a "gazelle" by industry leaders.

## Changing the Organizational Paradigm

As a result of the dramatic changes undertaken to develop a new learning vision, culture, strategy, and structure, companies transform their rigid, management-focused, short-term competitive orientations and become

### TABLE 4
#### Changing Organizational Paradigms

| Present Paradigm | New Paradigm |
| --- | --- |
| Short-term goals | Corporate and individual vision |
| Rigid culture | Flexible culture |
| Product orientation | Learning orientation |
| Regional emphasis | Global emphasis |
| Management direction | Employee empowerment |
| Procedure bias | Risk bias |
| Analysis only | Analysis, creativity, intuition |
| Competition | Collaboration and cooperation |

dynamic learning organizations. Table 4 provides a comparison of these paradigms.

## Corporate Learning at Motorola

For more than eighty years, Motorola has been recognized as a world-class leader in a wide range of communications and electronics markets. 2010 revenues exceeded $20 billion, and the company has more than 60,000 employees around the world. Its products include mobile phones, smartphones, two-way radios, networking systems, cable television systems, and wireless broadband networks. And for more than twenty years, Motorola has been recognized as a pioneer in its commitment and its endurance as a learning organization. Its commitment to learning, quality, innovation, and customer service has resulted in numerous awards, including the Malcolm Baldridge award for quality and the top learning organization by ASTD. Other awards include *Electronic Engineering Times* recent award as the leading supplier in the worldwide embedded systems industry for its worldwide launch of the Digital DNA brand. The company won this award by being best in class for 16 supplier attributes, including documentation, pricing competitiveness, application support, customer orientation, and technology leadership—a truly phenomenal achievement.

Since the early 1980s, companies from all over the world have made pilgrimages to Motorola's headquarters in Schaumburg, Illinois, to explore the high-performance work practices at Motorola. They have discovered that Motorola's success is built on a foundation of corporate-wide learning that is leveraged to create new products and services, delight new and existing customers, quickly respond and adapt to the rapidly changing global environment, and develop high-impact teams. The cornerstone for this corporate learning is Motorola University, an institution that has helped propel the firm to its position among the top global companies.

### COMMITMENT TO QUALITY AND CONTINUOUS INNOVATION

The commitment to ongoing innovation in products and services continues to the present day. Motorola's successes over the years cannot be ascribed purely or even primarily to the desire to beat the competition, although that has often been the outcome. The company's most important motivation is the technical objective of constantly trying to improve its performance. Mobilizing the entire firm around apparently impossible goals has long been a central part of Motorola's corporate strategy.

Since quality is a way of life at Motorola, everything from the antenna on a two-way radio to accelerometers on automobiles is subject to the company's drive to attain perfection. Targets such as the Six Sigma quality goal of reducing the error rate in every process to fewer than 3.4 mistakes per million operations have helped create a common vocabulary and sense of purpose. Even more important, workers who are constantly thinking of ways to improve the company's performance fuel Motorola's momentum and search for new opportunities.

## A CULTURE OF LEARNING AND TRAINING

Some of the best training in the world takes place at Motorola. The tradition of training began in the 1920s and has continued to grow in importance. Until the early 1980s, Motorola Corporation had its own array of traditional employee development activities, of which training was a key component. The firm's decision in 1980 to build its own university outside the corporation's human resources department was a radical one. The university was not intended to replace training within the company; rather, training would continue as a department within the human resources area.

By the end of the 1980s, Motorola University had expanded its operations in the United States and around the world. The university also began offering new and more comprehensive services, such as online learning systems, translation and cultural training, and an expanded portfolio of executive education programs. Nearly all Motorola training organizations are integrated and serving businesses. Every one of its 60,000 employees are expected to receive forty hours of training a year. Today, Motorola University offers more than 3500 "learning interventions" at its twenty-three branches with an investment of over $200 million per year.

At Motorola University, factory workers study all types of business-related topics, from the fundamentals of computer-aided design to robotics, from communication skills to customized manufacturing. They learn not only by reading manuals and attending lectures but by inventing and building their own products. The university does not employ many professors. Instead, it relies on a cadre of outside consultants—including engineers, scientists, and former managers—to teach most of its courses. The instructor's role is to guide people into thinking as well as remembering. In a class on reducing manufacturing cycle time, for example, senior managers formed teams to devise new ways of getting a product to market faster. Motorola later organized a course that dramatically reduced time spent on product development.

Thousands of workers have learned skills at Motorola University that help create new, or improve existing, businesses. As a result, hot-selling products pour off Motorola's assembly lines. The company became the first American electronics firm to defeat the Japanese, even in their home market.

## TRAINING AND BUSINESS SUCCESS

It was determined early on that Motorola University was to have its own board of trustees (general managers of the corporation) and would be chartered to address issues of imminent business need. The university's job was not so much to educate people as to be an agent of change, with emphases on retraining workers and redefining jobs. Thus, while other companies may also offer generous amounts of training, Motorola stands out in its aim of binding education to business targets, as when it set the goal of reducing product-development time and then created a course on how to do it.

In corporate circles, Motorola's training program is considered a model because of its strong link to the company's business strategy. "Motorola's whole system is driven from the shop floor," explains Antony Carnevale, a former labor economist with the Committee for Economic Development in Washington, D.C. "The company trains to solve performance problems. It doesn't just put a little red schoolhouse in the workplace."

Experts also point out that Motorola extends its training programs to every worker worldwide. In contrast, most companies provide training only for certain employees, such as general managers or technicians. Motorola is further recognized for the way it monitors its training programs. For example, in order to move training efforts closer to operations, the company now offers an increasing number of on-the-job apprenticeships.

Motorola calculates that every $1 it spends on training delivers $30 in productivity gains within three years. Motorola cuts costs not by taking the usual route of firing workers but by training them to simplify processes and reduce waste. Motorola executives believe that the company's sizable training commitment has contributed to strong financial results. Already in the 1990s and continuing into the twenty-first century, Motorola has spent as much as 4 percent of its payroll for training, far above the 1 percent average invested by American industry.

## THREE KEY PRINCIPLES OF LEARNING

Over the years, Motorola University recognized three key principles about learning and how it can affect business success.

The first principle is that learning and change must go hand in hand. Motorola's early experience with training initiatives yielded little or no change in business operations. Why? Employees were uninterested in change because they did not see why it mattered. In addition, mixed messages from managers regarding quality principles undermined the momentum of change. The company addressed these problems by letting employees know that unwillingness to change was considered poor performance. Accountability, or what was termed "shared responsibility for change," was developed across the entire organization, including the top levels. Motorola firmly believes that change must begin at the top. With the help of Motorola University, the organization began to see change, not as a requirement mandated by some for the benefit of a few, but as a collective effort undertaken for the benefit of the whole.

The second principle is that innovation is much likelier to occur when people participate in the solution instead of having it handed to them. Although change affects an entire organization, everyone must be responsible for the details that apply to his or her sphere. Senior managers may be accountable for setting a strategic direction, but they are too far removed from daily operations to dictate the specific changes that will achieve the firm's strategic objectives. In the mid-1980s, for instance, Motorola established an eighteen-month time frame for designing a new product, down from its standard of three to seven years. The firm developed a two-week course that brought marketing, product development, and manufacturing managers together to meet, argue, and reach agreement about the needs of the market, the right new product, and the schedules and responsibilities of each production group. This action learning format overcame the problems that traditionally arose when the three departments met and agreed on plans but proceeded with their work as if they had made no agreements. Action learning did not begin as an effort to improve educational delivery systems but as an outgrowth of the firm's strategic agenda. Motorola wanted to use the training to send a message about achieving quality by integrating efforts across functions, a message that went beyond quality of product to include the quality of people, service, and the total organization. Thus, organizational context dictated learning strategy, which in turn evolved models of educational implementation.

The third principle is that it's important to balance single-mindedness of purpose within the organization against a broader frame of reference that extends beyond the organization. Learning is about inquiry, and even within an organization as large as Motorola, the internal conversation may become fairly one-sided, with questions that all begin to sound the same and lead to uncreative answers. Without balance, intense focus may also lead to tunnel vision

## EMPLOYEE DEVELOPMENT AND BUSINESS REDEFINITION

Throughout most of the 1980s, Motorola University built credibility within the organization by developing educational experiences that addressed a number of imminent business needs. Education was linked to key strategic objectives, such as reductions in operating costs, product improvements, or acceleration in new product development.

In today's uncertain and turbulent business environment, Motorola University concentrates on raising questions before answers exist. The university's role—which parallels the changing competency requirements of individuals within the organization—is to raise the level of inquiry inside the company through a diversely structured dialogue with customers, experts, and industry representatives such as suppliers, regulators, policymakers, and special-interest groups.

Motorola University's initiatives in recent years look more like new business development activities than classic educational programs. Developing new business in an era of discontinuous change is not the same process it was in the past. And while it appears at first blush that Motorola University is merely serving as an incubation center for the company's entrepreneurial activities, knowledge creation is a more deeply rooted focus of change. In raising questions that have no answers, Motorola University is creating a forum for exploring beyond the boundaries of the company's existing business and industry. The university's objective is to develop the company's critical competencies so that it can generate new models or maps with which to make sense of uncertain or ambiguous business environments. Over the years, computer-based learning has continued to expand. The company has developed many short desktop tutorials to help employees work through the process-mapping problems and to eliminate wasteful extra steps in such areas as manufacturing, distribution, and administration. Internet training, however, is not seen as a complete replacement to onsite classroom programs. Rather, Motorola sees that people need support in their learning. Thus, although they may do pre-work on the Internet, employees generally move into classroom training situations where they share experiences with each other and get coaching from an instructor.

## RESEARCH

Motorola University created a research agenda that resembles the classic university charter, but an agenda based on the evolution of learning within the corporation. As the company shifts its inquiry into its future outside the context of its well-defined customers and into ill-defined or even undefined markets, it must develop a correspondingly critical set of new competencies within the organization and among its stakeholders.

During the past fifteen years, the university has hosted many global research conferences. The gatherings look much like the conferences organized by academic universities: a sharing of new knowledge derived from the research of individuals and colleagues. All presentations are delivered by Motorola employees for Motorola employees and invited guests.

## TECHNOLOGY FOR GLOBAL LEARNING AND HIGH PERFORMANCE

Another important initiative at Motorola University has created an institute that develops educational delivery systems around satellite, Internet, and virtual reality technologies. Learning solutions include web-based systems, instructor-led training, online communities of practice, video, and satellite conferencing with Motorola employees worldwide. The College of Learning Technologies (CLT) is a department of Motorola University and employs a cadre of experts in instructional, multimedia design, and educational technology. The institute develops courses, learning tools, and methodologies and conducts applied research to ensure that its services are the best available. Through CLT, Motorola is exploring ways to develop a new worldwide market in educational products for Motorola technology.

As Motorola University continues to pursue its comprehensive learning strategy, CLT is at the forefront in providing learning solutions for all Motorola employees with "the right knowledge, at the right time, anywhere in the world." Employee training is now so deeply ingrained at Motorola that all employees—from top executives to factory workers—are responsible for identifying courses they want to study every year. If supervisors spot performance deficiencies during annual reviews, they offer recommendations and develop appropriate remedial plans. CLT makes ongoing individual learning possible for every Motorola employee.

## RESTRUCTURING FOR QUICK AND AGILE CRISIS RESPONSE

The 1990s created tremendous challenges for Motorola. The European telecom giants Nokia and Ericsson were rapidly leapfrogging past Motorola in telephone technology and design. The Asian financial crisis affected manufacturing and sales for many Motorola products. The company responded quickly by instituting several renewal programs built around four processes.

First, Motorola sought global leadership in core businesses by realigning its business groups to provide even better customer experiences. The restructuring enabled greater market-focused delivery of products.

Second, the company encouraged fuller participation in partnerships and alliances. Motorola recognized that it could no longer provide total customer satisfaction on its own. Today's customers are wary of becoming trapped in an inflexible relationship or a single-technology road map. The future belongs to those who view the business world as an ecosystem—a business community that thrives or dies by virtue of the overall health of its participants. An increasing number of Motorola's corporate customers indicated that in order to stay competitive, the company needed both competition and more cooperation with its suppliers and partners.

Third, Motorola built platforms for future leadership. The company recognized that the days of closed, turnkey architecture were gone and began switching to an open, extensible structure on which other companies could build and add value. As a result, Motorola has recently and successfully created more integration components.

And, fourth, Motorola has undertaken additional initiatives to improve quality and reduce cycle time. Global competition has resulted in renewed urgency, both in terms of the manufacturing process and the time involved in creating new products and bringing them to market. The Six Sigma quality standard has been extended to the realm of consumer preference.

Thanks to these tremendous innovations and the agility created by its corporate learning culture and enhanced by Motorola University, the company successfully weathered various crises over the past twenty years.

## PREPARATION FOR FUTURE CRISES AND CHAOS

Motorola realizes that it must be prepared for ongoing challenges and crises in the highly competitive and chaotic telecom field of the twenty-first century. Thus, leaders and staff throughout the company are continuously assessed and trained in a large variety of categories such as overall performance, teamwork and cooperation, vision and strategy, communication skills, creativity and risk taking, flexibility, integrity, objectivity and practical intelligence, company loyalty, initiative and commitment, diversity, empowerment, customer satisfaction, humility, and business knowledge. They are challenged to consider the following questions:

- What will our organizational structure look like in 2025?
- What structural changes must we make in order to support our vision?
- What new technologies will we need?
- What skills should our managers develop for the growth and world changes we are experiencing?
- How can we attract the worldwide talent we need for this outstanding growth?

Motorola's formula for success has been quite simple: Generate and maintain an extensive knowledge base that enables the company to project the most effective areas and methods for leveraging current core competencies in light of trends in both supply and demand. Then, search constantly for ways of improving your product lines, processes, and people so that you can capitalize on identified trends and opportunities. Finally, have the courage and passion to reinvent your company or product line by putting knowledge into action.

Learning and an emphasis on quality are not the only reasons for Motorola's bottom-line success, but experts contend that the company's focus on continuous education and innovation are crucial advantages in today's marketplace. "Training," declares Carnevale, "is the strongest variable we see contributing to higher returns, and its importance grows over time." And there is growing financial proof at Motorola that continuous learning may be one of the smartest investments employers and employees ever make. By investing heavily in its belief that better-educated employees are better competitors, Motorola is staying on the cutting edge.

---

## Top 10 Strategies for Becoming a Learning Organization

### 1. USE FUTURE-SEARCH CONFERENCES TO DEVELOP VISION

Changing an organizational vision may feel like changing the tire on a moving car, but it is a critical first step. To begin, involve leadership and as many shareholders as possible—employees, customers, suppliers, and partners—in recreating the company as a learning organization. Future-search conferences are one method of doing this. Such conferences can, as Marvin Weisbord and Sandra Janoff (2000) note, "bring people together to achieve breakthrough innovation, empowerment, shared vision, and collaborative action" (p. 3).

Leaders should consider a number of principles and procedures as they plan and conduct a search conference.

- Explore—together—the whole system, its history, ideas, constraints, opportunities, global trends, sources.

- Try to achieve common ground without using force or compromise, empha-size validating rather than reconciling polarities, and remain focused on mutual development.
- Reinforce learning before and after the future search.
- Implement and maintain learning through understanding and capitalizing the resources of the entire environment and all systems.
- Create structures that facilitate relationships.
- Act locally to cause change in large systems because everything is connected.

Before future-search conferences begin, companies should confirm the neces-sary core values. The corporate culture must ensure that knowledge can be collec-tively and meaningfully organized by people—who are, in fact, extraordinary sources of information about the real world. People in such companies are empowered and enabled when creating their own futures. They want opportunities to engage their heads and hearts as well as their hands. Cooperation, equality, and empowerment help them feel more knowledgeable about and in control of their futures.

Well-planned and well-managed future-search conferences can be an effec-tive tool in shaping learning organizations. A new shared vision will undoubtedly influence organizational policies and practices, align learning with organizational goals, and maximize knowledge to improve product and service quality.

## 2. GAIN COMMITMENT AND SUPPORT FROM TOP-LEVEL MANAGEMENT TO BECOME A LEARNING ORGANIZATION

Once the company has decided to become a learning organization, it is impor-tant to disseminate this vision and its corresponding values within and outside the organization, using methods such as announcements, posters, newsletters, videos, and symbols. Assign financial and human resources to the task of making the vision a reality.

Top managers should not only articulate the vision but be active early partici-pants in its actualization. Senior-level managers acting as advocates of corporate-wide learning efforts are the most powerful means of informing and inspiring others within the company.

## 3. CREATE A CORPORATE CLIMATE OF CONTINUOUS LEARNING AND IMPROVEMENT

A corporate environment that supports and rewards learning encourages people to participate enthusiastically in the rigorous challenges of a learning organization. The following factors are helpful in developing such a climate:

- Establish learning as the key to the organization's purpose and success.
- Create a culture of continuous improvement.
- Value mistakes and performance shortfalls, both for the effort expended and for the learning gained.
- Emphasize that problems and errors should be shared and not hidden.
- Show concern for development of the whole person.
- Widen the accessibility of information.
- Help make learning a habit.

## 4. SIMPLIFY POLICIES AND STRUCTURES AROUND LEARNING

Learning organizations work best when boundaries are minimized so that knowledge and ideas can move quickly and efficiently within and outside the organization. Reengineering to increase learning involves the following actions:

- Cut unnecessary restrictions and procedures.
- Shrink the size of working units.
- Decrease restrictive control of policies and allow greater flexibility.
- Streamline structures and create a company with fewer boundaries.
- Flatten hierarchy.
- Move toward project-based operations.
- Enable departments and units to act on their own initiative.
- Root out bureaucracy and unnecessary rules.

## 5. REWARD INDIVIDUAL AND TEAM LEARNING

"That which is rewarded gets done" is one of the most powerful management principles in the world. We should also be mindful of its antithesis: "That which goes unrewarded is soon abandoned." Therefore, it is vital for an organization to identify as many ways as possible of rewarding individual and, even more important, team learning. Reward actions that directly or indirectly contribute to organizational learning, such as risk taking, commitment to learning and personal mastery, teamwork, encouraging new experiences and ideas, being a teacher or trainer, and transferring acquired knowledge to teammates and the broader network.

Rewards can and should be financial whenever possible. But doesn't learning have to be measured before it can be rewarded? Yes, and surely an individual's or a team's learning and the bottom-line effect of that learning are measurable—much like many elements evaluated during performance appraisals. The quantity and quality of learning that benefits the company can be seen in terms of new and improved products, services, and relationships as well as documented knowledge acquired, created, stored, and/or transferred by individuals and groups.

## 6. INCORPORATE LEARNING IN ALL POLICIES AND PROCEDURES

In order to systematically transform a company into a learning organization, it is absolutely essential to integrate learning as an automatic part of all operations, including production, marketing, managing, finance, and human resources, among others. The following policies exemplify this integrative approach:

- Learning acquired from all projects is captured and transferred throughout the company.
- Managers are hired or promoted based on their learning and their ability to enhance the learning of those around them.
- All employees are responsible for acquiring and transferring information.
- The firm recruits employees who have the characteristics of good learners, such as desire for personal mastery, initiative and persistence, listening ability, and openness to change.
- All employees are trained in core workplace competencies, including learning capability, creative thinking and problem solving, self-development, and leadership and vision.

## 7. ESTABLISH CENTERS OF EXCELLENCE AND DEMONSTRATION PROJECTS

Centers of excellence are a valuable strategy used by many learning organizations. By practicing systematic job rotation into and out of the centers, companies are able to develop and circulate best practices and know-how throughout the organization.

Demonstration projects in all areas of the organization are a related approach. In these locations, the company can devote more energy to experimenting with different ideas, policies, procedures, products, or services.

## 8. MEASURE FINANCIAL AND NONFINANCIAL AREAS AS A LEARNING ACTIVITY

"That which can be measured gets done" is another key principle of management. Therefore, learning organizations measure the relationship of expenditures on learning not only to financial areas—profits, return on investments, expenditures—but also to other sectors such as quality and customer satisfaction. Motorola, for example, calculates a 3 to 1 return on each dollar spent on training and actually seeks to spend as much as possible on learning; it knows these expenditures will increase the bottom line and the quality line.

In addition, discourses about metrics—for example, whether they should be focused internally or externally, the degree of specificity sought, the use of custom-built or standard measures—are all-important learning activities. And the process of searching for the most appropriate metrics can in itself be a valuable aspect of learning.

## 9. CREATE TIME AND SPACE FOR LEARNING

Organizational learning cannot be pushed. Despite a person's natural creativity, there are times when the necessary idea doesn't emerge immediately. Pushing too hard for innovative ideas may create stress that inhibits, rather than helps, the desired breakthrough.

Although a committed group may want to move quickly to reach its learning destination, it is important to remember there are some inherent speed limits. People need time to plan and reflect; they need physical, social, and mental space in which to listen and be creative. Sometimes, slowing down leads to faster resolutions. In their commitment to providing time for reflection and learning, some firms have gone so far as to offer three- to twelve-month sabbaticals during which staff may visit, work with, or study at academic institutions and the sites of industry leaders.

Recognize also the importance of architecture and physical surroundings in creating an environment that is more conducive to thinking, learning, and sharing knowledge.

## 10. MAKE LEARNING INTENTIONAL AT ALL TIMES AT ALL PLACES

There are a variety of other ways to make learning a way of life throughout the organization.

- Institute success-sharing meetings.
- Practice action learning as much as possible.
- Set aside time at meetings and programs to reflect on accumulated knowledge.
- Introduce new ideas into the organization by hiring or contracting outsiders for key positions.
- Generate as many explicit learning strategies as possible that are appropriate for your organization.

# CHAPTER 5

# Empowering and Enabling People

The need to pursue work-related learning in today's knowledge organization is among the many revolutions of the New Economy. The heart, growth, innovation, and distinctiveness of learning organizations derive from the ability to utilize human capital. And the fundamental business challenge is how to attract, deploy, develop, adapt, and retain it better than anyone else. The strategic argument has shifted from "managing knowledge" to "managing people with knowledge" and acquiring and growing that knowledge superbly (Manville, 2001).

People are pivotal to learning organizations because only people have the capacity to learn. People are the masters who take information and transform it into valuable knowledge for personal and organizational use. In the Systems Learning Organization model, the people subsystem includes the following six elements: managers and leaders, employees, customers, business partners and alliances, suppliers and vendors, and the community (see Figure 11).

In order to contribute to organizational learning, each of these groups must be empowered and enabled. If they are empowered but not enabled, they will have the necessary resources at their disposal, but not the knowledge to effectively use them. Groups that are enabled but not empowered will have the necessary knowledge, but not the ability to apply it. Let's explore some ways in which each group can become qualified for and proficient at organizational learning.

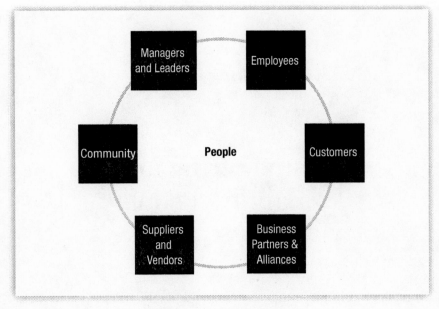

**FIGURE 11**   People Subsystem

## Managers and Leaders

Many leaders whose tactics may have been acceptable to organizations in the past will find that the same approaches are unacceptable in learning organizations of the future. Hard-nosed managers who single-handedly determine team direction, make key decisions, and push employees may prove destructive in today's organizations. Such managers have not realized that the organization has evolved from a structure based on steady-state control to one that thrives on learning, empowerment, and continuous change (see Table 5).

Managers must abandon controlling in favor of empowering, become less commanders than stewards, and exchange approaches of transitional managers for those of transformational leaders. The new organization requires a new type of leader who can play new kinds of roles with new kinds of skills.

---
**TABLE 5**
### The Move From Steady-State to Continuous Change

| From | To |
|------|-----|
| Continual change | Transformation |
| Quality improvement | Process engineering |
| Matrix | Network |
| Performance appraisal | Performance management |
| Technophobia | Application of technology |
| Functions | Process |
| Control | Empowerment |
| Employment | Employability |

---

## NEW LEADERSHIP ROLES

Let's explore some of the new roles required of managers in a learning organization.

### Instructor, Coach, and Mentor

The most important responsibility for managers today is enabling others to learn. This task requires a variety of approaches, those of instructor, coach, and mentor. The choice of role in any situation depends on the focus of help, time available, approach to helping, associated activities, and ownership, as shown in Table 6.

## Leaders as Teachers at Becton, Dickinson and Company (BD)

Becton, Dickinson and Company (BD) is a global medical technology company that manufactures and sells medical devices, instrument systems, and reagents. Founded in 1897 and headquartered in Franklin Lakes, New Jersey, BD does business in nearly fifty countries and has nearly 30,000 employees worldwide. Eight full-time staff members oversee strategic enterprise learning and development by embracing Noel Tichey's "leader as teacher" model; Tichey advocated that all leaders must have a teachable point of view to develop other leaders.

RD began applying the leader as teacher model in the early 2000s. The company's CEO, Ed Ludwig, notes that "when we recruit, we definitely want people to know that teaching will be part of their success factor. They will be expected to take time to develop people and get into a formal training mode" (ASTD, 2007b).

Since the creation of BD University in 2000, its staff has trained over 600 leader-teachers across the company's three major segments in the fifty countries in which BD operates. The strategic-level training is disseminated through five colleges: leadership, business skills, sales, career, and operations effectiveness. Leader-teachers are both self-selected and recruited, and can be managers at any level.

> "Our leaders-teachers must possess the desire to teach, credibility, the respect of their employees and peers, and some skills in teaching and facilitation," says Joe Toto, director of leadership development and learning. "They bring unique value to employee development by providing credible information—but they also model and live the process that they're teaching. Further, it's two-way learning, which benefits the leaders because they are exposed to viewpoints they might not otherwise encounter" (ASTD, 2007b, p. 39).

BD employees can be involved in teaching as classroom instructors, guest speakers, peer coaches, subject matter experts, or program champions who are responsible for the course content. Over 90 percent of the company's leaders participate as instructors or speakers.

Ongoing success of the company, according to BD leaders, is based upon the role of leading and development in the company. Wendy Wittershein, senior business partner for leadership development and learning, notes, "Our senior leaders have raised the bar to direct our company into new, higher-value products that will require new and more robust skills sets. To meet the challenge, BD University has engaged more leader-teachers who are affiliated with global product development and are working on the front lines of innovation" (ASTD, 2007b, p. 40).

---

### Knowledge Manager

Since the learning organization will increasingly consist of knowledge specialists, it will be an organization of equals, of colleagues and associates. No knowledge or area will necessarily rank higher than another; each will be judged by its contribution to organizational learning and success. Information-based, egalitarian companies require leaders who motivate and assist colleagues in the collection, storage, and distribution of knowledge inside and outside the unit. Knowledge managers will help select data for organizational

## TABLE 6

### Managers as Instructors, Coaches, and Mentors

| Dimension | Instructor | Coach | Mentor |
|---|---|---|---|
| *Focus* | Task | Results of job | Development of person throughout life |
| *Time available* | Day or two | Month or year | Career or lifetime |
| *Approach to helping* | Show and tell; supervise practice; set up opportunities to try out new skills | Explore problem together | Act as a friend; listen and question to enlarge awareness |
| *Associated activities* | Analyze task; give clear instructions; supervise practice; provide feedback on results | Jointly identify problems; create development opportunities; review | Link work with other parts of life; clarify broad and long-term aims and purpose in life |
| *Ownership* | Instructor | Shared | Learner |

memory, confirm mechanisms for gathering and coding knowledge, and encourage people to both use and share this valuable information.

### Co-Learner and Model for Learning

Leaders are not there simply to tell others what to learn. They encourage, motivate, and assist workers in learning and continuously improving their skills as well as their learning abilities. Managers assist workers in identifying learning resources. Leaders must be devoted learners themselves, taking time for and demonstrating a love for learning. By practicing action learning, taking risks, seeking innovative answers, and asking fresh questions, managers display solid learning practices and skills to others.

### Architect and Designer

Given the new technologies, structures, environments, and resources of learning organizations, leaders must be architects who can fit or sculpt these elements into a system that will thrive in the rapidly changing marketplace. Leaders help redefine their organizations, reshape networks and teams, and reinvent new methods for selecting, training, and rewarding people so that everyone can participate in the global business environment. Leaders must also help create and design new and appropriate policies, strategies, and principles.

### Coordinator

Like an orchestra conductor who enables each musician to play his or her instrument more magnificently, the learning leader empowers people to perform at their best. A leader is also like the coach of a soccer team who melds players into a cohesive unit so that each player is responsible for the team's success and at the same time understands how his or her play affects the game.

### Advocate for Learning Processes and Projects

Robust organizational learning requires more than one advocate, or champion, if it is to succeed. This is particularly true of learning that will lead to changes in a basic value or long-cherished approach. The greater the number of advocates for a new learning idea or program, the more rapidly and extensively organizational learning will take place. Although it should be possible for anyone to champion learning processes and projects, managers are often the best and most likely candidates; they should welcome, even solicit, the opportunity to be learning advocates.

## Leadership Development at InterContinental Hotels Group

InterContinental Hotels Group (IHG) is the largest hotels company in the world measured by number of rooms (with 646,000 as of January 2010), and has more than 4,500 hotels in over 100 countries. Its brands include InterContinental, Holiday Inn, and Crowne Plaza. To improve leadership training, IHG launched a virtual leadership development community in 2009 called "Leaders Lounge." The corporate intranet-based portal is available by invitation to unit managers, corporate directors, and those in higher positions. The portal features information and insights on leadership, including shared practices within the organization. Also included are timely tools, tips, articles, and videos to reinforce company strategies. Readers are free to employ social media and other informal leaning tools as they post tips and react to content (Harris, 2010, p. 34).

Dedicated areas within the lounge include the "Leadership Gym," which features tools designed to give leaders' skills a workout. Another area, called "Problem Solver," solicits input on strategies and leadership issues. "The Academy" includes sections for users to access in-depth e-learning opportunities on key business topics, including finance, branded customer experience, and coaching skills. The contents are easily accessed from the global learning management system used by IHG. Information is available on a synchronous and an asynchronous basis, and its content has now expanded into a number of foreign languages (Harris, 2010).

## NEW LEADERSHIP SKILLS

In addition to taking on new roles in learning organizations, managers must accomplish new tasks.

### Build Shared Vision

Learning leaders must envision, along with fellow employees, the type of future the company desires, one that is exciting and challenging enough to attract and retain the best and brightest knowledge workers. The extent to which managers are able to build a vision of shared goals for an organization determines employees' commitment and willingness to carry out the vision. Leaders should attempt to blend extrinsic and intrinsic visions, communicate their own vision, encourage the personal visions that give rise to a shared vision, and maintain an ongoing vision process.

### Coordinate Multiple, Task-Focused Teams

Due to the learning organization's increased use of project teams, managers are likely to be leading and coordinating a number of different task-focused teams, each carrying out a variety of activities on different schedules. Managers must be able to quickly enter into and become trusted partners of the teams. Planning and managing these multiple responsibilities requires an agile, caring, and well-organized individual.

### Acknowledge and Test Mental Models

Many of an organization's best ideas are never put into practice because they conflict with established mental models or processes. Leaders must be able to confront existing assumptions without provoking defensiveness or anger. Specific abilities in this area include balancing inquiry and advocacy, distinguishing between what is espoused and what is practiced, recognizing and dismantling defensive routines, and seeing and testing leaps of abstraction.

*Engage in Systems Thinking*

Leaders in learning organizations must help people see the big picture, with its underlying trends, forces, and potential surprises. They must be able to engage in systems thinking, which enhances their ability to foresee the effects on the organization of both internal and external factors. Deciphering and analyzing massive amounts of sometimes contradictory information demand patience and persistence. Some key capabilities include avoiding symptomatic solutions and focusing on underlying causes, distinguishing detail complexity from dynamic complexity, seeing processes instead of snapshots, focusing on areas of high leverage, seeing interrelationships rather than things, and realizing that we and the causes of our problems belong to the same system.

*Encourage Creativity, Innovation, and Risk Taking*

Jack Welsh, former CEO of General Electric, challenged his managers with the following questions: Are you dealing with new things? Are you coming up with fundamentally new approaches for getting work done? Are you generating new programs?

For GE and other learning companies, a constant flow of new ideas is the lifeline to continued success. Although everyone is encouraged and expected to be creative, managers are best equipped to create this environment by encouraging risks as well as protecting and supporting those whose risks have not led to successful outcomes. Managers can be leaders in trying out new ideas and challenging old ways.

*Conceptualize and Inspire Learning and Action*

The ability to conceptualize complex issues and processes, simplify them, and inspire people to learn and succeed is a necessary competency for the transformational leader. Charisma may be helpful, but leading by showing concern for and confidence in employees and associates is more effective. Leaders require solid facilitating and coordinating skills if they are to gain workers' participation in challenging, sometimes unenjoyable, tasks. And no task is more important than encouraging and inspiring learning (Belasen, 2000).

# Employees

There are several principles and guidelines to consider when empowering and enabling employees. The first step toward becoming a learning organization is to treat employees as adults with the innate capacity to learn, who have the skills necessary to handle problems, and who enjoy responsibility and recognition.

Once employees are perceived as capable learners, they need freedom and support. Enthusiastic and energetic employees are more creative and committed to learning and productivity. Peter Senge (2006), whose ideas on the subject of learning organizations have attracted wide attention, has described these organizations as places where people can "continually expand their capacity to create the results they truly desire, where new and expansive patterns of thinking are nurtured, where collective aspiration is set free, and where people are continually learning how to learn together" (p. 3).

## Engaging Honda Employees on the Factory Floor

At Honda, the saying goes that there is "more knowledge on the factory floor than in the office." Therefore, the allocation of power is commensurate to the high level of commitment, creativity, and intellectual capacity of associates. (As at many learning organizations, all Honda employees, including the company president, are called *associates*.) But Honda does not just talk empowerment; it permits people to actually create a new car. That's empowerment, enablement, and a whole lot more!

Honda managers believe that associates are the people most qualified to decide how their jobs should be done. If managers notice a problem, they ask associates for their input, involvement, and advice. The Honda attitude toward worker-learners is, "We have a goal here. If you can do it better—do it. If you fail, we'll pick you up, dust you off, and encourage you to keep trying."

One key to Honda's success is *gemba*, a Japanese word that means "the place of action," which is commonly the shop floor. At Honda, *gemba* means that the people involved with a particular project or process gather together when they need to take some action. This is more than simultaneous engineering and cross-functional teamwork. It is instead more like spontaneous action learning.

The power and effectiveness of *gemba* were demonstrated at the Marysville, Ohio, plant during the development of the Honda wagon. At some point in the initial development process, workers discovered that installing the wiring harness in the tailgate required ten minutes, which was too long. All the Honda people involved—design engineers, assemblers, and employees from stamping—arrived in the area where the prototype was being built. It was up to them to make the changes needed to install the harness quickly and efficiently. They soon discovered a solution, which involved switching to a different wiring harness and changing the diameter of the hole through which the wiring was fed.

People at Honda talk often about the concept of matching power with ability. Confidence, responsibility, pride, and, most of all, accomplishment are also important factors on the factory floor. Honda people are learning together because they have been given the opportunity to use their own creativity and imaginations (Marquardt, 2002).

## DELEGATE AUTHORITY AND RESPONSIBILITY

Learning organizations reduce dependency and push as much responsibility as possible toward the point of action and decision making. Power and learning are thus located where the best information and the greatest need exist. Operations and power are decentralized and delegated to equal the responsibility and learning capacity of the individuals and teams involved. Empowerment and accountability should be correlated, and employees should have appropriate levels of influence, trust, and ability to get exceptions.

## Career Development and Employee Retention at T. Rowe Price

Nearly 5,000 people are employed by T. Rowe Price around the world in Baltimore, Buenos Aries, Sydney, Toronto, Copenhagen, Hong Kong, Tokyo, London, Luxembourg, Amsterdam, Singapore, and Zurich. The company's high expectations for client satisfaction and employee retention has recently spurred a cluster of innovative new learning programs. T. Rowe Price has made a strong commitment to retain employees in a time and an environment with the following internal and external challenges: rapid expansion, need to maintain high standards, increased complexity, and a need for standardization of the learning function, as well as the emotional component of the investor relationships during these turbulent times.

One valuable tool is *Discovery*, a wiki-based collaborative knowledge management tool created by the firm's IT group. It incorporates Web 2.0 tenants, including forums, RSS feeds, bookmarking, and tagging. *Discovery* enables associates to capture knowledge and create emerging categories of information. Answers to difficult research questions and now flow through the organization more quickly. New associates can quickly gain proficiency by taking a well-based course inserted into their introductory training curriculum. This program has resulted in a significant decrease in turnaround time for research items, including completion of service level agreements in less than two hours. Other benefits include greater transparency of ideas, increased ability to update and publish information, and improved capacity to implement contingency plans (ASTD, 2008).

## INVOLVE EMPLOYEES IN DEVELOPING STRATEGIES

In this increasingly dynamic, interdependent, and unpredictable world, it is simply no longer possible for someone at the top to figure it all out. The old model of organization leadership—the top thinks and the bottom acts—must give way to a structure in which everyone is thinking and acting at all levels at all times. Sharing power with employees makes business sense as well as personal sense.

Accordingly, employees should be empowered to participate in the development of strategy and tactics, especially in areas that affect them professionally. Learning organizations clearly realize that empowered workers can make decisions that are as good as, if not better than, those of managers, simply because they have the best information.

## A Community of People at DaVita

DaVita, a kidney dialysis company with $6 billion in annual sales and more than 35,000 employees (who are called *teammates*) is guided by a learning and development philosophy that truly places its people at the top of the list. At DaVita, according to Steve Priest, Director of the Chief Wisdom Office, "we strive to do things the DaVita way, with the full engagement of our heads, hearts and hands in the work we do. Why? Quite simply it is the right thing to do for a care-giving company. Dialysis is an intense, time-consuming process by which we are literally saving peoples' lives. Being able to come from a place of deep commitment to service is critical to the job" (Priest, 2010, p. 44).

At DaVita, the focus is on the whole person, to provide educational programs that develop teammates holistically. The company also delivers training in people skills such as conflict resolution, effective communications, team building, and emotional intelligence. Priest continues, "We believe that helping our teammates to become better human beings will create a ripple effect that extends to our patients. Work helps shape our identities, and it is where we often overcome limiting beliefs and personal challenges. In doing so, we learn about ourselves and how our interactions with other human beings help shape society as a whole" (p. 45).

## EMPLOYEE SELF-SERVICE

One valuable tool that learning organizations provide for their employees is an Employee Self-service System (ESS), which offers them the opportunity to make choices and register the results of those choices immediately.

Isenhour (2009) notes that there are four categories with various features within an ESS system:

1. Development
   - Enroll in training courses
   - View completed training
   - Access e-learning internal/external courses
   - View/apply for internal job vacancies
   - Complete employment tests for new jobs
2. Communications
   - Review company communications
   - Access company policies or procedures
   - Access HR policy manuals and e-mail inquiry/help request
   - Complete employee surveys or 360-degree feedback data
   - View/respond to personal information requests from HR
3. Benefits Services
   - Research and view plan rules and requirements
   - Enroll in cafeteria-style programs (medical, dental, insurance)
   - Add and/or delete dependents
   - Model retirement and/or access 401K savings investment records
   - Model health plan alternatives' costs (e.g., HMO, PPO)
4. Personal Data
   - Correct errors in personal data (degree, graduation date)
   - Update emergency contact, address, telephone information
   - Change W-4 withholding forms
   - View previous/current pay and performance information
   - Enter time reports, vacation/sick days, and travel expense reports

## Career Advancement at Credit Suisse

Siegfried Hoenle, Head of the Credit Suisse Business School, describes the importance of systematic talent management and lifelong learning at Credit Suisse, noting that "talented employees can rest assured that they will receive specific support in their development. In 2009, we further improved and harmonized our processes globally in this field as well as introducing an online application. This gives our managers systematic access to our global talent pool as well as transparent and consistent succession planning" (Credit Suisse, 2011).

At Credit Suisse, decisions concerning promotion are also taken on the basis of a globally consistent process. A key topic at the Credit Suisse School in 2010 was "increasing internal employee mobility." The company believes that employees should benefit from the global and wide-reaching activities of Credit Suisse, and be in a position to move their own careers forward more actively. Thus, the company strives to give its employees opportunities to gain experience in various regions and business areas in order to develop their potential in the global arena.

## BALANCE INDIVIDUAL AND ORGANIZATIONAL NEEDS

Learning organizations balance the individual's and the organization's development needs in order to properly address both. Organizational productivity and profits matter as much as the quality of employees' working lives. Leadership fully recognizes that better organizational results are built on happy, productive individuals.

Companies should seek to develop the full range of human potential—to respect social and spiritual needs as well as economic ones. Learning organizations have a high regard for human dignity and delight in (not merely tolerate) ethnic and cultural differences.

Workers often feel overwhelmed with all they need to learn for their jobs, especially as knowledge demands grow exponentially. An organizational learning culture helps ease those feelings because learning responsibilities are shared equitably within the organization. Also, when organizations support continuous growth and learning, the possibility of greater self-actualization and fulfillment at work increases.

Learning organizations are also aware of the growing pressures, and conflicts, of family and job obligations, so they try to develop pro-family company policies, such as flexible work arrangements, dependent-care services, and wellness programs. Capital One, Hewlett-Packard, and Texaco, for example, have made such programs integral parts of their human resources and learning support policies.

# Balancing Employee Development and Healthy Lifestyles at Janus Group

Janus Group manages approximately $160.8 billion in assets under management for more than four million shareholders, clients, and institutions around the globe. Executive, managerial, and supervisory development account for 20 percent of Janus's learning programs, which occur through two signature programs:

- The *emerging leader* program is designed for high-potential individual contributors and future leaders. It consists of four days of training for four weeks, plus an action learning project. Participants come from all departments, helping to build cross-functional relationships and to enhance cross-departmental business knowledge. Each group has a senior leader (vice president and above) as the sponsor.
- The *corporate athlete* program is a science-based method for helping people align their personal and professional goals, manage their energy with fitness and nutrition planning, and craft a strategic action plan for leading their lives. Participants begin with a 360 evaluation, which seeks feedback not only from coworkers and supervisors, but also from family and friends. All participants in the corporate athlete program also get a personal coach/trainer who works with them throughout the program (ASTD, 2008a).

The balance model in Figure 12 demonstrates equilibrium between the needs of the individual and those of the organization. In order to perform, the organization must continually build the performance capability of indi-

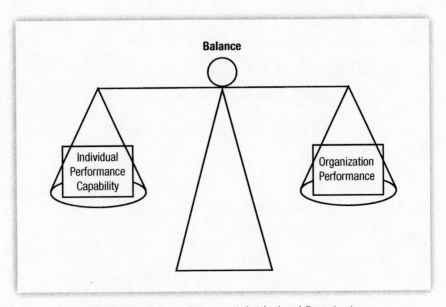

**FIGURE 12** Balance Between Individual and Organization

viduals along with that of the organization. Performance and performance capability should therefore be viewed as two separate but integrated dimensions that are in balance.

## Customers

Learning organizations recognize that customers can be a fertile source of information and ideas and should be closely linked with organizational learning systems and strategies. Conversing with and gathering information from customers invariably provide new knowledge, for customers, after all, have direct knowledge about their purchases and behavior. They can provide up-to-date product information, competitive comparisons, insights into changing preferences, and immediate feedback about service and patterns of use.

Learning organizations typically adopt one or more of several approaches toward educating their customers. They may provide ongoing, accessible training and learning opportunities (video training, embedded technology, classroom instruction) to educate customers about their products. This not only creates informed customers who can provide better ideas and insights on improvements to products or services but also cultivates greater loyalty among fellow learners and partners. Canadian Bank of International Commerce (CBIC) recognizes the critical importance of customer learning. While the bank's staff requires information about customers and their evolving needs, customers may also benefit from learning about the bank's products. Taking customer education a step further, the Dana Corporation and Ford Truck offer courses to improve their customers' business performance. Dana's program addresses generating repeat business, and Ford's covers consultative selling skills.

Learning organizations also encourage and support customers' expectations of improved quality, innovation, and greater speed, which serve as incentives to constantly improve and therefore learn. Milliken's staff accompanies the first shipment of every company product in order to observe its use; they are then better able to develop further improvements to products.

Another strategy is to actively seek feedback and suggestions from customers and suppliers. Senior executives at Motorola, including the CEO, meet personally and regularly with customers. Worthington Steel machine operators make periodic trips to customers' factories to gather firsthand knowledge about their needs.

## Business Partnerships and Alliances

The growth of global competition and virtual organizations has drastically increased the occurrence of short-term alliances and partnerships among companies. Most companies use these alliances and partnerships to increase profits and market share or to cut expenses, time, duplication of services, and political maneuverings.

Learning organizations, however, seek to add another important, long-term benefit to the alliance: learning. At the beginning of their relationships, learning companies consider the possible knowledge to be gained from their allies, such as customer intelligence, process and operations policies, and cultural nuances. They may even build these learning objectives into their agreements. Learning companies then provide for adequate exchange of personnel so that valuable learning is captured and brought back to their organizations. The short-term partnership therefore becomes a profitable, long-term investment that can be used to leverage future successes.

## Suppliers and Vendors

Learning organizations realize that success depends to a large extent on the success of a company's entire business network, not just its employees and customers. When others in the business chain are learning together about commitments and policies as well as appropriate management or technical skills, the results can be especially beneficial in the long run. Companies may offer staff learning resources to their valuable, long-term partners.

Manville (2001) notes that organizations must embrace the extended enterprise. Companies have become increasingly virtual through such mechanisms as outsourcing, focus on core competencies, and a host of alliances, joint ventures, and partnerships. People—be they employees, suppliers, vendors, or partners—work together in value chains that deliver goods and services to customers. Although the chains are linked by contractual bonds, they are also defined by relationships, knowledge exchange, and other intangibles. Learning has become a critical process that occurs across boundaries as well as within them.

This means that suppliers, vendors, partners, and others are all part of an overall learning environment, along with core employees. Companies that recognize this new reality are using certifications to qualify their suppliers and vendors as well as their own staff members. Ford provides learning to ensure appropriate procedures, technical expertise, and brand management among its dealerships. Anheuser Busch trains distributors in the handling of food and beverage products in the interests of maintaining quality and brand integrity. Cisco Systems is creating higher customer satisfaction and support for faster product rollout by offering learning programs and tools to its channel partners, who provide 70 percent of revenue. Toyota pioneered the use of learning in qualifying and aligning its suppliers, and the "work with us, learn from us, teach us" principle now governs thousands of manufacturing and supplier relationships around the world.

In the new economy, companies are beginning to see that training, learning, and knowledge services must be developed, pursued, and packaged as part of their overall relationship with customers and partners. And as we will explore in chapter 7, they are using the Internet and management systems to systematically provide, track, and integrate learning into those relationships.

## Community

Learning organizations are aware of the many benefits that accrue when communities become part of the learning process. Positive results include enhanced image in the community, greater interest among residents in working for or buying from the company, improved quality of life in surrounding areas, preparation of a future workforce, and the opportunity to exchange and share community resources.

Learning organizations might engage in the following types of community education efforts: encouraging teachers, parents, and other interested community members to participate in corporate training programs; tutoring or co-teaching in classrooms; sponsoring learning events in partnership with other corporations, academic institutions, or agencies.

National Semiconductor, in Santa Clara, California, has actively involved the community in its organizational learning efforts. The company runs numerous programs for local schools, county school superintendents, high school teachers, and elementary school science teachers. By being a good community member, National Semiconductor learns and gains as well. Early entrance into a new market can build a good image for the company. The company established a branch of National Semiconductor University, which trains the upcoming workforce in the school system and thus prepares future engineers for semiconductor technology. In this way, according to Kevin

Wheeler, former director of National Semiconductor University, "We have a trained workforce ready, willing, and able to work for National. The community benefits by learning about technology, electronics, and American management styles. And National benefits by learning a lot about the local culture and needs of people in that culture" (Marquardt, 2002, p. 126).

The demarcations between management and employees, departments and units, employees and customers, the company and its vendors, and even the company and its competitors have become less permanent and more flexible. Empowering and enabling these various groups of people extend and strengthen the learning enterprise.

## Empowering People at Whirlpool Corporation

Whirlpool Corporation has annual revenue of approximately $18 billion, more than 70,000 employees, and more than seventy manufacturing and technology research centers around the world. After acquiring the Maytag Corporation on March 31, 2006, Whirlpool Corporation became the largest home appliance maker in the world.

### COMMITMENT TO PEOPLE

One of Whirlpool's greatest achievements as a company has been its commitment to people—its 70,000 employees, its millions of customers, its numerous partners, and the global community. This commitment to developing and caring for everyone inside and outside the company and helping them learn is expressed clearly in Whirlpool's values statement.

#### Our Values

How do you become one of the world's most trustworthy, knowledgeable, and resourceful companies? You hire people who adhere to these values daily. Our core values, Respect, Integrity, Diversity and Inclusion, Teamwork, and the Spirit of Winning, bring innovative solutions to our customers.

Our goal is to be known, trusted, and respected as one of the world's top corporate citizens. The values listed below allow us to maintain doing business the best way we know how: the right way.

#### Respect

At Whirlpool, we encourage employees to share their beliefs, perspectives and opinions. And with components such as diversity networks and our emphasis on social responsibility, people at Whirlpool know they are in an environment where others value and admire them. We demand that everyone be treated like the valuable individuals they are. This value has helped us succeed for almost a century.

## Integrity

From the employees we hire to how we run our business, integrity factors into everything we do. We produce the highest quality products at the best possible prices for our customers with honesty and admiration and take pride in our work and in what we produce.

## Diversity and Inclusion

Having a plethora of people with different backgrounds offers Whirlpool the unique perspectives we need to succeed on a global level. We believe in Diversity and Inclusion and support it by promoting educational, professional and social activities that foster an inclusive work environment.

The only way to succeed is if everyone feels like they can contribute to the business and their voices are heard. That is why we constantly seek fresh approaches, new ideas and different outlooks to achieve success.

## Teamwork

We succeed because we work together to get the job done. Teamwork is apparent in all we do from the very first idea generation sessions to the manufacturing, marketing and delivery of our products. At Whirlpool, you'll rarely hear the word "I." We work together to makes things happen.

## Spirit of Winning

It begins with the belief that setting and achieving ambitious goals is key to extraordinary performance. Sticking to the status quo, or being just a little better than last year, is not good enough. There is no room for the "fear of failure." Whirlpool's culture and values will enable individuals and teams to appropriately reach and take pride in extraordinary results and further inspire the 'Spirit of Winning' in all of us.

In the Spirit of Winning culture, everyone is a leader, responsible for his or her own actions. With a full awareness and understanding of Whirlpool's strategic aims, these individual and team actions will drive outstanding performance.

Whirlpool hires and develops employees who demonstrate the following five attributes:

- Integrity: Behave honestly
- Commitment: Express their full potential and energy at work

- Reliability: Can be counted on consistently to do what is expected or required
- Initiative: Originate new ideas or methods without being asked
- Cooperativeness: Work together for a common purpose

These valuable qualities all contribute to being a learning employee and building a learning organization.

## COMMITMENT TO QUALITY LEARNING FOR ALL EMPLOYEES

Whirlpool believes that it cannot expect continuous improvement in its key business processes without investing in the systematic education and training of all its people at all levels. Whirlpool's state-of-the-art, $5.5 million Corporate Development Center near corporate headquarters in Brandywine Creek, Michigan, is a manifestation of its conviction.

Tom Helton, former director of human resources and the driving force behind the center's development, described it as a critical "vehicle to help further the business agenda of the corporation and carry out our company's strategic design. Through this construction, Whirlpool has demonstrated its commitment to the lifelong learning of its employees" (Marquardt, 2002, p. 128).

The 56,000-square-foot building features video and broadcast systems, breakout rooms, and an amphitheater with a computerized projection screen. Proximity to Whirlpool's administrative center allows executives to teach classes at the center; in fact, half the classes are taught by headquarters leadership. Helton praised the involvement of top-level managers in guiding the learning process: "It sends a tremendous message about the importance of learning to participants when they see the CEO of a company teaching."

The major mission of the Corporate Development Center is to provide Whirlpool with a visible point from which to drive a single, integrated, worldwide training and education agenda. It develops highly effective individuals, teams, and organizations capable of winning in every region and market in the world. The site also enables professionally competent leaders of character to serve the company's customers, shareholders, and other stakeholders.

Inherent in this mission are three goals: to develop a global mind-set; to align the organization with Whirlpool's vision, strategic design, and business strategies; and to build the knowledge and skills necessary to win.

Whirlpool's learning programs, according to Helton, contain a "bold, new strategy" of consistent application, organizational impact, and rapid execution. Acquiring, leveraging, and transferring knowledge, skills, capabilities, and best practices will be critical for learning throughout the organization.

One program at the Corporate Development Center is the Whirlpool Leadership Academy, which offers a core curriculum designed to provide the knowledge and skills necessary to develop and strengthen leadership capabilities. The Whirlpool Excellence Academy is another major program, designed to support the Whirlpool Excellence System and other business strategies by enabling people to acquire, improve, and maintain job-related knowledge and skills.

## EMPOWERING WHIRLPOOL'S PEOPLE

Whirlpool has set a high standard of commitment to its employees and expects the same level of commitment in return. The company's High-Performance Partnership represents a promise to all employees that Whirlpool will encourage and enable contributions and commitment from each individual and team and will provide a dynamic and diverse work environment that is valued by all. Whirlpool has set a clearly defined goal of achieving eighty-five (out of one hundred) on the corporate people commitment index, which represents a high level of mutual company and employee commitment. For Whirlpool, people commitment means living shared values in the workplace, recognizing and rewarding performance, training and educating, listening to concerns and ideas, and contributing and sharing ideas.

As former CEO Dave Whitwam noted, "One of the approaches ... to help employees feel like owners is to give them responsibility. We need their heads thinking as well as their hands working. In some of [the] factories today, there is no supervisor on the floor. Teams made up of hourly workers hire new employees, create production line layouts, decide on production levels, and even make employee termination recommendations. They drive the quality process. That's a real change from how industrial companies have traditionally been managed."

Another demonstration of Whirlpool's commitment to empowering and enabling employees is its compensation system, which is driven by the principle of "pay for performance." Essentially, all Whirlpool employees received stock options in 1991. Some operations provide gain-sharing programs that allow employees to benefit directly from their own productivity and quality improvements. Being stockholders as well as stakeholders has given workers even more incentive to become active learners.

In one annual report, Whitwam remarked that the commitment and effort of the people employed by Whirlpool worldwide "were crucial to our performance ... and we have many programs in place to further encourage going forward. Whirlpool Excellence Systems (WES) has helped our men and women understand the need to make decisions and carry out their jobs for the purpose of satisfying customers—and to challenge those decisions that they believe fall short of the mark. So, too, have innovative performance-based compensation systems at all levels within the corporation. Whirlpool has made substantial progress toward becoming an integrated global home-appliance company, one in which its people share the best of what they know and do with colleagues worldwide" (Marquardt, 2002, p. 129).

Whirlpool seeks to tap the creativity and skills of its employees around the world to provide quality and competitive prices for all its customers. Cost and quality improvements, higher customer satisfaction, and the efficiencies resulting from sharing best practices in areas such as product development, engineering, procurement, manufacturing, marketing, sales, and distribution contribute to Whirlpool's strong global performance.

## EMPLOYEE LEARNING FOR COMPANY SUCCESS

At Whirlpool, line managers run action learning groups composed of frontline workers. Close to 100 percent of line managers actually conduct the action training. The role of training and HR people has become largely one of training line managers to be trainers.

Whirlpool is dedicated to building a perfect product for its customer. With that as the point of departure, you can indeed take the notion of satisfying the customer to a completely different plane, and that's where breakthrough learning has become possible for Whirlpool.

In one annual report, employees from around the world were cited for significant benefits to Whirlpool customers resulting from their knowledge and initiative: A cross-functional team developed Whirlpool's award-winning, super-efficient refrigerator; a learning group devised a just-in-time system to supply product kits and components; a project team leveraged knowledge captured in North America into a new dryer designed for European customers; and cross-functional employee groups in Europe refined complex manufacturing processes.

## EMPOWERING CUSTOMERS

Whirlpool has emphasized the importance of learning from its customers if the company is to develop the ability to delight them. Success means understanding better than anyone in the industry the present and future needs of consumers and trade partners. Whirlpool believes that its research in these areas is the most exhaustive in the home-appliance industry.

By paying consumers to "play around" with appliances at its Usability Lab in Comerio, Italy, Whirlpool discovered that microwave oven sales would improve if it introduced a model that browned food. The result: Whirlpool developed the VIP Crisp, now Europe's bestseller, which is also gaining popularity in the United States.

Whirlpool realizes that doing business successfully in a given geographic region requires a thorough understanding of consumers and the market as a whole. In Asia, for example, Whirlpool conducted focus group sessions with 1,000 consumers in nine countries, surveyed 6,500 households, engaged in 700 consumer discussions in four countries, and performed other extensive research studies with economic, diplomatic, and regulatory sources. Whirlpool also benchmarked other Western companies that have been successful in the Asian region, among them: AT&T, Emerson, Hewlett-Packard, McDonald's, Motorola, Procter & Gamble, and Westinghouse.

## LEARNING WITH AND FROM PARTNERS

Whirlpool has also developed close learning relationships with organizations in related businesses, such as Procter & Gamble and Unilever. In these and other partnerships,

Whirlpool not only exchanges basic information and ideas but shares more intensive involvement at developmental, engineering, and technological levels.

As part of its global strategy, Whirlpool seeks to learn and work closely with its worldwide partners. Recently, Whirlpool incorporated specially designed agitators into its washing machines when it sold them in India. This helped Indian women wash saris without the five-foot-long sari getting tangled. Whirlpool formed a joined venture with a local partner to produce the redesigned washing machine to suit local taste and culture (Casestudyinc.com, 2011). Whirlpool is a world leader in establishing trade partnerships, and it maintains strategic agreements with the top major retailers in North America, Europe, and South America. These partnerships have produced significant learning and driven Whirlpool's business success.

## PEOPLE AND THE CORPORATE COMPETITIVE ADVANTAGE AT WHIRLPOOL

As a result of its learning prowess, Whirlpool has had significant global success. Whirlpool people know, said Whitwam, that the company's vision of "reaching worldwide to bring excellence home" depends on their ability to provide "continuous quality improvement and to exceed all of our customers' expectations. We will gain competitive advantage through this, and by building on our existing strengths and developing new competencies."

This vision and those capabilities are becoming more of a reality every day for this emerging learning organization. Whitwam and the people of Whirlpool have wisely recognized that "continuous change is the essence of the global market," and that only by empowering and enabling people from throughout the organization and across the business chain can they achieve worldwide success (Marquardt, 2002, p. 131).

### Top 10 Strategies For Empowering And Enabling People

#### 1. ENCOURAGE LEADERS TO MODEL AND DEMONSTRATE LEARNING

Because actions usually speak louder than words, managers can demonstrate their appreciation and love of learning by their attitude and behavior. Spending time reading, listening, reflecting, studying, and attending learning programs sets a good example. And the important leadership skills of visioning, mental models, and systems thinking require consistent development and practice.

Leaders should learn from employees and take their ideas seriously. It's important not to filter out bad news; instead, leaders must remain open to data about the organization, industry, markets, competition, and customers. When channeling information to the appropriate employees, it's best to pass it along without adding managerial spin. Networks of learners and leaders from learning organizations can provide inspiration. Leaders must be able to acknowledge and be open about their own mistakes and those of others. Mistakes are best viewed as opportunities for learning.

## 2. INVITE LEADERS TO CHAMPION LEARNING PROCESSES AND PROJECTS

The primary responsibility of managers in learning organizations is to create a climate that promotes learning. Managers can develop such an environment in some of the following ways:

- Encourage employees to volunteer problem-solving ideas.
- Respond to employee ideas and suggestions in a timely way.
- Support the people you have empowered.
- Promote partnerships and teams that include you.
- Commit to openly discussing differences and working through conflicts.
- Advocate and reward learning.
- Encourage experimentation and reflection on acquired knowledge so that new knowledge can be created.
- Talk publicly and often about learning.
- Generate and enhance learning opportunities wherever and whenever possible.
- Listen to your staff, but don't always provide the answers; encourage them to solve problems themselves.
- Avoid teaching and controlling.
- Slow down and encourage reflection.

## 3. EMPOWER EMPLOYEES TO LEARN AND TO INNOVATE

Empowerment is often nothing more than a slogan espoused but not practiced by top management, particularly when major planning and decision making are under way. Employees quickly grasp this distinction and put less energy and creativity into implementing company operations. The organization's brainpower is barely tapped.

Learning organizations, however, empower and educate their workers about financial, technical, and other pertinent data that can lead to wiser decisions. These companies then entrust employees with the responsibility of achieving success. Truly empowering organizations realize that it is essential to place responsibility as close as possible to points of action. They involve employees in planning, evaluating, and determining responsibilities and profits.

## 4. INSTITUTE PERSONNEL POLICIES THAT REWARD LEARNERS

Many organizations do not practice their stated value of recruiting and rewarding people who are learners. In learning organizations, however, people who learn and help people around them to learn are promoted, rewarded financially, and given better career opportunities. The company looks for potential leaders among staff who take advantage of learning opportunities, ask fresh questions in attempts to optimize learning from experience, and learn well in team settings.

## 5. BUILD AND SUPPORT SELF-MANAGED WORK TEAMS

Probably the most direct way for an organization to demonstrate its confidence in the level of employee empowerment and enablement is by using self-managed work teams (also known as *self-directed work teams* or *high-involvement teams*). Several learning organizations—Microsoft, Colgate-Palmolive, and Novartis—have had great success with this kind of unit. Self-managed work teams are built and supported by a number of important factors.

For team members, these include the following:

- Clear goals and a thorough understanding of the team's power and decision-making authority
- Well-defined time frames
- Strong intergroup skills
- Understanding of group processes and functions
- Well-defined procedures for working within and communicating outside of the group

For the organization, these include:

- Policies, procedures, and systems that are compatible with team-based management
- The confidence to react with equanimity to the team's mistakes or slow pace
- The flexibility to allow the team to explore beyond its original boundaries

## 6. BALANCE FAMILY, WORK, AND LEARNING NEEDS

A learning organization must continually build the performance capabilities of individuals along with those of the company. It is important to ensure that organizational requirements do not overwhelm the personal and performance capabilities of employees. Otherwise the "well-learned" person will either collapse or leave for another company.

In respecting the whole person—personally, physically, spiritually, socially, and economically—as well as his or her family needs, a learning organization tries to be humane and family friendly. Wellness and physical fitness programs, counseling services, flexible work arrangements, and dependent care services all enable workers to focus energies on being more proficient learners and more productive workers.

## 7. ENCOURAGE AND ENHANCE CUSTOMER PARTICIPATION

Customers are a vital source of information and represent a tremendous impetus toward quality and continuous improvement. Learning companies get help with continuously improving services and products by actively sharing information with customers in order to obtain their ideas and inputs. Learning companies encourage customers to be part of their organizations. As fellow team members, customers can help identify needs and inadequacies, offer recommendations, and ensure quality.

To maximize their customers' involvement in learning and knowledge exchange, companies must offer opportunities to learn about products, services, vision, and collaboration options. Banks can provide information about different types of loans and investments. Zoos can educate the public about the environment as well as the care and feeding of animals. Computer companies can use embedded technology to train, as well as learn from, customers.

Learning exchanges such as these not only build customer loyalty and profits in the short term but also augment the learning resources of the organization in the long term.

## 8. MAXIMIZE LEARNING FROM BUSINESS PARTNERS AND ALLIANCES

For most U.S. firms, forming alliances with other companies represents primarily an opportunity for increased profits and greater market share over a limited period of time. Learning companies, however, see a much greater long-term benefit of partnerships—the opportunity to acquire valuable learning. To maximize their learning, they:

- Make up-front assessments of the alliance's learning potential, which might include such considerations as specific kinds of knowledge to be gained, core skills that could be built during the process, and the best approaches to developing these skills

- Build learning objectives into the agreement, and specify responsibilities for learning
- Involve human resources staff in facilitating learning
- Arrange for exchanges of personnel who can bring back learning

## 9. BUILD LONG-TERM LEARNING PARTNERSHIPS WITH SUPPLIERS AND VENDORS

Members of a company's business chain represent resources for new ideas, information, and programs as well as opportunities to explore programs or services that the company itself cannot try out, due to financial, political, or human resources reasons.

Purchasing educational resources, contracting expertise, and renting facilities can often be not only feasible but much more cost-effective when undertaken with partners. Reflecting with partners on experiences and possibilities can also add to overall learning.

## 10. PROVIDE EDUCATIONAL OPPORTUNITIES FOR THE COMMUNITY

There are a variety of ways in which companies can provide learning opportunities for the communities in which they operate. Learning organizations can include local teachers and community workers in in-house management and technical courses. The diversity of perspectives will enrich the discussion. They can invite membership from outside the organization into action learning groups. They can jointly sponsor learning events with other corporations, academic institutions, and government agencies. They can also identify community learning needs that can be provided by corporate staff. Community service opportunities can be highly motivating and can give workers a greater sense of purpose.

Providing learning opportunities for the community benefits both the company and the community. The organization's image is enhanced and appreciated. There is greater interest in working for or buying from the company. The quality of life in the community may be enhanced. Resources can be shared rather than hoarded or unnecessarily consumed. As a result, learning becomes a community-wide as well as a company-wide endeavor.

# CHAPTER 6

# Knowledge Management in Learning Organizations

Knowledge is power, and it can change the world. Frappaolo (2006), Awad and Ghaziri (2010), and others have written on how organizational knowledge has become the most valuable asset of an organization, more important than finances, current market position, equipment, and other resources. In the February 11, 2011 issue of *The Economist*, Thomson Reuter advertises with the slogan The Knowledge Effect, and notes how "knowledge allows us to steer the course of events, to grow economies, promote justice, even save lives." The ad continues, "From a trader in Sydney to a hospital worker in Illinois to a scientist in Beijing ... the knowledge we provide helps to 'spark ideas and action that affects millions.'"

In today's world of work, knowledge is now seen as the primary resource for innovation and success in the workplace. An organization's knowledge, more than anything else, determines its current value in the stock market and/or in the community.

Only through new knowledge can organizations increase their ability to improve products and services, thereby benefiting clients and consumers. Improved products and services must be accompanied by changes to systems, structures, and ways of communicating solutions to problems (Hughes and Morton, 2006). Knowledge is the food of the learning organization; its nutrients enable the organization to grow. Individuals may come and go, but if valued knowledge is lost, the company will starve to death.

An organization's use of technology to manage knowledge has quickly emerged as the most important discriminator between success and failure in the intensely competitive global economy. Nonaka (2008) proclaims that a company's ability to create, store, and disseminate knowledge is absolutely crucial for staying ahead of the competition in areas of quality, speed, innovation, and price. Only by developing and implementing systems and mechanisms to assemble, package, promote, and distribute the fruits of its thinking will a company be able to transform knowledge into corporate power.

Yet, most companies are incompetent at managing knowledge. It is totally uncharted territory. Managing know-how may be different from managing cash or buildings, but managing the intellectual investments of a company needs to be treated every bit as painstakingly. Acquiring the ability to manage knowledge should become the primary job of every worker and every organization.

Organizations must learn how to manage the mechanics of knowledge, just as they learned how to manage the mechanics of production in the industrial era. In the next chapter, we will discuss steps and strategies for managing knowledge that are only possible through the adroit use of technology. To better understand and apply these steps, however, we first need to look at different ways of defining knowledge.

## Hierarchy of Knowledge

Unless and until a company determines its own definition of knowledge and identifies the kind of knowledge that is organizationally important, it will not be able to manage its corporate knowledge. Obviously, not all knowledge is of equal value. Figure 13 presents a hierarchy or continuum of knowledge. At the upper levels of the hierarchy, there is an increase in breadth, depth, meaning, conceptualization, and value. Let's briefly examine each level, beginning at the bottom.

*Data* include texts, facts, interpreted images, and uninterpreted numeric codes without context and therefore without meaning.

*Information* is data imbued with context and meaning, whose form and content can be applied to a particular task after being formalized, classified, processed, and formatted.

*Knowledge* comprises bodies of information, principles, and experience that actively guide task execution and management, decision making, and problem solving. Knowledge enables people to assign meaning to data and

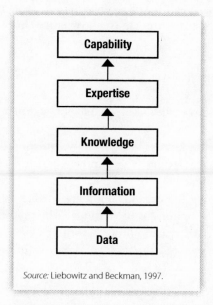

**FIGURE 13**   Hierarchy of Knowledge

thereby generate information. With knowledge, people can deal intelligently with available information sources and then take action.

*Expertise* is the appropriate and effective application of knowledge in order to achieve results and improve performance.

*Capability* encompasses the organizational capacity and expertise to create a product, service, or process at a high level of performance. It requires the integration, coordination, and cooperation of many individuals and teams. Capability is more than just current performance; it is the ability to learn, innovate, and create.

## Types of Knowledge

Knowledge can also be classified by type:

- "Know what": Knowing which information is needed
- "Know how": Knowing how information must be processed
- "Know why": Knowing why certain information is needed
- "Know where": Knowing where to find certain specific information
- "Know when": Knowing when certain information is needed

Wiig (1997) further distinguishes knowledge through the following characteristics:

- Goal-setting or idealistic: Vision, "care why" knowledge, or self-motivated creativity
- Systematic: "Know why" knowledge for acquiring systems understanding
- Pragmatic: "Know how" knowledge for acquiring advanced skills
- Automatic or tacit: "Know what" knowledge for routine working

While developing the organization's knowledge-based system or corporate memory, it is important to recognize different kinds and values of knowledge. Companies that are prepared with such an understanding will be able to effectively address the needs of their organizations.

## A Systems Model for Managing Knowledge

Let us now look at a comprehensive systems approach to managing corporate knowledge. The knowledge subsystem involves six stages, which cover the transition of knowledge from source to use:

- Acquisition
- Creation
- Storage
- Analysis and data mining
- Transfer and dissemination
- Application and validation

The knowledge subsystem is illustrated in Figure 14.

Organizations learn efficiently and effectively when these six processes are ongoing and interactive. They are not sequential or independent: Information should be distributed through multiple channels, each with often differing time frames. The management of knowledge must be subjected continually to perceptual filters as well as both proactive and reactive activities. Managing knowledge is at the heart of building a learning organization. Successful learning organizations systematically and technologically guide knowledge through each and all of these six stages.

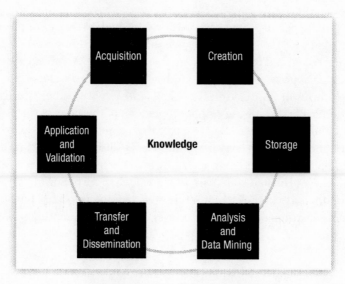

**FIGURE 14**   Knowledge Subsystem

## Knowledge Acquisition

People increasingly need an overwhelming volume and variety of knowledge from all over the world in order to adequately perform their work. Organizations build their knowledge bases by collecting information from many internal and external sources.

### INTERNAL COLLECTION OF KNOWLEDGE

One major complaint of workers is that their organizations do not tap a significant portion of their knowledge. Companies are often startled to discover the amount of intellectual capital present in the brains of their own employees, what Nonaka (2008) calls "tacit knowledge."

Sources of tacit knowledge include an individual's expertise, memories, beliefs, and assumptions, all of which may be valuable to the organization. This kind of knowledge is usually difficult to communicate or explain but can result in tremendous benefits to companies. Alcoa, Panasonic, and McKinsey & Company have demonstrated remarkable capability and creativity in collecting the knowledge of their workers.

Organizations may also adopt either an active or a passive mode of scanning their internal environments. On the one hand, they may allow information to percolate up or trickle down through the organization; on the other, they may actively scan their own internal environments for information, reflect on it, and convert it into usable knowledge. An excellent example of the latter approach is 3M Corporation, which has developed its ability to ascertain information from bench scientists within the organization. Through flexible structuring and reinforcement of the value of sharing work data, the company has benefited from a wealth of information, which in turn has been converted into innovative knowledge and marketable products.

The ability to learn from activities in other parts of an organization can become a principal source of added value for corporations. Organizations may acquire knowledge internally by tapping into the knowledge of their staffs, learning from shared experience, and implementing continuous change processes.

## EXTERNAL COLLECTION OF KNOWLEDGE

The pace of change is so rapid today that no single organization can ever control all effective operating practices and good ideas. Being a marketplace leader requires an organization to look outward for constant improvement and new ideas. The old school of thought, which held "if it isn't invented here, it can't be any good," is a curse in today's high-velocity markets. Organizations don't need to reinvent what others have done: Today's rallying cry is "acquire, adapt, and advance." Companies can capture external information using some of the following methods:

- Benchmarking other organizations
- Attending conferences
- Hiring consultants
- Reading newspapers, journals, and documents on the Internet
- Viewing television, video, and film
- Monitoring economic, social, and technological trends
- Collecting data from customers, competitors, suppliers, and other resources
- Hiring new staff
- Collaborating with other organizations, building alliances, and forming joint ventures

One of the most popular and valuable external sources of knowledge is benchmarking. Let's examine this widespread approach in more detail.

## Benchmarking

Companies generally assign benchmarking teams to look far and wide for better operating practices. Benchmark teams sound the alarm at the first sign that an organization has fallen behind the competition or failed to take advantage of important operating improvements developed elsewhere. The search for best practices quickly draws a firm outside the confines of its own culture and personal habits.

Best-practices benchmarking provides an organization with the rationale and process for accepting change as constant, inevitable, and beneficial. Organizations that engage in ongoing adaptation of best practices are often able to avoid being ambushed by unexpected change. They speed up their rates of improvement by systematically studying others and comparing their own internal operations and performance with the best practices of highly innovative and successful companies. This kind of benchmarking is strategically oriented and represents a pragmatic approach to change management and performance improvement. Other kinds of benchmarking may be process oriented—focused on discrete processes and work systems—or performance oriented—focused on assessment of their competitive position through product and service comparisons.

Tomorrow's best practices will inevitably evolve beyond or diverge from those of today. By their nature, best practices are dynamic and progressive. For this reason, best-practices benchmarking is often called an *evergreen* process because it renews the organization each time it is repeated. As an ongoing business process, it integrates fully with continuous improvement in the organization.

Benchmarking benefits organizations in these areas:

- Setting and refining strategy
- Continuously improving work processes and business systems
- Setting goals
- Solving problems
- Increasing education and idea enrichment
- Comparing and evaluating market performance
- Acting as a catalyst for change

Many of the learning companies mentioned in this book, such as Whirlpool, Caterpillar, National Semiconductor, and Accenture, consider benchmarking one of their most effective tools for acquiring high-quality and highly relevant knowledge.

There are two important points to keep in mind relative to knowledge acquisition. First, information, whether acquired from an internal or external source, is subject to the perceptual filters of corporate norms, values, and procedures. These filters influence the organization's decisions on the relevance and usefulness of collected information. Second, acquiring knowledge is not always intentional; much of it is accidental or a by-product of organizational actions. Learning organizations tend to be intentional about acquiring knowledge.

## Gathering Knowledge at PricewaterhouseCoopers

PwC (officially PricewaterhouseCoopers) is a global professional services firm headquartered in London. It is the world's second-largest professional services firm (after Deloitte) and has offices in nearly 800 cities across 150 countries. PwC employs more than 163,000 people. Total revenues in 2009 were $26 billion.

PwC is recognized as having one of the most mature knowledge management systems in the world and estimates that up to 99 percent of its revenue is generated from knowledge-based professional services and products. Its employees spend up to eighty hours a year creating and sharing knowledge. Why is knowledge management so critical to PwC? Among many significant reasons, the company's geographic dispersion and global clientele require timely coordination and information sharing among the different subsidiaries. Employees must be familiar with previous projects and work conducted in other areas of the organization. Similarly, rapidly changing information on topics such as tax policies, legislation, banking, and financial requirements must be quickly captured and disseminated to appropriate sectors. Another driving force is an employee turnover rate of 15 to 25 percent per year, which means PwC requires systems for storing knowledge instead of letting it walk out the door. Knowledge management also enables PwC to discover and constantly share best practices throughout the firm. A tendency toward silos of knowledge activity would create inefficiencies and duplication.

KnowledgeView, PwC's proprietary best-practices repository of information, contains over 4,500 entries gathered from more than 2,200 companies worldwide, with references to more than 350 internal and external benchmarking studies. KnowledgeView's goal is to support the firm's core competency of being business advisors: including the accumulation, analysis, creation, and dissemination of value-added information and knowledge that PwC professionals can use to improve business performance of clients, and ultimately increase the value of PwC's services.

KnowledgeView is Lotus-Notes based rather than CD-ROM based, which permits daily information updates as well as the capacity to access and share knowledge instantaneously worldwide. The databases in KnowledgeView incorporate the following information:

- Best practices as identified in PwC and non-PwC programs
- Benchmarking studies from internal and external sources
- Expert opinions synthesized from both the industry and process subject matter
- Abstracts of books and articles on business improvement
- PwC database of staff biographies with résumés, arranged by country, industry, skills, language, and so forth
- Views and forecasts from PwC experts

KnowledgeView is classified by industry, process, enabler, topic, and measurement so that PwC consultants can target and find the knowledge they are seeking. The format used for containing the information is an important feature of KnowledgeView. For example, in the best-practices database, the format is set up to answer the following questions:

- What caused the change?
- What old process needed improvement?
- What is the new process?
- What is the new performance and how is it measured?
- What lessons were learned?
- What are the future directions?

KnowledgeView is maintained and updated at knowledge centers located in Dallas, London, Sao Paulo, Moscow, and Sydney. Offering local staff immediate access, these regional centers help stimulate knowledge sharing. Due to its knowledge management values, goals, and achievements, PwC has been ranked as one of the world's "Most Admired Knowledge Enterprises" (MAKE) in the 2008 Global MAKE study.

## Knowledge Creation

Knowledge can be created through a number of processes ranging from daring innovation to painstaking and diligent research. It can also arise from the "uncanny ability people have to see new connections and combine previously known knowledge elements through complex inductive reasoning" (Wiig, 1997). The kind of knowledge discovered through problem-solving, experimental, and demonstration projects can be extremely valuable for organizations.

Whereas knowledge acquisition is generally adaptive, knowledge creation is generative. Creating new knowledge involves not only group-developed external information but tacit and highly subjective individual insights and intuitions as well. It is about using ideals as well as ideas to fuel innovation. Creating new knowledge is traditionally thought to be the province of the research and development department, but the task truly belongs to every unit and person in the organization.

For example, at National Semiconductor, management knows that it must shape and move knowledge throughout the organization if it is to be a leader in shaping and moving technologies. The company has initiated ongoing efforts to identify best practices and new concepts from all over the world, which are then systematically disseminated throughout the entire organization. National uses the following keys to encourage innovation:

- A corporate culture that emphasizes diversity in ideas, skills, and people and that makes innovation a top corporate goal
- Open attitudes that tolerate risks and convert failure to a learning opportunity—in other words: projects fail, people don't
- A clear, funded, and supported innovation process
- Corporate labs where development of patents and other intellectual property is highly valued
- Project champions who work with small, dedicated, multifunctional teams
- A workplace that stimulates new ideas and does not minimize any contribution
- Innovation measurement performed at all levels and considered important to corporate success
- Reward systems that provide clear-cut, significant, and timely benefits—such as money, position, or control—for innovators

## FOUR PATTERNS OF KNOWLEDGE CREATION

Ikujiro Nonaka (2008), professor of management at Hitotsubashi University in Tokyo, writes that "successful companies are those that consistently create new knowledge, disseminate it widely throughout the organization, and quickly embody it in new technologies and products." He goes on to state that knowledge creation should be at "the epicenter of a company's corporate strategy" (p. 96).

Nonaka identified four patterns of interaction between tacit knowledge and explicit knowledge in building or augmenting organizational knowledge. Tacit knowledge is the knowledge we hold inside and may have difficulty expressing. Explicit knowledge is formal, systematic, easily shared knowledge, such as product specifications, scientific formulas, and computer programs.

*Tacit to tacit:* This form of knowledge growth occurs when an individual passes on knowledge to another individual, as in a master-apprentice relationship. By working closely with the master, the apprentice absorbs the master's tacit knowledge. This is a limited form of knowledge creation because the knowledge of both people is never made explicit and cannot be leveraged by the organization as a whole.

*Explicit to explicit:* This kind of knowledge comes from combining and synthesizing existing explicit knowledge, as when the company controller gathers and synthesizes company information. This pattern represents a limited form of creating new knowledge because it uses learning that already exists.

*Tacit to explicit:* This pattern of knowledge creation occurs when an individual takes existing knowledge, adds his or her tacit knowledge, and creates something new that can be shared throughout the organization, as when the company controller comes up with a new system of budget control.

*Explicit to tacit:* This form of knowledge creation takes place when new explicit knowledge is internalized by the members of the organization to create new tacit knowledge, as when the controller's new budgeting process becomes the company's standard way of doing business.

In the knowledge-creating company, all four patterns exist and work dynamically together in a kind of knowledge spiral. These patterns become a powerful force for creating new knowledge as the various interactions generate much personal commitment and energy.

## KNOWLEDGE-CREATING ACTIVITIES

An organization may engage in a number of activities to promote knowledge creation.

### Action Learning

This approach to knowledge creation, which is discussed in more detail in chapter 8, involves a group of people working on real problems, learning while doing so, and incorporating that learning to more quickly and creatively solve problems and develop breakthrough strategies (Marquardt & Yeo, 2011). Action learning builds on the experience and knowledge of an individual or group by adding skilled, reflective questioning that results in new knowledge.

## SYSTEMATIC PROBLEM SOLVING

Although most problem-solving programs and tools are relatively straight-forward and easily communicated, the "necessary mind-set," according to Garvin (2009), is "more difficult to establish. ... Employees must become more disciplined in their thinking and more attentive to details." They must continually press for accuracy and "push beyond obvious symptoms to assess underlying causes, often collecting evidence when conventional wisdom says it is unnecessary" (pp. 81–82).

Xerox is a learning company that has mastered this approach to advancing its knowledge base. All employees have been trained in problem-solving techniques and using appropriate tools in four areas: generating ideas and collecting information, reaching consensus, analyzing and displaying data, and planning actions.

### Experimentation

This form of knowledge creation differs from action learning and systematic problem solving because it is motivated not by current situations or difficulties but by opportunity and expanding horizons. Examples of experimentation include the development of original innovations through research and development, pilot projects, and autonomous, on-the-side research efforts (i.e., "skunk works"). Experimentation may take the form of ongoing programs or one-of-a-kind demonstration projects.

Ongoing programs involve a continuing series of small experiments that are designed to produce incremental gains in knowledge. This form of knowledge creation is the mainstay of many programs for continuous improvement and total quality and are usually found on the shop floor. Learning organizations such as Corning and Chaparral Steel have successfully created new technologies through this technique.

Demonstration projects are usually larger and more complex; they generally require holistic, system wide changes undertaken with the goal of developing new organizational capacities. Garvin (2009, p. 83) notes that demonstration projects share a number of distinctive characteristics:

- Systematic principles and approaches that will be adopted later on a larger scale
- Learning by doing and making midcourse corrections
- Severe tests of commitment for employees who may be wondering if rules and operations have, in fact, changed

- Development by multifunctional, multilevel teams
- Explicit strategies for transferring learning required to produce significant effects

## Capturing Knowledge at Grant Thornton LLP

In an attempt to capture knowledge from seasoned employees and pass it down to those with less experience, Grant Thornton developed and deployed what it calls *K-Source*. This integrated knowledge management platform was designed to meet the key business goals of driving sales growth, strengthening client service, improving efficiency, and supporting firm values. It features an online community for every service line, industry, and geographic area. Each is overseen by a knowledge manager who actively seeks contributions. Participation is part of every employee's performance evaluation goals, and the CEO has a blog on the front page.

Employees can create personal profiles; set up personalized news feeds from Dow Jones Factiva; access courses, e-books, and webcasts; and participate in online discussions that facilitate information knowledge collection. Additionally, new instant messaging technology being deployed permits video phone conversations using built-in webcams.

### Learning from Past Experiences

Learning companies create knowledge by reviewing their successes and failures, subjecting them to systematic assessment, and transferring and recording what is learned in a way that will be of maximum benefit to the organization. According to Garvin (2009), research on the development of new products shows that the knowledge gained from failure was often "instrumental for organizations in achieving subsequent success. In the simplest terms, failure is the ultimate teacher" (p. 89).

Boeing is one learning company that expects its managers to systematically think about the past and learn from successes and mistakes. The company's 737 and 747 planes were introduced with serious problems. To ensure that those problems would not be repeated for the upcoming 757 and 767 planes, Boeing commissioned a high-level employee group, called Project Homework, to examine the development processes of the 737 and 747—as well as the 707 and 727, two of the company's most successful planes. After three years, the group identified hundreds of improvements that were then transferred to the 757 and 767 startups. Guided by the review, Boeing was able to produce the most successful, error-free launches in its history.

While some companies build much of their success on acquiring knowledge from others and improving on it, other companies focus almost entirely on creating new knowledge. These organizations—such as Merck, Rubbermaid, 3M, and Walmart—find success by being innovators rather than imitators.

## Moving from Knowledge to Sales at Panasonic

Founded in 1918, Panasonic has grown to become the largest Japanese electronics producer. In addition to electronics, Panasonic offers non-electronic products and services such as home renovation services. With nearly 400,000 employees worldwide, Panasonic was ranked the 89th-largest company in the world in 2009, with over $80 billion in revenues.

In the 1990s, Panasonic (known as Matsushita at that time) decided to become "a possibility-searching company" with goals in the following four areas:

- *Human innovation:* Business that inspires new lifestyles based on creativity, comfort, and joy in addition to efficiency and convenience
- *Humanware technology:* Technology for human innovation businesses
- *Active heterogeneous group:* A corporate culture based on individuality and diversity
- *Multilocal and global networking management:* A corporate structure that enables both localization and global synergy

Panasonic took the knowledge it created in various projects and spiraled the information throughout the company. Learning that took place in the Cooking Appliances Division eventually affected corporate strategy. The company was thus better able to identify the type of knowledge required in the changing competitive environment and could continuously enhance the enabling conditions.

Leveraging the tacit knowledge base of an individual and making use of socialization to transfer it throughout the organization is a highly valuable activity. For example, a head baker's kneading skill led to the development of Matsushita's bread-making machine. By its very nature, tacit knowledge is hard to communicate but is nonetheless critical. Socialization is an important means of sharing tacit knowledge between individuals. Tacit skills are learned by observation and imitation, and engineers had to experience the actual bread-making process to learn kneading skill. Nonaka (2008) postulated that the company's success points out four key aspects of knowledge creation.

First, amplifying knowledge creation across different levels in the organization led to the creation of Human Electronics and a series of successful products embodying that concept. Only by cross leveling can companies obtain the true benefits of organizational knowledge creation. The knowledge created in developing the Home Bakery unit spiraled beyond the unit to create new knowledge at the corporate level.

Second, enhancing enabling conditions promotes the four patterns of knowledge conversion. Matsushita increased redundancy and variety by providing research and development with up-to-date sales information, bringing autonomy to the divisions by restructuring the organization, and instilling intentions and creative chaos by setting challenging goals such as shifting to multimedia or improving productivity by 30 percent. Redundancy helped team members by providing a common language with which to share their tacit knowledge.

Third, continuously creating knowledge requires uninterrupted innovation. Because the competitive environment and customer preferences are always changing, existing knowledge quickly becomes obsolete. Constant upgrading of organizational intentions or values is important because new knowledge must be measured constantly against the company's latest intention.

Fourth, Panasonic recognized the value of self-organizing teams to the organizational learning process. Knowledge creation begins when members of each team share tacit knowledge on the types of work the employees at Panasonic should and should not do to fully utilize their creativity. The teams also analyzed existing work patterns and uncovered causes of inefficiencies. Panasonic realized that teams must be given full autonomy to develop ideas for improvement.

## Knowledge Storage

Before organizations begin to store knowledge for later retrieval, they must identify important information and determine the best method for retaining it. Organizations give meaning to data through reflection, research, and experimentation. Knowledge storage utilizes technical systems, such as records and databases, and human processes, such as collective and individual memory and consensus. A knowledge storage system should have:

- A structure that permits the system to find and deliver information quickly and correctly
- Categories such as facts, policies, or procedures divided on a learning-needs basis
- Ability to deliver requested information in a clear and concise form
- Content that is accurate, timely, and consistently available

Knowledge storage systems are not new. In fact, the concept first emerged in the 1980s. The thought was that after data were in place and cataloged, managers could help themselves to whatever slice of the data pie they needed at that moment. The idea sounded good. In practice, however, the size and complexity of the resulting data warehouse meant that maintenance costs were too high for everyone except a few banks and airlines.

Within the past few years, the concept of data warehousing has reappeared, and it is now traveling quickly around the world. Why? The answer has to do with competition as well as dramatic reductions in cost and increases in the power of today's computers. Thus, comprehensive repositories—online, computer-based storehouses of expertise, information, experience, and documentation in which knowledge is collected, summarized, and integrated across all sources—are emerging in organizations around the world. Cheaper UNIX systems are replacing the expensive proprietary mainframes of first-generation data warehouses. Web technologies such as ActiveX, CGI, Java, and JavaScript as well as GB Oracle databases have also emerged.

With a knowledge storage system, an organization is capable of retaining knowledge; it becomes company property. It doesn't go home at night or become lost to the company when an employee leaves. Unfortunately, knowledge (also referred to as *intellectual capital*), although far more important than physical material, may be scattered, hard to find, and liable to disappear without a trace because it is not stored. Storage is obviously important, but what kinds of knowledge should be stored?

## WHICH KNOWLEDGE TO STORE

Stewart (1997) has proposed five general categories for knowledge storage.

- *Corporate yellow pages:* Capabilities of employees, consultants, and advisers to the organization—who speaks Thai, who knows JavaScript, who has worked with certain clients
- *Lessons learned:* Checklists of successes, mistakes, or failures that might be applied to other projects
- *Competitor and supplier intelligence:* Continuously updated company profiles and news from commercial and public sources and wire services, call reports from salespeople, attendees' notes from conferences and conventions, an in-house directory of experts, and news about regulations.
- *Company experiences and policies:* Process maps and work-flows, plans, procedures, principles and guidelines, standards, policies, performance

measures, stakeholder and customer profiles, products and services (including features, functionality, pricing, sales, and repair)
- *Company products and processes:* Technologies, inventions, data, publications and processes, strategies and cultures, structures and systems, effective organizational routines and procedures

## HOW TO STORE KNOWLEDGE

Knowledge is nothing more than unusable data unless it is coded and stored in a way that makes sense to individuals and their organizations. Many companies are overwhelmed, inundated with the vast amounts of data that clutter up the information highway. Irretrievable, distorted, fragmented, or inaccurate information will not produce learning. To determine what data can be used, organizations must determine what is of value and then code the data based on learning needs and organizational operations. In addition, companies must establish well-defined criteria for identifying new knowledge, develop plans for formulating knowledge, and select efficient storage locations.

Store acquired learning by methods that enable workers to:

- Decide which coworkers might have the knowledge needed for a particular activity
- Decide which coworkers would be interested in a lesson learned
- Enter a lesson learned into the corporate memory

For example, Cigna Corporation, a leading insurance company, knows that excellence comes from making knowledgeable choices. Cigna realizes that significant latent knowledge and expertise exist throughout the organization but initially, the company did not have a good means of extracting and publishing this know-how. The company assigned home-office managers the job of building and maintaining a knowledge base—basically a collection of checklists, rules of thumb, formal guidelines for risk assessment, and names of experts. The collected knowledge was installed in the software used by underwriters to process applications. Now, if a nursing home in California wants insurance, the custom-built software tells the agent the location of the nearest geological fault line along with estimates of its threat level provided by the company's experts. When new information comes in, if it is sound, the managers evaluate it and promptly add it to the database.

## CHALLENGES IN STORING KNOWLEDGE

It is important to repeat that knowledge storage involves both technical and human processes. As organizations become physically and geographically diffused as well as more specialized and decentralized, their storage systems and memory may become fragmented, and the corporate benefits of the knowledge may be lost. And as work becomes more computer oriented, information from different occupational specializations is potentially available across functional boundaries. Networked information technology must be utilized so that fragmented information can be reinterpreted and readily exchanged internally and externally.

Given the fact that new technology is able to store and provide more information, consideration must be given to the potential of data deluge or information overload. The amount of information stored should not exceed the company's human capacity to process it.

## Analysis and Data Mining

Over the past thirty years, organizations have become skilled at capturing and storing large amounts of operational data. Until recently, however, we have not seen corresponding advances in techniques for analyzing this data, to reconstruct, validate, and inventory this critical resource. New approaches and tools have become available to mine and analyze large databases and interpret their contents.

Data mining is the latest analytical tool to enable organizations to find meaning in their data. By discovering new patterns or fitting models to data, employees can store and later extract information to aid in developing strategies and answering complex business questions. Software has been developed that can analyze huge volumes of data and identify hidden patterns. Whereas OLAP (online analytical process) can answer the questions managers ask, data mining software answers the questions managers haven't even thought of yet.

There are several data mining tasks, such as classification, regression, clustering, summarization, dependency modeling, and change and deviation detection. Data mining methods include example-based methods, decision trees and rules, nonlinear regression and classification, probabilistic graphical dependency models, relational learning, and intelligent agents.

## DATA MINING TOOLS

Data mining tools are software components and theories that allow users to extract information from data. The tools provide individuals and companies with the ability to gather large amounts of data and use it to make determinations about a particular user or groups of users. Some of the most common uses of data mining tools are in the fields of marketing, fraud protections, and surveillance.

Fayyad et al. (1996) note that data mining commonly involves four classes of tasks:

- *Clustering* is the task of discovering groups and structures in the data that are in some way or another "similar," without using known structures in the data.
- *Classification* is the task of generalizing known structure to apply to new data. For example, an email program might attempt to classify an email as legitimate or spam. Common algorithms include decision tree learning, nearest neighbor, naive Bayesian classification, neural networks, and support vector machines.
- *Regression* attempts to find a function that models the data with the least error.
- *Association rule learning* searches for relationships between variables. For example, a supermarket might gather data on customer purchasing habits. Using association rule learning, the supermarket can determine which products are frequently bought together and use this information for marketing purposes. This is sometimes referred to as *market basket analysis*.

A growing number of data mining tools are being developed for navigating data, discovering patterns and creating new strategies, and identifying underlying statistical and quantitative methods of visualization. Platforms to support these tools, techniques for preparing the data, and methods for quantifying the results are also emerging.

Data mining is being utilized by a growing array of organizations.

*Retailers:* The universal adoption of EPOS and the spread of loyalty cards are fueling rapid need for knowledge analysis. Key benefits are the abilities to understand customers' buying behavior and rapidly identify unprofitable lines. W. H. Smith is reported to have weeded out 20,000 of its least profitable products as a result of knowledge analysis, and the biggest U.S. retailer, Walmart, is investing in the world's biggest data warehouse to handle data on customer buying patterns from its 9,000 stores worldwide.

*Financial services organizations:* These institutions have long seen the potential of knowledge analysis to obtain an integrated view of their customers. High-payoff areas include targeted database marketing-and-risk analysis. Capital One Financial Corporation has virtually revolutionized the credit card business by using data mining to do highly sophisticated customer profiling and targeting. As a result, it has been able to develop a portfolio of literally hundreds of segmented credit card products.

*Manufacturers:* Some of the latest data mining techniques are being used by manufacturers. Downtime—for instance, when a paper roll breaks in a paper mill—is expensive, but by analyzing the data from previous stoppages, companies have been able to predict the combinations of circumstances that are likely to result in downtime. Organizations then match this knowledge with current operational conditions and act to avoid potential breakdowns, which represent prevention rather than a cure.

*Telecom companies:* These firms generate huge volumes of customer and operations data. Telecom operators analyze call data in ever more sophisticated ways for the purposes of determining competitive pricing, developing new price tariffs, and designing highly segmented marketing campaigns. Knowledge analysis technologies have also been applied to improving network utilization; for example, a company can analyze the amount of uncompleted calls to specific customers that may result from an insufficient number of lines.

## Knowledge Transfer and Dissemination

Knowledge transfer and dissemination involves the organizational and technological movement of information, data, and knowledge. An organization's capacity to move knowledge is also the capacity to transfer and share power and is indispensable for corporate success; knowledge must be disseminated accurately and quickly throughout the organization or the company fails.

Knowledge retrieval may be either controlled or automatic. Controlled retrieval utilizes individual and group records and memories; automatic retrieval is triggered by various events or situations. Weick (2009) warns that information retrieved from organizational memory may bear little resemblance to the original material due to the transformational nature of storage and retrieval processes, the normal integration of human memory, the impact of perceptual filters, and the loss of supporting rationales. It is therefore important to develop a corporate memory and design processes that ensure accurate and timely knowledge retrieval.

Accessing required information just in time extends an individual's long-term memory and reduces workload memory requirements. The corporate knowledge base consolidates information in a central location, thus liberating a person's working memory from such menial data as resource location. This creates the right conditions for rapid sharing of knowledge and sustained, collective knowledge growth. Lead times between learning and knowledge application are shortened throughout the organization. Human capital will also become more productive through structured, easily accessible, and intelligent work processes.

When structuring knowledge, it is important to consider how and why the information will be retrieved by different groups of people. Functional and effective knowledge storage systems are categorized with the following elements in mind:

- Learning needs
- Work objectives
- User expertise
- Function or use of information
- Location and method of information storage

Several companies have made great strides in developing their knowledge-sharing systems. Accenture, for example, uses Knowledge Xchange, which allows more than 50,000 professionals around the world to utilize the system to access knowledge bases and share knowledge. Chevron employs intranets, groupware, data warehouses, networks, bulletin boards, and videoconferencing to distribute stored knowledge. In addition, Chevron utilizes knowledge bases, lists of experts, information maps, corporate yellow pages, custom desktop applications, and other systems. Bell Atlantic uses CYLINA (Cyberspaced Leveraged Intelligent Agent), which acquires knowledge through interactions with large numbers of users. The company supplements this approach with Auto-FAQ, a system that helps users retrieve knowledge from CYLINA in response to their questions.

## Collecting and Disseminating Knowledge at McKinsey & Company

McKinsey & Company is a global management consulting firm of over 17,000 employees that focuses on solving issues of concern to senior management. 2010 revenues exceeded $6 billion. McKinsey serves as an adviser to the world's leading businesses, governments, and institutions. The company has developed the following principles relative to organizational learning and knowledge management:

- Knowledge-based strategies must begin with strategy, not knowledge or technology.
- Strategies need to be linked to organizational performance and success.
- Executing a knowledge-based strategy is not about managing knowledge, but nurturing people with knowledge.
- Organizations leverage knowledge through networks of people who collaborate, not through networks of technology that interconnect.

In the past, McKinsey associates had to rely on their personal network of contacts when meeting client requests for information and/or help that fell outside their own individual realm of expertise. The sources for new information were limited by the size of a consultant's personal network. By electronically linking every associate together with LANs and WANs, and at the same time developing knowledge databases containing previous consulting experiences, industry information, and expert contacts, the number of sources for new information available to any single McKinsey associate has been greatly increased. Additionally, discussion databases organized around specific topics have allowed ongoing knowledge sharing between geographically distant employees of the firms. Anyone at anytime in any location can monitor ongoing discussions, take away new insights, or join in and add new knowledge throughout the computer-assisted learning system.

### INTENTIONAL TRANSFER OF KNOWLEDGE WITHIN THE ORGANIZATION

Knowledge may be transferred intentionally by a variety of means. Written methods include individual communications such as memos, reports, and open-access bulletin boards as well as internal publications of all kinds, using video, audio, and print media. Internal conferences, briefings, mentoring, and training with internal consultants or perhaps in formal courses offer additional opportunities for exchanging information. Job rotation or transfers can be planned to disperse knowledge to other areas of the organization, although large corporations comprising many divisions may provide short-term tours tailored for specific audiences and needs.

## UNINTENTIONAL TRANSFER OF KNOWLEDGE WITHIN THE ORGANIZATION

Organizations may also transfer knowledge unintentionally in a number of ways. Routine job rotation, stories and myths, task forces, and informal networks all send knowledge to different areas of the organization. Much informal learning takes place as a function of daily and often unplanned interactions among people. The less intentionality or planning there is to the process, the more potential knowledge is lost.

## Knowledge Cafés at Datatel

Datatel, a leading provider of technology solutions and professional business services to higher education institutions throughout North America, recently created a virtual knowledge café. The café includes learning paths tailored to roles as well as discussion forums, FAQs, and tips and tricks to share knowledge. Datatel encourages people to help themselves to knowledge and to engage in any conversation that interests them in any area.

Another way of sharing internal knowledge is via the company's *Discovery Week*, a five-day offsite conference at a local hotel. In 2009 it was attend by 88 percent of the employees and 100 percent of the executive team. The company provided a cyber café, wireless Internet access and ad hoc meeting rooms, and tables in the hotel's central atrium to encourage networking and enable sharing of knowledge. The days were filled with ninety-five learning sessions given by employees, executives, and professional trainers, as well as by external and internal keynote speakers and community of practice meetings.

Datatel's culture supports a core value of sharing information early and often. Other special events include:

- A wellness fair, a showcase in which teams educate other employees on their business and support strategies
- Innovation challenges in which employee teams present their most innovative ideas to move the company forward (the top three are then funded)

- Special cafés on special topics (e.g., launching a SharePoint intranet to facilitate document sharing and discussion boards)
- "Ask the experts" discussion board, job aids, and document libraries (Salopek, 2010b)

## BARRIERS TO SHARING AND TRANSFERRING KNOWLEDGE

Insofar as releasing information releases power, the transfer of knowledge is indispensable for learning organizations. Knowledge should be disseminated appropriately and quickly. However, three major conditions create bottle-necks in the timely and effective transfer of knowledge:

- Critical business processes are available only to a few people.
- Knowledge is not available at the appropriate place and/or time.
- Transfers and restructuring increase the difficulty of securing knowledge.

## Capturing and Transferring Knowledge at NASA

As organizations age, so do the individuals within those organizations. Of course, at some point, the individual can retire or leave the organization. This is what happened to the National Aeronautics and Space Administration (NASA). The people who formed and developed the organization began to retire after thirty years of creating the knowledge of the agency. NASA became concerned because their organizational knowledge, which was stored in the individuals, was "retiring out-the-door."

The agency began a program to transfer the knowledge of its senior engineers to the more junior engineers. The engineering directors' workforce is made up of engineers, scientists, and computer scientists. Management structure is lean and most work is accomplished through the collaboration of these individuals. The age distribution of the workforce in the engineering directors could be characterized as bi-modal. There were a number of people hired in the late 1960s and another group hired in the late 1980s, so there were few employees who were in the middle of their career. Most were either thinking about retirement or just beginning their careers. As a result, the leaders and the engineering directors were concerned that the loss of the more experienced individuals would leave a void that could impact the development of future systems.

The goals of the engineering directors were to:

1. Capture and transfer to the younger employees scarce knowledge and skill
2. Develop ways to maintain knowledge and skills apart from experts

3. Create a culture of learning among experts in younger employees
4. Create a culture in which ongoing debate, discussion, and inquiry about technical methods was encouraged

Specifically, it appeared that most knowledge in organizational memory about technical approaches was stored with specific individuals. Because of a culture that produced minimal interaction between senior experts and younger employees and the non-routine nature of the information, exposure to this knowledge was limited. There was also an apparent resistance by senior experts to documenting organizational memory in accessible forms such as manuals, training courses, or expert system databases. Finally, the structuring element was also targeted for improvement. In fact, less experienced employees stated that they felt that they lacked an appreciation about the total approach to engineering processes and the directors. This, as well as specific expertise, had never been systematically shared. Communication had been limited due to the small amount of informal interaction with other departments, management, and most important, senior technical experts.

Because of the diversity in missions, each team developed a plan for the dissemination and diffusion of technical information. They included formal and informal methods designed to transfer information from the senior technical experts to younger employees as well as methods for exchanging information among the younger employees and with other organizational units.

There were a number of formal strategies adopted by the teams. They included electronic bulletin boards that would be updated monthly to focus on new techniques, lessons learned, and other important technical information. Many teams opted for a series of "brown bag" meetings once a month to discuss technical problems and issues among themselves and senior experts. These were advertised across departments to maximize exposure and information exchange. Other teams selected more standard approaches, including training and documentation of procedures and processes. Some teams used a combination of methods and instituted a formal lessons learned program that made technical information available to other teams as it came online through a combination of lunch meetings, electronic bulletin boards, training, and memos. Finally, one team instituted a program for senior experts and younger employees to come together, on an ongoing basis, to hear about current technologies outlined in journal articles or at conferences.

In the teams that were the most active, it was the younger employees who took a vigorous role in the process, including scheduling meetings and ensuring that technical experts were available. Teams that focused on less formal activities, such as brown bag lunches and development of guidebooks and procedure manuals, seemed to make more progress than teams that had planned to develop more formal and complicated processes, such as an expert system or databases. After six months, many of the younger employees stated that they felt better apprised of non-technical activities that only a few months ago they considered the domain of senior experts. They also reported a perceived increase in dialogue and team meetings that question established assumptions about doing business.

## BARRIERS TO RETRIEVING AND TRANSFERRING KNOWLEDGE

Four factors may limit the transfer of knowledge within organizations and thereby affect its availability, form, accuracy, and meaning:

- Cost
- Cognitive capacity of the recipient
- Message delay caused by prioritized sending
- Intentional or unintentional message modification or distortion of meaning

One learning company, Blanchard Training and Development (BTD), has become a leader in knowledge transfer. Each year, the company sponsors a conference for its international licensees. One of the biggest payoffs has been the wealth of knowledge exchange and sharing of techniques for enhancing the effectiveness of managers. BTD also sponsors staff exchanges. Under this program, an employee from a licensee organization works for a six-month period at BTD. This fosters a better understanding of Blanchard's approaches, products, and personnel. Likewise, BTD places its employees at various internships with licensee organizations, where they can learn more about those companies, their programs and products, and the organizational and local cultures.

Knowledge sharing and management has always been a major part of the corporate learning culture at Accenture. Previously, the company relied on individual and team knowledge sharing via a network of strong personal relationships. With the advent of technology, however, the firm extended its focus through groupware technologies and the creation of knowledge-sharing applications. In addition, Accenture created four interrelated teams to disseminate and diffuse knowledge:

- People Team, which continues to evolve the firm's understanding of the competencies, roles, rewards, measures, and learning needed to support knowledge sharing
- Process Team, which concentrates on knowledge-sharing processes and their integration into business processes, along with the functional requirements and design of KnowledgeSpace

- Technology Team, whose mandate is to define the technical architecture to support Accenture's knowledge-sharing needs
- Leadership Team, whose task is to implement the required structures, processes, and technology and to serve as role models

## TECHNOLOGICAL MODES OF TRANSFERRING KNOWLEDGE

A comprehensive, wide-scale transfer of knowledge is accomplished most efficiently through the intelligent use of technology, which makes knowledge available anywhere, anytime, and in any form. Information communications software—including e-mail, bulletin boards, and conferencing—enables interactions in person and among dispersed groups. It also provides an electronic learning environment in which all members have equal access to data and are able to communicate freely (see chapter 7).

Search engines now allow for searches of all files located on a LAN or WAN, using criteria found in many web browsers. Current groupware offers the incorporation of expert or decision-support systems into a standard graphical user interface and enables individuals to access imported knowledge as well as capture congenital and experiential knowledge within the organization.

## Knowledge Sharing at Hewlett-Packard

Hewlett-Packard (HP) is a technology company that operates in more than 170 countries around the world. The company was founded in a one-car garage in Palo Alto, California, by Bill Hewlett and Dave Packard, and is now one of the world's largest information technology companies, operating in nearly every country. Headquartered in Palo Alto, HP serves more than one billion customers across the world, with approximately 300,000 employees worldwide. In 2010, the company was ranked at number ten, with revenues of over $125 billion.

Lew Platt, HP's former chairman, president, and CEO, recently stated that "successful companies of the twenty-first century will be those who do the best jobs of capturing, storing, and leveraging what their employees know." In keeping with this philosophy, the firm's consulting unit, HP Consulting, has undertaken a knowledge management initiative, aimed at transforming the decentralized knowledge of its consultants from a latent asset into a resource available to everyone within the organization. Previously, knowledge sharing at HP Consulting was informal and serendipitously based on personal networks or accidental encounters at meetings. But the unit recognized that success was highly dependent on the ability to manage and leverage organizational knowledge—and that this knowledge, appropriately leveraged, was as valuable as financial assets.

In order to accomplish greater dissemination and diffusion of knowledge, HP Consulting had to create an environment in which everyone is enthusiastic about sharing knowledge. HP has learned that the human side of knowledge management is the hard part since it involves creating a strong foundation where an organization must move from individual knowledge to organization knowledge. It must energize itself to create knowledge sharing and reuse behaviors to tap its collective wisdom. Sharing, leveraging, and reusing knowledge must all become part of HP's culture.

HP Consulting's knowledge management initiative has three key objectives:

- To deliver increased value to customers by bringing more intellectual capital to solutions, not by adding work hours
- To create an environment in which everyone is enthusiastic about sharing knowledge and leveraging the knowledge of others
- To leverage and reuse knowledge

HP Consulting launched its knowledge management initiative using pilot programs that focused on the following behavioral elements:

- Taking time to reflect and learn from successes and mistakes
- Creating an environment that encourages sharing of knowledge and experiences among consultants
- Encouraging the sharing of best practices and reusable tools and solutions that can be leveraged by other consultants

Leadership also identified four attitudes that sustain knowledge sharing, leverage, and reuse at HP Consulting. First, leveraging other people's knowledge, experience, and deliverables is regarded as desired behavior. Second, the results of innovation, both successes and failures, are equally shared. Third, time spent increasing personal and group knowledge and confidence is considered a highly valued activity. And fourth, consultants who actively share their knowledge and draw on the knowledge of others dramatically increase their worth.

The results have been extremely profitable for HP. Along the way, knowledge management has progressed from being an initiative to becoming a means of leveraging HP Consulting's transformation into a knowledge-based business.

## Knowledge Application and Validation

The systematic application of knowledge creates long-term value to organizations. This is accomplished through the continuous recycling and creative utilization of the organization's rich knowledge and experience. Technology enables optimum application of corporate knowledge. A company's ability to provide customer service through diagnosis and troubleshooting is a good example of knowledge application and validation.

With a well-developed knowledge system, a company can put its best people at the front line and keep their expertise available to the entire organization. Charles Paulk, chief information officer of Accenture, notes that, because of Knowledge Xchange, "When one of our consultants shows up, the client gets the best of the firm, not just the best of that consultant." Paulk lists the following among the many benefits of Accenture's knowledge management system (Schwandt and Marquardt, 2000):

- Savings in areas such as shipping costs of physically transferring knowledge
- Improved ability to tap into colleagues' knowledge
- Capacity to work globally
- Forum for mapping corporate brainpower
- Ability to cope with growth and staff turnover, since newcomers who quickly learn organizational knowledge can contribute that much faster to its success

## Top 10 Strategies for Knowledge Management

### 1. SHARE RESPONSIBILITY FOR COLLECTING AND TRANSFERRING KNOWLEDGE

In learning organizations, everyone is encouraged to become adept at gathering data. All employees should be aware of the importance of collecting and sharing knowledge, and they should be informed as to how such knowledge can be collected and transferred. This knowledge may be obtained through formal channels such as conferences, the Internet, or newspapers and journals as well as through informal channels such as social gatherings, museums, and movies.

Some companies promote and reward research among staff, realizing that in-depth analysis can be leveraged into significant learning power. One learning organization even encourages employees to use part of their vacation time to augment corporate learning. For example, a hospital asked an employee who was vacationing in Singapore to visit hospitals and learn about their personnel policies. Of course, the company paid for part of the employee's airfare.

## 2. SYSTEMATICALLY CAPTURE RELEVANT KNOWLEDGE FROM OTHER COMPANIES AND OTHER SOURCES

Learning organizations avoid the "not invented here" syndrome and systematically look outside themselves to gather valuable information. These external ventures may include initiating study missions designed to understand the performance and distinctive skills of other organizations, benchmarking best practices in the industry, and attending conferences and forums.

For example, Whirlpool, which has made benchmarking an important tool of knowledge acquisition, benchmarks the world's most successful and admired companies: those in the top 25 percent in areas such as total quality, people commitment, innovation and growth, and customer satisfaction.

## 3. ORGANIZE INTERNAL LEARNING EVENTS

Learning organizations have developed many tactics to encourage the sharing of internal learning. Fraser and Neave, for example, has created a culture in which each employee "shares, learns from each other, recognizes, and creates a cycle of continuous learning." One powerful and vibrant technique is the "sharing rally," which is held at every site, with winning ideas moving up to regional and, eventually, global levels. Sharing rallies are conferences at which employees or teams are encouraged to share their improvement programs, successful and unsuccessful risks, and quality enhancements with fellow employees. Other internal company strategies can include:

- Strategic reviews that examine the changing competitive environment in light of the company's product portfolio, technology, and market position
- Systems audits to review the effectiveness of large, cross-functional processes and delivery systems
- Internal benchmarking reports, which identify and compare best-in-class activities within the organization
- Jamborees or symposiums that bring together customers, suppliers, outside experts, and internal groups to share ideas and learn from one another

## 4. ENCOURAGE CREATIVITY AND PROVIDE OPPORTUNITIES AND REWARDS FOR BEING CREATIVE

Albert Einstein once wrote that "imagination is more important than information." Increasing a company's knowledge by learning only from others generally leads to gradual, quantitative improvement. However, quantum improvements result when an organization generates new thinking and consequent knowledge.

Consider some of the following activities to encourage generative thinking and creative learning in your organization:

- Install small-scale experiments and feedback loops to increase learning processes and achieve continuous improvement.
- Reward imaginative and risky efforts.
- Conduct workshops on creativity and right-brain thinking.
- Utilize action learning to achieve breakthrough thinking and innovation on your most complex and difficult problems.

## 5. ENCOURAGE AND REWARD INNOVATION

Organizations cannot survive unless they continuously develop new products or services. *Companies will die unless they can create a continuous stream of new products and services.* Survival in the global marketplace means continually creating new ways of producing better products and services. Inventions and innovations will be imperative because no existing market share is permanent and no product life is indefinite. Yet, too few of our organizations have stressed the critical significance of inventing new knowledge.

Learning companies emphasize the vital role played by generative learning in achieving organizational learning and success; based on this understanding, they encourage experimentation and reflection. 3M allows employees to devote up to 10 percent of their time to inventing. Goodrich, Kirin Brewery, DuPont, and PepsiCo encourage experimentation whenever possible. Sony sets a "sunset," or end-of-life, date whenever it introduces a new product, thereby triggering immediate work on developing replacement offerings. The company's objective is to create three new products for every one that it phases out, whether incrementally improved old products, new spinoffs from the original, or an entirely new product.

## 6. DEVELOP CORPORATE CAPABILITY IN DATA MINING AND ANALYSIS

More and more data mining tools are being developed that can analyze, dissect, and categorize data so as to convert it into valuable knowledge for the organization. Learning organizations should constantly be on the lookout for the best tools for their particular industry as well as benchmark what are the best practices in other industries in terms of data mining and analysis.

## 7. MAXIMIZE KNOWLEDGE TRANSFER ACROSS BOUNDARIES

Job rotation and team mixing are two of the most effective ways to transfer knowledge in an organization because the people involved not only carry knowledge with them but also are in place to ensure successful transmission of their knowledge. Another benefit of people transfer is the fresh approaches and perceptions that transferees bring to their new situations. They are likely to raise the "dumb" questions that lead to new insights.

Genpact has developed a knowledge platform that enables all employees to grow and collaborate. Every employee is invited to leverage the portal at his or her own discretion by storing documents, creating wikis, writing blogs, conducting surveys, searching for information, and creating communities of practice. More than 750 communities make use of Genpact's Knowledge management tool to collaborate and disperse information across the organization.

## 8. DEVELOP KNOWLEDGE BASE AROUND ORGANIZATIONAL VALUES AND LEARNING NEEDS

Knowledge is ineffective unless it is coded and stored in a way that makes sense to individuals and organizations. Too many companies are overwhelmed by vast amounts of data. Organizations must identify useful information by assessing its value and then coding it based on learning needs and organizational operations.

The stored knowledge should be easily accessible across functional boundaries. Store the knowledge not only by topical categories but also according to learning needs of staff, organizational goals for continuous improvement, and user expertise.

## 9. CREATE MECHANISMS AND REWARD SYSTEMS FOR COLLECTING AND STORING LEARNING

Many of us barely appreciate, much less understand, the tremendous power of computers for coding and storing organizational knowledge. Because we are not fully aware of the memory and value systems of the organization, we do not know which data to retain and which to store in centralized information systems. In addition, we may not realize the potency of knowledge and therefore do not take the time either to add knowledge to the organization or to seek it inside and outside the company's computer base.

As a result, all too often, valuable learning never leaves the minds of the individuals or groups involved. Learning organizations know how to capture this knowledge through various methods of positive and negative reinforcement. Consider some of the strategies used by global consulting giant McKinsey & Company, one of the best knowledge management companies in the world:

- A director of knowledge management coordinates company efforts to create and collect knowledge.
- Knowledge transfer is seen as a professional responsibility and part of everyone's job.
- Knowledge development is included in the personnel evaluation process.
- An employee does not get a billing code without preparing a two-page summary of how and what he or she has learned from the project.
- Every three months, each project manager receives a printout of what he or she has added to the company's Practice Information System.
- An online information system called the Practice Development Network is updated weekly and now has more than 6,000 documents. In addition, the Knowledge Resource Directory, McKinsey's yellow pages, is a guide to who knows what.
- Each of McKinsey's practice areas maintains a list of members, experts, and core documents.
- Each practice area publishes a bulletin two to three times a week, featuring new ideas and information that it wants the rest of the company's staff to know.

## 10. IMPROVE THE TRANSFER OF TRAINING TO ON-THE-JOB UTILIZATION

According to Mary Broad (2005), less than 10 percent of corporate classroom learning is ever transferred to the job. This percentage can be significantly increased by implementing a deliberate strategy that includes specific steps for managers, participants, and trainers. Examples of possible actions include:

*For managers:*

- Before: Become familiar with the course and plan use of learning.
- During: Protect learners from work-related interruptions.
- After: Develop opportunities for learners to use new behaviors immediately.

*For learners:*

- Before: Confer with manager and previous trainees on course objectives, content, process, and application to job.
- During: Record key concepts and applications to the job.
- After: Regularly assess your performance and acknowledge any progress made.

*For trainers:*

- Before: Confer with supervisors on possible barriers to on-the-job transfer of training and identify ways to reduce or eliminate them.
- During: Help learners form mutual support groups for learning together and helping one another back on the job.
- After: Maintain contact with learners and provide support and help with transferring new skills to their jobs.

# CHAPTER 7

# Technology for Building the Learning Organization

Olivier Serrat (2009), Head of Knowledge Management at the Asia Development Bank, notes that great learning organizations learn faster and better, and that the necessary speed and accuracy involved is possible only through wise use of technology. Effective use of technologies requires an understanding not only of information technology and computer science but of the arts and sciences of learning, discovery, and communications as well. Organizations that know how to harness technology to enhance their learning capacity have a decided competitive advantage over those that are still using relatively Stone Age tools.

The technology subsystem of the Systems Learning Organization model is made up of supporting, integrated technological networks and information tools that enable access to and exchange of information and learning. It includes technical processes, systems, and structures for collaboration, coaching, coordination, and other knowledge skills. It also comprises electronic tools and advanced methods such as computer conferences, simulation, and computer-supported collaboration. All these elements work to create knowledge freeways.

In this chapter, we will explore the two key dimensions of technology as they support learning organizations:

- *Technology to manage knowledge:* Computer-based technology for gathering, coding, processing, storing, transferring, and applying data among machines, people, and organizations

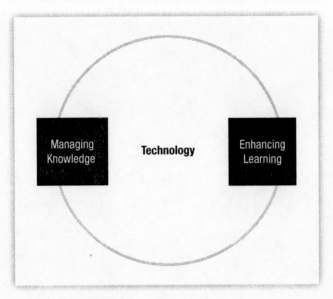

**FIGURE 15**   Technology Subsystem

- *Technology to increase the speed and quality of learning:* Video, audio, and computer-based multimedia training for delivering and sharing knowledge and skills anywhere, anytime

Figure 15 illustrates the technology subsystem of the learning organization.

## Technology to Manage Knowledge

Information technology presents organizations with new strategic opportunities for learning throughout the corporation. It enables companies to automate, educate, and transform themselves. Information technology permits the redistribution of power, function, and control to locations where they will be most effective. Production, coordination, and management can be accomplished more efficiently and thoroughly.

Technology allows organizations to break many old rules of management, change, development, and learning. Added capabilities include the following:

- Information appears simultaneously in as many places as it is needed.
- Generalists are able to do the work of experts.
- Organizations can reap the benefits of both centralization and decentralization.
- Decision making becomes part of everyone's job.
- Field personnel can send and receive information from any location.
- Plans can be revised instantaneously.

## TECHNOLOGY AND KNOWLEDGE FLOW

Technology can be a key mechanism for improving organizational communication and knowledge transfer. Information technology in particular improves communication by blurring the boundaries within the company and increasing the range of possible relationships beyond hierarchies. It also permits easier direct communication across time and space by electronic bulletin boards, mail, and conferencing. Communications software creates electronic learning environments in which all members have equal access to data. With every personal computer networked through the mainframe, with relevant external systems, any person in the organization can take part in gathering and transferring knowledge. Remote access to national and global knowledge networks is available at any time.

Information technology reduces the number of management levels needed in the hierarchy, yet at the same time provides enhanced potential for span of control. Empowered with information, frontline workers gain increased autonomy. For example, Buckman Laboratories, a leading-edge chemical company, has made the front line the focus of almost all its knowledge management and e-learning. Cisco equips sales representatives on their way to client meetings with new product information via Internet, teleconferencing, and even wireless transmission.

Information technology contributes to flexibility. A computer-mediated communications system utilizes its own storage, processing, and retrieval capabilities for internal and external communications. Databases, texts, articles, reports, manuals, and directories can be held for quick and easy access by all workers. All of Cisco Systems' sales and technical staff learn online. The company's approach keeps employees constantly up-to-date and has reduced training expenses by 60 percent.

Sharing information on a real-time basis and encouraging wider access to information requires the following strategies:

- Creating online databases for use across functional boundaries
- Hooking into online databases and electronic bulletin boards outside the organization, such as those at universities and other learning centers
- Installing an e-mail culture where its use is widespread
- Using electronic data interchange to create comprehensive network systems

## Prudential's LaunchPad Training Program

The Prudential Insurance Company of America is a Fortune Global 500 whose subsidiaries provide insurance, investment management, and other financial products and services to both retail and institutional customers throughout the United States and in more than thirty other countries. Prudential is composed of hundreds of subsidiaries and holds more than $2 trillion of life insurance. In 2010, the company had over 40,000 employees and revenues of $35 billion.

Through its LaunchPad Training Program, Prudential equipped its field associates with laptop computers and provided a custom-tailored training program to help them incorporate the new technology into their daily business practices. With laptop computers, representatives are able to conduct business with customers while maintaining access to current information, thus ensuring customer satisfaction, increasing customer loyalty, and encouraging repeat business. LaunchPad achieved unprecedented success in workplace learning and development, as demonstrated by the following statistics:

- 100 percent of the field force now using a single technology platform
- Satisfaction rate of 93 percent for workplace learning and development among the field force
- Industry recognition in 11 prestigious national awards

Prudential's LaunchPad, according to ASTD's Award Committee, set a new standard for workplace learning and development by creating the best technically trained field force in the financial services industry. Barbara Koster, Senior Vice President and Chief Information Officer, cites the success of the LaunchPad program as her biggest professional accomplishment because it has dramatically improved the way in which Prudential does business.

### ORGANIZATIONAL EFFECTS OF TECHNOLOGY

Hughes and Morton (2006) emphasize the importance of integrating technology with an organization's strategies, structures, and employees. Viewed through this integration, it becomes clear that companies that have exploited information technology as part of remaking themselves have done so by changing each of these elements in a dynamic and balanced way that recognized their essential complementarities. Information technology has six major effects on the workplace, learning, and employees:

- Fundamental changes in work processes
- Integration of business functions at all levels within and among organizations
- Shifts in the competitive climate of many industries
- New strategic opportunities to reassess missions and operations
- Basic changes in management and organizational structure
- Organizational transformation by managers

Let's examine each of these effects.

### Changes in Work Processes

Information technology results in basic changes in production, coordination, and management areas. *Production* is affected by physical supports such as robotics, process control instrumentation, and intelligent sensors. Other changes may include information production through data processing and introduction of knowledge resources such as mobile phones and intranet technology. *Coordination* changes when distance and time differences become irrelevant. The organization's memory (command database) can be maintained over time, accept contributions from all parts of the organization, and be available to a wide variety of authorized users. *Management* becomes more flexible because information technology can better sense changes in the external environment and maintain close contact with members' ideas and reactions. Pertinent, timely information represents crucial input for the organization's direction-setting process.

Technology also allows more control of two key aspects: measuring the organization's performance against the appropriate critical success factors and interpreting such measures in relation to the plan in order to determine future actions.

### Integration of Business Functions

Business functions can be integrated at every level within the organization and among organizations. This integration takes four forms.

1. *Links within the value chain* extend the team concept to all parts of the organization. For example, Xerox connects design, engineering, and manufacturing personnel within its system of local area networks to create a team that focuses on one product. This type of team finishes tasks in less time and with greater creativity while maintaining higher morale.
2. *End-to-end links of value chains* connect organizations through just-in-time and electronic data interchange.
3. *Value chain substitution* is effected via subcontract or alliance.
4. *Electronic markets* are the most highly developed form of electronic integration. For example, travel agents may perform price comparisons and reserve seats electronically.

These four forms of electronic integration effectively remove buffers, to varying degrees. They also leverage organizational and individual expertise.

### Shifts in the Competitive Climate

Many industries experience climate shifts. Information technology heightens the importance of such critical functions as scanning and monitoring the business environment. Effective scanning and monitoring enable an organization to deal proactively with the turbulent world of technological changes.

### New Strategic Opportunities

Technology offers organizations the ability to easily reassess their missions and operations. Automating processes will reduce production costs, and utilizing technology to informate will inevitably increase efficiency and generate new information as a by-product. In these ways, organizations will be able to transform themselves.

### Basic Changes in Management and Structure

When successfully applied, information technology affects management and organizational structure. Hughes and Morton (2006) see information technology as a critical enabler in the re-creation and redefinition of the organization as we know it. Information technology redistributes power, functions, and control to the most effective locations according to each company's mission, objectives, and culture. For instance, an organization may link all its engineers on the same network, allowing individuals to share information, ask for help, or work collaboratively on projects. In this way, information technology increases the speed of information transfer and decision making.

### Organizational Transformation by Managers

Information technology enables and compels managers to lead their organizations through a process of complete transformation in order to prosper in a globally competitive environment.

## TECHNOLOGICAL SUPPORT FOR KNOWLEDGE MANAGEMENT

To ensure effective collection, storage, and transfer of knowledge, learning organizations must implement the following four procedures, in sequence.

First, establish a networked infrastructure of information technology for all employees. The platform should support knowledge systems across the organization, enabling every worker to communicate electronically with all other employees, both individually and in groups. Provide each employee with a workstation that can handle complex computational, informational, and communication needs. Powerful exploration and system navigation tools that use flexible keyword search, hypermedia, dynamic visual querying, and decision trees should be available, along with a range of standard office automation software such as text processing, presentation graphics, spreadsheets, rational DBMS, web browsers, and e-mail.

Second, create enterprise-wide data, object, and knowledge repositories. At this stage, learning companies are creating and regulating relational and object models and data dictionaries across the organization. Reformat existing online information before inserting it into the company-wide databases. Smart data-entry templates should be available to check for validity, consistency, and accuracy. Include software for translating media into text.

Third, automate and enable operations, management, and support activities. With the aid of electronic systems, automate all operations within the organization. For example, in marketing and sales, use technology to more accurately match products to customer needs, and increase profit margins through improved pricing.

And fourth, develop integrated performance-support systems and applications for knowledge discovery and data mining. In this last stage, learning organizations form centers of expertise that are responsible for collecting, storing, analyzing, and distributing knowledge. Additional tasks include training and certifying workers in their specialties and providing qualified online and onsite workers and consulting services.

The most dramatic and successful applications result from the deployment of integrated support systems that provide employees with coordinated task information, advice, training, job aids, references, and administrative resources. These centers of expertise serve several purposes, such as:

- To create, research, improve, and manage the knowledge repository
- To establish and enforce standards, methods, and practices
- To align and coordinate interests with related centers
- To assess workforce competency and performance
- To identify gaps and remedy deficiencies in the content and processes of the knowledge repository
- To provide training and consultancy services
- To supply competent workers for staff projects and processes

## Customer or Client Relations Management (CRM)

According to Waddill and Marquardt (2011), *Customer or Client Relationship Management (CRM)* involves using technology to organize, automate, and synchronize business processes such as sales activities. It is also useful for customer service and marketing. Salesforce, Microsoft, and SAP are three well-known CRM vendors. The data collected through a CRM provides insight into the habits, preferences, and needs of the client. CRM can identify, draw, and attain new clients, cultivate and retain those the company already has, and reengage former clients, while reducing costs of marketing and servicing the client. A CRM can supply valuable information for knowledge management. AVAYA is a world-class organization that uses CRM as part of their knowledge management system.

## Navigating for Knowledge at Deloitte

Deloitte Touche Tohmatsu is the largest private professional services organization in the world. Deloitte has over 170,000 staff at work in more than 150 countries, delivering audit, tax, consulting, enterprise risk, and financial advisory services through its member firms. One of Deloitte's most innovative learning initiatives is the Cultural Navigator, a package of tools and resources that present a wide range of intuitive, easy-to-use learning, consulting, and assessment solutions. Elements include a cultural profile tool that allows users to compare their personal profiles with those of other cultures and identify areas of commonality and difference. A cultural simulator tests and reinforces awareness and learning by creating online simulations around a variety of management topics pertaining to a specific country or region.

In order to get new employees up to speed more quickly, Deloitte has designed a new, high-intensity live simulation that places learners in close approximation of real work. Participants and coaches play roles that reflect actual responsibilities and challenges of working at a client site while coaches guide teams through the project process and provide skill tutorials based on their own experiences. The simulations are offered quarterly and are reinforced with performance support materials and e-learning modules.

The results are impressive. An employee who has completed the learning experience averages 30 to 40 percent more business than those who have not.

## Technology-Based Learning

Workplace learning in the new millennium will be just in time, just what's needed, and just where it's needed. In other words, it will be customized, digitized, and optimized for each individual, thanks to the ever-increasing power of technology and its growing applicability to learning in the workplace.

At the Boeing Training Center in Seattle, Washington, for example, pilots and ground crew technicians utilize ten full-flight simulators that feature fixed-base simulators, flight training devices, several modern computer-equipped classrooms, and multiple computer-based training (CBT) areas. Training modules are downloaded into the network. Each training carrel is equipped with a Windows-based PC, where laser animation and audio can be overlaid on a computer-generated graphic to simulate changing scenery or weather conditions. Other programs simulate pilot–copilot interaction for flight training; the modules are so realistic that pilots can be certified for flight without ever logging a minute in the air. This form of technological learning achieves maximum training flexibility in a constantly changing environment. The old method of using trainers and training manuals is too cumbersome, unreliable, and expensive in today's competitive marketplace. Technology simply does the job faster and better.

### INCREASED USE OF LEARNING TECHNOLOGIES

One of the most striking workplace phenomena is the unrelenting demand for increased knowledge and speed of learning. A small but growing number of companies worldwide are recognizing technology as the key to achieving better and faster learning. Worldwide corporate e-learning has grown to over $48 billion (E-learning, 2011).

Companies now invest in a wide variety of rapidly diversifying electronic-learning technologies. Use of computer-delivered training, Internet- and network-based distance learning, electronic performance support systems (EPSS), virtual classrooms, and interactive or multimedia computer-based training is surging. Organizations are spending more than $10 billion a year on software for intranets. And, thanks to rapid technological advances, once separate learning technologies are no longer as distinct in process and capabilities as in the past.

E-learning can either be *synchronous*, which provides immediate interactions and is facilitator-enabled (graphics and programming tend to be less complex with the synchronous design) or *asynchronous*, which typically requires more time to develop because the content must be perfect. E-learning should be graphic and interactive intensive; normally a team of designers, graphic artists, programmers, and others create the program (Waddill & Marquardt, 2011).

## Web-Based Learning at Credit Suisse

The Credit Suisse Group is a financial services company, headquartered in Zurich, Switzerland, with more than 50,000 employees worldwide. In 2009, Credit Suisse was recognized as "Bank of the Year" by the International Financing Review. In 2009, the use of e-learning methods virtually doubled at Credit Suisse, with approximately 500,000 log-ins to web-based training courses. Without e-learning, Seigfried Hoenle, Chief Learning Officer at Credit Suisse observed, "We could not train our employees in important business concepts such as Legal and Compliance. This is the only way for us to ensure that all employees receive the most up-to-date information on regulatory requirements in order to incorporate it fully into their work. We have recently begun to make short and ultra-short learning modules available to our employees online for daily use. Every two weeks, we supply employees with short, entertaining learning units on business basics and personal effectiveness via the intranet. With "Experts' Insights," short internal expert videos dealing with topical internal and external developments, all of our employees have access to the wealth of knowledge that exists within our bank"(Credit Suisse, 2011).

## TYPES OF LEARNING TECHNOLOGIES

Learning technology includes both presentation and distribution. Let's look at the various presentation and distribution learning technologies as categorized and defined by the ASTD

*Presentation technologies* include:

- Podcasts/Vodcasts
- CBT: Computer-based training
- Multimedia: Computer application that uses text, audio, animation, and/or video
- Television: One-way video that may be combined with two-way audio or other electronic response systems
- Teleconferences: Instantaneous exchange of audio, video, or text between individuals or groups, at two or more locations. A *videoconference* or *video teleconference* is a set of interactive telecommunication technologies that allow two or more locations to interact simultaneously via two-way video and audio transmissions. With this software the user need only have a webcam, computer, and Internet connection. It allows the users to see each other as they interact. A simple example of this form of conferencing appears in the open source product named Skype (Waddill & Marquardt, 2011).
- Virtual reality/Virtual worlds: Computer application that provides an interactive, immersive, and three-dimensional learning experience by using fully functional, realistic models
- Electronic performance support system (EPSS): An integrated computer application using expert systems, hypertext, embedded animation, and/or hypermedia to provide assistance in performing tasks
- Mobile devices such as iPhone and iPad

*Distribution technologies* include:

- Cable TV: Transmitting television signals via cable technology
- CD-ROM: A format and system for recording, storing, and retrieving electronic information on a compact disc that is read by an optical drive
- Electronic mail (e-mail): Exchanging messages through computers
- Extranet: A collaborative network that uses Internet technology to link organizations with suppliers, customers, or other organizations that share common goals or information needs

- Internet: A loose confederation of worldwide computer networks that are connected through several overarching networks
- Intranet: Computer networks within an organization
- Local area network (LAN): A network of computers sharing the resources of a processor or server within a relatively small geographic area
- Wide area network (WAN): A network of computers sharing the resources of one or more processors or servers over a relatively large geographic area
- Satellite TV (also called *interactive business TV*): Transmission of television signals via satellites
- Simulator: A device or system that replicates or imitates a real device or system
- World Wide Web: All Internet resources and users employing hypertext transport protocol (HTTP)

Each presentation technology could use a number of distribution technologies. For example, computer-delivered training could be accomplished using LANs or WANs, the web, the Internet, intranets, CD-ROMs, and computer disks.

## Sharing Learning and Technology at National Semiconductor

National Semiconductor is a semiconductor manufacturer headquartered in Santa Clara, California, that specializes in analog devices and subsystems. The products of National Semiconductor include power management circuits, display drivers, audio and operational amplifiers, communication interface products, and data conversion solutions.

National Semiconductor holds annual in-house International Technology and Innovation Conferences for the purpose of encouraging National's technologists to create and share core technologies to build National's technology roadmap. Papers were recently presented in the following areas:

- Circuit design and simulation
- Manufacturing
- Device technology and architecture
- Process technology
- Packaging

- Test systems and methodologies
- System and software development

## VIDEO COMPRESSION TECHNOLOGY FOR LEARNING

National Semiconductor has invested intensive creativity, time, and research in the development of video technology. Why is video compression so important to National? Because the interactive video capabilities of the new products, such as document-sharing on real-time, would not be possible without video compression. The available bandwidth of telephones are too narrow to send real-time motion video, and video data takes up too much storage space. Video compression is a critical innovation for video playback, video conferencing, and videophones.

With this technology, National is able to develop a document or share information with co-workers halfway around the world in real-time. The data is entered on a PC and it appears instantly on their screens. The team members receive feedback immediately. Together they can finalize specifications for a new run of chips or create a proposal for a new customer more quickly and conveniently than was ever thought possible before.

## MANAGING THE LEARNING TECHNOLOGY

E-learning can be managed through a Learning Management System (LMS). The LMS enables the user to design curriculum and author courseware. According to Deb Waddill, a leading practitioner and theorist in the field of learning technologies, LMS also offers all of the course-related functions such as registering, tracking course completion, grading, and receiving grades. Those with HR oversight can observe patterns in elective courseware. HR personnel can track employees' completion of required courseware or select electives.

With the advent of Learning and Course Management Systems (LMS/CMS), many of the previously tedious logistics of course management can be handled online and as a self-service function. Typically, a learning management system will have specific features for the learner and a separate set of features for the instructor. Features for the student that can be expected from a standard LMS include threaded discussion, file sharing, assignments, resources (such as hyperlinks, files, documents), synchronous chat, and multimedia (audio, video, hyperlinks, simulations). The administrator or instructor features may include the ability online to track participant progress; to grade participants; to author courseware, modules, and lessons; to exchange files; to create and issue tests and surveys; and to generate reports.

Waddill and Marquardt (2011) note that some of the most widely used Learning Management Systems include Blackboard, Virtual Classroom System, Lotus Learning Space, Saba, and Moodle. However, many organizations develop their own LMS in-house because it may be more cost effective than using or leasing one of the larger-scale systems. Further, some larger systems, such as an Enterprise Resource Planning (ERP) system, contain modules for course design, offering, and management.

## Learning Management Systems at Sanofi-Aventis

Sanofi-Aventis, the result of a merger between two European companies in 2004, is the fourth largest pharmaceutical company in the world, and has over 100,000 employees working worldwide. The Learning Management System (LMS) closely aligns with corporate values, key productivity measures, and core competencies. Curriculum maps that identify the training programs for each of these areas are available through the company's learning management system. Once a developmental area has been identified, employees can easily locate an appropriate training course using the maps. Courses are accessed via the LMS and organized by functional area as well as by core competency. Because of the self-directed nature of the learning and the on-demand availability of most of the courses, developmental plans can be as dynamic as the business environment.

According to Mike Capaldi, associate vice president of sales, training, and leadership development, "The employees needed training within sixty days, so we leveraged new systems—including our LMS and virtual classroom to deploy cross-training" (ASTD, 2007a). A web-based platform integrated with the LMS was designed and implemented to communicate the logistics of study requirements, timelines, registration, and travel. Self-paced, web-based technology was used to accelerate the initial training process by providing coursework and content online. Training staff used Brainshark Rapid Learning, an asynchronous development tool, to create online learning objects and to track learners' progress.

Employees at Sanofi-Aventis complete more than forty hours of training per year, and the company invests nearly 3 percent of payroll in learning and performance improvements. In 2006, the company made a major capital investment in learning in the form of a 30,000-square-foot, state-of-the-art training center. The center includes 22 classrooms, a 200 seat auditorium, 5 conference rooms, a 48-seat assessment center, 32 simulation rooms, a creativity center, and a production facility for virtual classroom offerings. The simulation rooms, which include equipment with digital video recording capability, allow trainers to observe trainees in role plays, provide coaching on their performance, and even download video clips to a flash drive for later use (ASTD, 2007a).

## Podcasts/Vodcasts

*Podcasts/Vodcasts* refer to audio and video files that are distributed by Internet to a computer or handheld device. Podcasts are easily created using open source software, and the recorded product can be exported in the format that is compatible with the device on which the podcast will be run. Podcasts are very easy for publishing audio and video files. Free audio recording tools allow the producer to create a variety of files that are compatible with any hardware. It is not necessary to have an Internet connection in order to listen to a podcast; a computer, MP3 player, or cell phone will suffice to play an audio file (Waddill & Marquardt, 2011).

## Virtual Worlds for Learning

Another emerging and powerful e-learning tool centers around the use of virtual worlds, which require participation using *avatars*, graphical representations of humans that appear three-dimensional. The learner logs in to what appears to be a three-dimensional world where the natural laws of the real world do not exist. The learner's avatar may walk, dance, run, fly, and make a variety of gestures initiated by the owner using keyboard codes. The learner can also make the avatar talk by using the microphone on the computer or the chat text-based feature.

According to Mansfield (2007), virtual worlds are an underused training environment. They present boundless opportunities for creative uses, including:

- Simulating business situations
- Conducting "office hour" discussions
- Using gaming as a learning device
- Testing a hypothesis in another world
- Practicing skills in a safe environment

## ADVANTAGES OF LEARNING TECHNOLOGIES

Learning technologies are growing in popularity because they increase the quality, relevance, and speed of learning. They also offer the following advantages.

*Available as needed and just in time:* Unlike traditional training, which is just in case, this type of training gives individuals the information they

**TABLE 7**

Strengths and Weaknesses of Technology-Based Learning Methodologies
(with permission from Waddill & Marquardt, 2011)

| Technology | Strengths | Weaknesses |
|---|---|---|
| E-Learning (Online Learning) | Inexpensive | Passive |
| | Reliable | Not designed with adult learners in mind |
| Threaded Discussion | Worldwide distribution | |
| Posting Assignments | Accessible any time | Software incompatibility |
| Video | Dynamic | Development time/costs |
| | Reaches large audiences | |
| Audio Podcasting | Global distribution | No interaction |
| | Inexpensive | Favors technology savvy |
| Web-conferencing | Audience participation | Complexity (some types) |
| | Immediacy (real-time) | |
| Multimedia | Interactivity | Development time/costs |
| | Highly appealing | |
| Networked Media | Interactivity | Expertise required to develop |
| | Updating | |
| Performance | High job relevance | Development time/costs |
| Support Systems | Uses existing systems | Expertise required |
| Simulations and Virtual Worlds | Authentic learning | Development time/costs |
| | Higher skill levels | Expertise required |
| | | Maximum bandwidth necessary |
| New Media (Twitter, Chat, Wikis, Blogs) | Immediate learning | Depends upon reliable connectivity |
| | Collaborative | |
| mLearner | Collaborative | Use of text, limited |
| | Ubiquitous (cell phone access) | |

need when they need it. Employees don't have to wait for an appropriate class; learning is ready when they are. Flexibility is such that the learning content can be a work in progress.

*Learner-controlled:* Employees have the freedom to initiate the types of learning experiences they need to achieve professional improvement. They also control where they learn, often at their worksites rather than in a distant corporate classroom. More and more courses are being automated using online documentation systems. Why is it so important for employees to control their own learning programs? Because most jobs within the corporation are becoming ever more complex and require higher levels of skills, only the workers are fully aware of what they need and why they need it.

*Self-paced and user friendly:* Learning technologies are becoming more accessible and easier to manipulate, which is essential to encourage worker use. Intranet applications, for example, typically utilize an interface that is conducive to simple point-and-click navigation. Learners can proceed at the pace they choose.

*Accessibility over a wide geographic area:* One of the greatest benefits of learning technology is its ability to provide learning when instructors and training sources are at some distance from learners. Learning via technology allows accessibility to any number of geographic areas, from different offices to different countries. Individuals and groups may engage in training at home, in the office, or on the road. In determining which distance-learning technology to employ, consider elements such as the learners' demographic, educational, and socioeconomic profiles and their level of motivation.

*Hands-on interactivity:* Technology such as touchpads, the Internet, and intranets permit hands-on, direct, and immediate interaction with instructors and/or fellow learners. Groupware, chat rooms, and other two-way communication tools can also be integrated easily into learning programs.

*Uniformity of content and delivery:* Consistency is improved because the same program is being offered by the same person and/or system throughout the company. Centralization of information and databases also helps ensure this uniformity.

*Adjustment to individual learning styles:* It is important to take into account participants' multiple learning styles, orientations, and preferences for problem solving. A number of models have been developed to classify learning styles, but among the best is Honey and Mumford's (2010) system of classification:

- **Activist:** Involves self fully in new experiences; enjoys the here and now; stays open-minded; finds implementation and longer-term consolidation boring
- **Reflector:** Stands back and ponders experiences from many different perspectives; collects data and thinks before reaching conclusions; values analysis; remains cautious and thoughtful; listens before commenting

- **Theorist:** Is good at adapting and integrating observations; takes a logical, step-by-step approach; proceeds as a synthesizer and systems thinker; displays rational objectivity
- **Practitioner:** Is interested in trying out new ideas, theories, and techniques; acts quickly on attractive ideas; is practical; sees problems as challenges

The wide variety of technologies enables the development of programs that appeal to each learning style and sometimes several at the same time. For example, artificial intelligence, which attempts to replicate the thought process of the human brain, can observe, guide, and coach users and modify its instructions according to the input it receives. It can adapt to each user's cognitive style, providing customized help that corresponds to the needs of trainees.

*Adjustment to learners' motivation levels:* Materials can also be adapted to learners' motivation levels. The best technologies for motivated learners appear to be videos, workbooks, audiotapes, and CDs. For these enthusiastic participants, self-paced programs, simple and low-key materials, and self-explanatory or self-help content will suffice. Less motivated learners prefer videoconferences, cable television, two-way audio, satellite broadcasts, interactive CDs, and kiosk systems. In designing programs for these students, it is important to incorporate monitoring and additional interactions with instructors and other participants. Mandatory attendance may be necessary, and content can be expanded and varied based on participant questions.

*Safety and flexibility:* Delivering training modules via virtual reality technology is especially useful when it allows trainees to view objects from a perspective that would be impractical or impossible in actuality. For example, it is not practical or safe to turn a drill press on its side in order to see the bottom as a front view. Cyber-training has applications beyond manufacturing or traditional blue-collar tasks, as in brokerage firms that now use virtual reality to train brokers.

*Ability to update continuously:* Technologies, especially those that deliver via the web, allow organizations to update easily and provide information to all employees. Intranet sites can also be amended inexpensively as often as needed.

*Availability of both push and pull approaches:* Too often, employees are provided with more information than they can possibly process or retain. Technologies like intranets allow companies to provide access to as little or as much information as employees wish to pull onto their desktops.

*Cost-effective:* Technology-based learning is significantly lower in cost. Savings occur because a smaller number of instructors are able to reach many more participants, whether at the same time or at different times, which reduces travel expenses and downtime. The process of developing and maintaining learning packages, databases, and intranet sites with a minimum of costs and time continues to become easier and simpler (Waddill & Marquardt, 2011).

## Using Technology for Learning at Ford Motor Company

Ford is the second largest automaker in the U.S. and the fourth-largest in the world based on annual vehicle sales. Ford is the eighth-ranked overall U.S.-based company in the 2010 Fortune 500 list, based on global revenues in 2009 of $118.3 billion. In 2008, Ford produced 5.532 million automobiles and employed about 213,000 employees at over 90 plants and facilities worldwide.

Ford recognizes that automotive engineering has become so complex that it is impossible to get the job done with group-based classroom training anymore. Several years ago, company leaders acknowledged that before Ford cars could gain acceptance from the general public, the company needed a well-informed sales force and technicians who were highly skilled and experienced in the new automotive technology. Dealerships could not afford poorly trained staff if they wanted to compete in the marketplace.

Faced with the paradoxical objective of reducing the cost of dealer training and communications while providing more learning within a shorter cycle, Ford elected to implement its own learning information superhighway on its FORDSTAR Communications Network.

### FORD'S LEARNING TECHNOLOGY NETWORK

FORDSTAR was initially created more than fifteen years ago to improve internal communications with employees. FORDSTAR is the largest interactive distributed training network in the world. Today, it broadcasts to more than 250 regional sales offices and is believed to be the most comprehensive internal daily television news service in the world. Yet FORDSTAR does much more; it has become the learning network of Ford.

Ford not only conducts training to its dealerships, but they also use their system as a real-time knowledge sharing infrastructure for both corporate communications and market research. For example, corporate marketing polls dealers on which features to bundle in upcoming products. Ford executives also use the network to conduct two-way discussions with thousands of employees simultaneously, facilitating greater communications and understanding throughout the organization (OneTouch, 2011).

Ford has spent more than $100 million to build this all-digital satellite communications network for training its dealers' employees throughout Canada, Mexico, and the United States. While the idea of company-to-dealer television networks is not new to the automotive industry, no other company is equipped to send more than one television signal at a time, none uses high-speed compressed digital video technology, and none is equipped to use interactive voice and data as the basis for training and communication. FORDSTAR can broadcast up to eight video channels simultaneously on a single transponder (eight different training courses can be delivered at the same time) and has another transponder dedicated to data transmissions.

## FORDSTAR'S FACILITIES AND RESOURCES

Each FORDSTAR classroom is equipped with a television, satellite reception equipment, and interactive keypads, which students use to call the instructor and answer multiple choice, yes/no, and numeric questions. Student interaction computers also monitor the sites and capture questions and quiz results from each student attending the broadcasts. The Dearborn, Michigan, learning center provides eight channels of training-oriented programming. Dealerships downlink the telecourses and learning materials so that technicians, salespeople, and other personnel may learn onsite.

The instructor's desk and broadcast facility put him or her in complete control of the various multimedia sources available, which include the following components:

- Standard computer for graphics and other computer-generated teaching aids
- Overhead camera to display props and other objects
- Switching console to show various tools
- Telestrator pen to write on the screen
- Camera focused solely on the instructor

Ford publishes the monthly *Star Guide* for dealerships, listing course descriptions and noting intended audiences and different time zones, making it easy for dealers to decide which courses best match their employees' needs and schedules. Course topics range from new-model overviews and warranty and policy administration to anti-lock brakes and service department town hall meetings.

## ONSITE COORDINATION

Onsite facilitators fill several important roles in implementing FORDSTAR's learning programs. Among other functions, facilitators may conduct orientation sessions designed to acquaint participants with the technology and methods they will use to interact with instructors. They sometimes act as contact persons to whom instructors send course materials and may communicate any issues or concerns that arise later during classes. Facilitators often administer and grade tests, review results with students, and summarize test results for instructors. Instructors can then use these summaries to identify areas in need of review during the next broadcast, while questions are still fresh in the students' minds.

## INTERACTION IS KEY TO FORDSTAR'S SUCCESS

FORDSTAR utilizes an interactive distance learning (IDL) system that features an automated, multifunctional control desk. To maximize interactivity, the control desk (multimedia interactive platform, or MIP) is operated by an instructor, and the response keypads allow continuous interaction with learners. FORDSTAR's programs are designed to call for some form of interactivity every ten minutes. This interactive capability is a key feature in FORDSTAR's success. Here's how it works.

Employees log in on response keypads at the beginning of class, thereby creating automated attendance records for Ford and the instructors. During class, instructors encourage interactivity by issuing preformatted questions from the host station. Employees view each question on their TV monitors and select from possible answers on their keypad displays. When instructors receive results from all participating classrooms, they broadcast these results back to their students. With the correct answer highlighted, learners are able to gauge their progress in relation to others in classrooms throughout the network.

In addition to monitoring the progress of the entire class, instructors can monitor each student's achievements. Student response to every question is logged in on the instructor's computer, making the system an effective tool for courses that require certification or grading. Individual performance records enable instructors to offer additional assistance to students in specific areas, thus ensuring overall success.

The keypads also provide data feedback from the dealerships, creating a valuable audio link between the students and the instructor. If students have questions or comments, they press the call buttons on their keypads to electronically raise their hands. The instructor recognizes callers by name and location within seconds and activates student microphones using the system's touch screen. The ability to have two students on the air at once facilitates interaction between the sites.

## IMPROVED DELIVERY AND PERFORMANCE AT LESS COST

Instructors are able to cover 20 to 30 percent more material during a telecourse, student grades are 20 percent better, and time away from dealership premises has been reduced by as much as 50 percent. Through FORDSTAR, the HRD staff is now able to reach the more than 45,000 technicians and 50,000 salespersons in a matter of days. Learning technology has cut classroom training from an average of thirty-one days to just nine, and larger numbers of people can be trained simultaneously.

There is also a higher quality of performance in the classroom because establishing a disciplined and consistent learning process is easier when information comes from a single course instead of from numerous courses throughout North America. In addition, instructors tend to be more organized when designing for distance learning, perhaps due to high expectations and substantial initial costs. It is wise to optimize the advantages of distance-learning technology by preparing for large numbers of learners who will be participating at the same time.

Another benefit to delivering courses led by multiskilled instructional teams is that leader-experts in particular fields are accessible to all participants, while other instructors are available both during and after courses. Students also tend to be more prepared and participative. Instead of experiencing several hours of classwork and lectures at a single time, they can learn at an incremental pace in the familiar surroundings of their offices.

Electronic distribution reduces the costs of course materials, and utilization of satellite networks and web-based learning significantly decreases per-student costs of faculty and facilities. Ford has expanded FORDSTAR into Australia, Europe, and South America. To spread distance learning to these sites more quickly, Ford has continued to expand its training via the network to employees at manufacturing and design plants. Using technology has indeed lifted learning, performance, and corporate success to world-class heights for Ford Motor Company.

## SUPPLEMENTING CLASSROOM TRAINING AND E-LEARNING

As business speeds up, the demands of customers, partners, and other value contributors change quickly, and workers need faster and more relevant knowledge at the front line. Several new trends are emerging, such as the perception of learners as customers. Companies that take this view design programs and systems centered on learners, providing choice and customization in balance with business needs. Another development is increasing use of the Internet for learning applications that supplement classroom learning: e-content matters, along with e-management, e-collaboration, e-mentoring, e-simulations, and webinars. Learning in general has evolved into a holistic culture of learning activities that involves much more than classroom activity. Training programs and classroom instruction will not disappear but will be complemented by many other approaches to learning and development, including self-study, simulations, coaching, and teamwork.

Manville (2001) notes that leading companies such as Amazon.com, Cisco, Ford, and Procter & Gamble are combining learning offerings through Internet portals with programs, assessments, and learner profiles tracked and delivered by learning-management systems organization wide. These companies take a learner-centered perspective and blend different opportunities to create a rich, mutually reinforcing blend of programs, information, and resources driven by each individual knowledge worker's needs.

Learning organizations are also combining skill listing, competency models, and focused curricula with both electronic and face-to-face learning. Experiences emphasizing individuals and groups, development and knowledge-transfer, both formal and structured as well as informal and unstructured, are appearing. Examples include Cisco's certification in new technology for its salespeople, or particular competencies achieved by dealers in the maintenance of cars and trucks at Ford (Manville, 2001).

## ELECTRONIC PERFORMANCE SUPPORT SYSTEMS

The electronic performance support system (EPSS) is one of the most powerful and effective uses of technology for managing knowledge and increasing the efficiency of learning. EPSS uses databases (text, visual, or audio) and knowledge bases to capture, store, and distribute information throughout the organization in order to help workers reach the highest level of performance in the shortest possible time, and with minimal personnel support. The system consists of several components, including, but not limited to, interactive training, productivity and application software, and expert and feedback systems.

EPSS has been called by many the learning tool of the twenty-first century (Nguyen & Woll, 2006; Rossett & Schafer, 2007). It is certainly essential to maximizing the power of the learning organization. But many of us are not familiar with the term, much less with the system's capabilities or even what EPSS looks like. So let's explore how this resource can support corporate-wide learning.

EPSS can and should provide whatever is necessary to generate performance and learning at the point of need. To do that, EPSS can take on many forms, including everything from computer systems that help a line worker in a potato chip factory run and repair any part of the manufacturing process to a customer service workstation that anticipates customers' problems and prompts the worker to ask the system the right questions.

### EPSS Components

It is important to remember that EPSS technology cannot work alone. Experts (internal or external) must be available to provide other than computer-related advice. The combination of human and machine blends creativity with vast information resources. A comprehensive and powerful EPSS includes nine key components.

1. *Competency profiles* are cumulative records of such factors as knowledge, attitudes, skills, and performance levels and may include performance appraisals. These profiles serve two functions: to ensure that workers with the right credentials, authorization, or training are engaged in decision making and to help HRD departments evaluate employees for new positions, assess performance problems in existing jobs, and identify employees who are ready for additional training or development.

2. *Expert knowledge bases* contain external information—such as industry, market, customer, and competitor data—and internal information—such as employee, policy, process, and financial data. Before it is stored in knowledge bases, all information must be arranged in formats that are usable by the electronic systems and the workers. This process is called *mapping and structuring the data*.

3. *Online help* provides screen- and field-specific assistance for each program or application of the EPSS and may be linked to any computer-based training or reference material in the knowledge base. Workers must be able to access online help through a simple, intuitive user interface.

4. *Integrated training and job aids* are part of an EPSS and include any items an employee might need to perform a particular procedure. The system may include explanations as to the reasons for certain decisions and the analytical steps involved in making those decisions. In this way, the EPSS serves as both a decision-support system and a problem-solving system.

5. *Electronic integrated reference systems* are capable of performing powerful online searches. These systems store an organization's complete documentation, including equipment maintenance manuals, detailed procedures, and process guides. References might also include names, phone numbers, and addresses of experts who can help workers gather new information or act as coaches. Users should be able to quickly and easily search any of this material as well as integrate it with other training or performance support before applying the referenced information. Information in the system should be organized around specific work requirements.

6. *Online documentation* includes any continuous improvements devised by employees. As new materials are created or updated, operators can

quickly map, structure, and integrate the data into existing knowledge bases.

7. *Monitoring, assessment, and feedback systems* check user activity and evaluate its appropriateness. Employees can find out immediately if something is wrong or out of specification and correct the problems. By accessing competence profiles, these systems may also indicate how well specific individuals fit particular jobs or tasks and may then offer suggestions for improving skills.

8. *Links to external applications* allow workers to jump easily from one application or software package to another. For example, workers should be able to use a word processing program to draft a report, draw in information from an existing database to make a spreadsheet, and then print, transmit, or store a final report.

9. *System information* utilizes user cues and tools to update the vast amounts of information in the knowledge base, including system changes, enhancements, and new products. Since all new information has to be mapped and structured, the EPSS should contain a utility that allows system administrators or end users to format information before it is entered. Maintenance tools should also provide information on how the system is being used, what works, what doesn't work, and what upgrades may be needed.

## Using Expert Systems for Retirement Planning at T. Rowe Price

EPSS can be productively applied in the area of financial analysis and planning. Because so many variables are involved in financial decisions, an expert system offers great benefits. T. Rowe Price, headquartered in Baltimore, Maryland, is one of America's largest investment management firms. Retirement planning represents an important segment of its business, and the company offers a number of analytical software tools to customers. Users provide background on their financial situations and goals by answering questions and choosing among options. The program then presents their best options as determined by the rules of the expert system. Such systems allow T. Rowe Price customers to explore various options independently and without the pressure of real-time, face-to-face interaction. Expert systems for consumer decision making and evaluation of options is an important, but relatively untapped, application of EPSS. The T. Rowe Price software is an interesting prototype that we may see more frequently as organizations look for ways of distributing their expertise throughout their customer base.

*EPSS and Organizational Learning*

Intelligent and appropriate use of EPSS increases organizational learning in a number of ways. It improves job performance as it enhances knowledge by providing help just in time and just where workers need it. The system furnishes instant access to information, methods, tools, and decision-making aids, and users may also utilize computer technology to leverage the expertise of coaches or mentors, thus increasing their self-sufficiency and sense of empowerment. EPSS accelerates on-the-job training and improves learning retention while significantly reducing training time, cost, and paper documentation such as user manuals, tests, and evaluations. Companies will also appreciate their increased flexibility with worker assignments and the ability to train employees located at remote or distant sites.

An EPSS can be valuable in building a learning organization because it provides the infrastructure necessary for effective functioning. Its performance-centered design propels individuals to the required level of performance quickly and as independently as possible (Waddill & Marquardt, 2011). Here are some of the most direct benefits.

*Performance:* An EPSS leverages a worker's inherent intellectual and social skills by presenting information, knowledge, advice, and support at the moment of need.

*Individual learning:* Workers who use an EPSS learn in three ways—changing behavior due to negative or corrective feedback from the system; reviewing EPSS modules on the job just before using them; and reviewing EPSS modules off the job when mistakes are less dangerous and costly.

*Generation of new knowledge:* Workers will develop new techniques, methods, and procedures on the job beyond those that were part of the organization's original knowledge base. In this way, learners create new knowledge.

*Knowledge capture:* As individuals or teams gain new knowledge, an EPSS captures it through a formal process, such as mail messages, shared databases, or interviews with expert workers.

## BALANCING ORGANIZATIONAL AND WORKER NEEDS FOR TECHNOLOGY

Manville (2001) notes the difficult but important task of balancing increased demand for collective innovation and output from the organization on one hand and increased demand for freedom and autonomy from workers on the other. Both demands are valid and necessary. Balancing entrepreneurial initiative with measurable creativity across the organization presents a formidable challenge.

Workers want to be able to take a course, attend a webinar, or work with a community of practice with the sole stipulation being that they receive certification or meet performance objectives. Predefined curriculum paths and tailored objectives help structure learning while allowing a generous degree of individual initiative.

E-learning offers many new options to the worker, including the freedom to engage in a class or an online exercise at work or at home, after hours, in installments. Depending on schedule, convenience, and opportunity, workers can also choose between immediate, performance-driven learning and longer-term developmental growth. As well, there are different methods for those who are visually oriented (simulations or web-based instruction) or those who need to interact with other people or learn best through conversation (communities of practice).

Technology also holds out the promise of personalization and mass customization. For example, Cisco's learning system allows movement from basic content delivery, to aggregation through portals, to role-specific portals, to profiling for individual learners based on their backgrounds, needs, and aspirations as well as on changing business requirements.

## Technology and Learning at Federal Express

Federal Express is the world's largest express transportation company. Headquartered in Memphis, Tennessee, the company delivers more than 8 million items in 220 countries each working day. All the numbers at FedEx are large and growing—with more than 280,000 employees, FedEx flies into more than 325 airports and maintains 1,400 staffed facilities and more than 50,000 drop-off locations. Sales for fiscal year 2010 approached $35 billion. The company prides itself on setting the standards in the shipping industry for reliability, innovative technology, logistics management, and customer satisfaction. FedEx has received numerous awards, including the Malcolm Baldridge National Quality Award.

Under the guidance of CEO Fred Smith, the company has made a conscious effort to build a learning organization. Since 1991, many staff members have worked with Peter Senge at the MIT Center of Organizational Learning. Action learning has recently become an important part of the company's efforts in building a learning organization. FedEx leaders quickly point out that in becoming a learning organization, it has boosted intellectual capacity, agility, and resourcefulness.

FedEx has devoted considerable resources to technology subsystems and attained significant success. Since its founding, the company has developed and implemented several new technologies with the goal of distinguishing all aspects of its business from those of its competitors. In addition, FedEx made a huge investment in interactive training resources—more than $100 million in 1,200 systems in 1,400 field locations.

## *SENSEAWARE* AND INNOVATION

FedEx operates at the leading edge of movement and technology. At this intersection, great innovation is occurring that has led to significant competitive advantages for FedEx. One recent innovation is *SenseAware*, a sensor-based logistics service that pairs a multi-sensor device with a web-based shipment monitoring and collaborations application. *SenseAware* enables customers to monitor their shipment in near real-time, with information such as temperature, location, and exposure to light, and share this information continually with FedEx's supply chain partners.

## TECHNOLOGY-BASED LEARNING FOR CUSTOMER SERVICE

In recent years, FedEx replaced some of its classroom training programs with a computer-based system that features interactive video on workstation screens. This training system captures and interprets input from learners to determine whether a task is being performed correctly. If a learner makes a mistake, the system recognizes the error, points it out, and shows the proper method.

The interactive video instruction system presents training programs that combine television-quality full-motion video, analog audio, digital audio, text, and graphics. Learners interact with the system using touch screens or keyboards.

The interactive video training correlates closely with job testing. Using the system, employees can learn about their jobs, company policies and procedures, and customer service issues by reviewing various courses. Currently, there are more than 1,200 interactive video instruction units placed at more than 1,400 FedEx locations. All workstations are linked to the Federal Express mainframe in Memphis. There is virtually no subject or job-related topic that customer-contact workers cannot find on the interactive video instruction platform.

Once the CD-ROM courseware is written, FedEx knows that it must be updated. The workforce relies on the system to provide accurate and current information. For them, out-of-date information is worse than no information at all. For this reason, new and updated interactive internal FedEx websites are available to employees as needed.

## IMPROVEMENT PROGRAMS FOR CUSTOMER SERVICE

FedEx's customer service representatives get thousands of telephone calls a day, all demanding ready answers. In the past, company representatives handled questions by passing along customers and problems to another representative. The EPSS, however, has enabled FedEx to resolve problems immediately and proactively without passing off any customers.

The EPSS permits customer service representatives to enter another computer application without closing down the first. For example, representatives do not have to exit the billing screen before accessing the customer service screen. They can retrieve information from several databases and place it promptly on their computer screens so they can address their customers' specific problems. Through prompts, the system enables workers to provide instructions on topics such as measuring a box and even converting pounds to kilograms.

Recently, FedEx created a mandatory performance improvement program for all employees who deal with customers face-to-face or over the phone. Its primary goals were to completely centralize the development of training content while decentralizing delivery and to audit employees' abilities to retain what they learned. The program consists of job knowledge tests linked to an interactive video instruction (IVI) training curriculum. FedEx customer-contact employees around the country are required to take the tests every year via computer terminals at their worksites. The tests measure knowledge of specific jobs and are reflected in annual employee evaluations, making up about one-tenth of the performance ratings.

By testing customer-contact employees on product knowledge, services, policies, and various aspects of their jobs, FedEx obtains two major benefits. First, all employees operate from the same book, which means that customers receive accurate and consistent information. This helps maintain the company's high service levels and commitment to quality. Second, managers have an objective method of measuring the job knowledge of all customer-contact employees.

FedEx offers many incentives to encourage workers to quickly increase their learning. For example, employees are paid for two hours of preparation before each test, two hours of test time, and two hours for post-test study. Workers use a variety of web-based learning programs so that no trainers are necessary, and no travel costs are incurred.

## VALIDATING ELECTRONIC TEST PROGRAMS

Federal Express also developed a test program called QUEST (Quality Using Electronic Systems Training) to ensure that all its learning tests are valid, relevant, and fair, and meet appropriate standards. The company implemented the program by creating focus groups composed of trainers, managers, and employees. The focus groups designed the tests, which consist of multiple-choice questions pertaining to all vital aspects of employees' jobs.

Based on their collective knowledge, the focus groups created surveys covering the critical tasks for each job. Workers were then asked to rate their own tasks in order of importance. The focus groups wrote the test questions based on those evaluations, being careful to include only questions that pertained directly to specific workers' actual activities.

Pilot testing was the final step before implementation. At this phase, subject matter experts and an on-staff industrial psychologist examined any questions that might be construed as unfair based on the number of workers who missed them. The entire process—from focus group formation through test validations to implementation—took approximately fifteen to eighteen months.

To keep the tests timely, FedEx scheduled quarterly meetings of the original focus groups. Group members discuss test questions to determine if they are still valid and also write new questions. Over a period of time, FedEx has built up a bank of several hundred questions for each test. Invalid questions are replaced with equally weighted questions on the same topics.

FedEx has found that the QUEST program saves hours in clerical and administrative activities because the computer does all the scoring, record keeping, item analysis, and score reporting. Additional features of the program are real-time registration, real-time score reporting, and item analysis.

## SIMULATION LEARNING FOR AIRLINE PILOTS

FedEx's rapid growth means that more than 350 new pilots are hired every year. Over 4,500 current and new pilots are required to attend a minimum of two training courses a year, with a minimum of twelve hours in simulated training and a four-hour check ride designed to test their defenses and teamwork skills. The company owns twenty simulators, costing between $15 million and $20 million each. Every year, over 60,000 pilot "training events" occur, involving everything from upgrades in technology to the two- or three-month immersions it take to learn the MD-11 or any new plane. FedEx owns two training centers, one in Memphis and one in Anchorage, and is leasing simulator time in Miami, Orlando, Minneapolis, Singapore, Bangkok, and Taipei.

## SUCCESS OF E-LEARNING

Federal Express has invested large amounts of money on technology-based learning but is quick to point out the many benefits and even greater savings that have resulted for the company. Internal studies at FedEx show that its system for just-in-time training is effective: Instruction time on some modules has been reduced by 50 percent, with no loss in retention or quality of training. Since the implementation of interactive video training, job knowledge test scores have increased an average of twenty points. Locations that make greater use of interactive video training report higher scores. When correlating scores and performance evaluation ratings, FedEx learned that the employees with the highest test scores are generally the company's better performers.

FedEx firmly believes that its philosophy of training to the job, performing to standards, and testing for competency provides customers with a value-added insurance program that translates into outstanding service, which gives the company a competitive edge. Well-trained, knowledgeable, and empowered employees support this philosophy as well as the company's goal of 100 percent customer satisfaction.

## Technology and Learning in Organizations Around the World

Technology utilization is a powerful resource in organizations. Information and multimedia technology, from cloud-based computing to web-based applications to mobile learning, are to the economy of today's world what the railroad was to nineteenth-century America. New technologies and their innovative use have enabled learning organizations to quickly leapfrog over their competitors. Organizations around the world are finding new ways of integrating multimedia in order to provide enhanced learning in ways that are more efficient, less costly, and more flexible and powerful than ever before.

### Top 10 Strategies for Technology Application

#### 1. ENCOURAGE AND ENABLE ALL STAFF TO CONNECT TO THE KNOWLEDGE AND LEARNING

Mobile learning and cloud computing have become part of everyday life and everyday learning inside and outside organizations. However, in many organizations, some workers, especially older employees, may be unwilling or unable to understand and use these and other technologies for personal and corporate success. A learning organization will dedicate time and energy to these people; after all, many are in senior positions and may be unintentionally slowing the use of technology, thereby limiting a company's ability to store and transfer knowledge. In doing so, they limit the firm's capacity to learn faster and better.

The information available in such abundance from electronic sources is too valuable to be neglected by even a few employees. Learning organizations encourage staff to tap into websites such as those maintained by universities, vendors, partners, and other learning resources. They can also examine research findings and new practices related to neuroscience, adult development, and psychology while keeping abreast of advances in computer software and hardware that may facilitate teamwork across geographic and discipline differences.

## 2. DEVELOP MULTIMEDIA, TECHNOLOGY-BASED LEARNING CENTERS

Many learning organizations maximize their formal learning efforts by incorporating computers, multimedia, interactive video, and distance learning into their facilities. Technology is being used to create and support learning environments that powerfully integrate art, music, and visuals, blending the most effective educational theories with state-of-the-art technologies.

In these learning centers, computer-assisted programs and tutorials greatly enhance the flexibility of individual learning, while group efforts enhance interpersonal, critical thinking, and generative learning skills.

With the vast array of learning technologies available, selecting the best medium becomes important. As a general rule of thumb, mobile and computer-based training are more effective for knowledge skills, whereas interactive technology usually is more effective for behavioral training.

## 3. DEVELOP AND USE A VARIETY OF DISTANCE-LEARNING TECHNOLOGIES

With its FORDSTAR program, Ford has successfully demonstrated the power and value of using a variety of distance-learning technologies. Here is a quick checklist to consider when developing distance learning for a given organization:

- Verify that distance learning is the right choice for the organization.
- Be prepared to define distance learning and communicate its benefits to key stakeholders within the organization.
- Integrate distance learning into the overall training strategy.
- Identify course objectives and methodology during the instructional design phase in order to select the appropriate technology.
- Form a course development team that includes the instructional designer, developer, trainer, and technological support. Identify a management sponsor, distant site facilitators, and materials and facilities support.
- Adapt traditional courses to fit distance-learning platforms based on technology needs.
- Use dress rehearsals and a pilot to test distance-learning classes.
- Use comprehensive evaluations systems to assess learning.
- Use cost-benefit calculations to illustrate the benefits of action learning.

## 4. USE TECHNOLOGY TO CAPTURE INTERNAL AND EXTERNAL KNOWLEDGE AND IDEAS

Using technology to gather knowledge from people both inside and outside the organization should be a high priority. Human resources department, for example, can videotape interviews with acknowledged experts; the tapes can then be made available to staff who might benefit from the expert's knowledge, ideas, and inspiration. Corning's Bill Whitmore even created a new name, *tecknowledgy transfer*, for this process, which is designed to identify technical experts, capture their knowledge, and then transfer that knowledge to strategic sites within the organization. Royal Bank of Canada also uses technology to expedite knowledge transfer through communication channels such as videoconferences between offices, a weekly worldwide conference call known as the President's Forum, and a corporate video network.

## 5. ACQUIRE AND DEVELOP COMPETENCIES IN GROUPWARE AND SELF-LEARNING TECHNOLOGY

Improving the quality of group decision making while decreasing the time required for the process is a valuable accomplishment for learning organizations. To this end, it makes sense to become familiar with various groupware software packages that can help manage group processes and learning in areas such as project planning, team development, and meetings management. Other specific software applications are designed to promote learning and assist with individual problem solving and decision making.

## 6. IMPLEMENT AND EXPAND ELECTRONIC PERFORMANCE SUPPORT SYSTEMS

The EPSS must be understood by people across the organization before it can be developed and used properly. Requirements include an adequate technological infrastructure, appropriate skills among employees, and management support for development and implementation.

All nine components of a comprehensive and solid EPPSmust be developed. In brief, these are competency profiles; expert knowledge bases; online help; integrated training and job aids; electronic integrated reference system; online documentation; a system for monitoring, assessment, and feedback; links to external applications; and system information.

## 7. PLAN AND DEVELOP A JUST-IN-TIME LEARNING SYSTEM

Much like the just-in-time inventory concept, the reasons behind just-in-time learning are to reduce waste and cost and increase productivity by making sure learning happens as close as possible to the time when workers need it. This is especially important because the shelf life of much current knowledge has become shorter than ever, often less than a few months in certain technical and service areas. Thus, the pressure is on learning organizations to develop innovative ways of providing learning at the most effective moments. To construct a just-in-time learning system, companies must integrate high-tech systems, coaching, and actual work on the job into a single seamless and rewarding process.

## 8. BUILD INTERNAL COURSEWARE TECHNOLOGY AND CAPABILITY

Learning organizations should acquire the technology and capacity to design software systems that support individual and collective learning. These might include self-development systems, open learning catalogs and live resources, career development systems, diagnostic instruments, decision-making aids, opinion surveys, and even methods of achieving instant and continuous feedback about the learning of teams, departments, or the company as a whole. These systems can then be integrated with other software tools, such as project managers, spreadsheets, databases, and word processors and become part of the everyday activity, language, and know-how of the organization.

## 9. USE THE INTERNET AND INTRANETS FOR TRAINING

Learning organizations reap tremendous benefits from using intranets for learning purposes. Positives include consistency, centralization, and convenience because the same training materials are drawn from a single database to be used by employees when and where they prefer. The interactive quality of tools such as Java and Shockwave enliven web-based training, making it fun and engaging. Most intranets can be created and maintained with minimal programming expertise, and once systems are established, updating intranet learning materials is easier and less expensive than revising print-based resources. And, as bandwidth increases and new technologies emerge, the potential of intranets continues to evolve. Last but not least, new learning technologies help organizations stay current with the younger workforce.

## 10. INCREASE CAPABILITIES OF MANAGEMENT AND HUMAN RESOURCES STAFF

To maximize the power of technology and enhance organizational learning capacity, managers and HRD staff should be knowledgeable about technology-based learning, and according to Waddill and Marquardt (2011), be prepared to assume key leadership roles in the following areas:

- Operating technological systems that support organizational learning
- Managing large and continuous organizational change processes
- Facilitating outsourcing processes for technological resources
- Facilitating structured on-the-job learning systems
- Integrating existing technologies with new technologies
- Redesigning business processes to incorporate the new technology
- Securing appropriate buy-in on technologies from the user groups

# CHAPTER 8

# Action Learning: The Cornerstone for Building a Learning Organization

Perhaps no tool is more effective in building a learning organization than action learning. Lex Dilworth (1995) called action learning "the DNA of a learning organization" since action learning enables organizations to continuously learn on an organization-wide basis, which makes them better able to adapt to the continuously changing environment. Reg Revans (1982), a pioneer in the development of action learning, notes that action learning creates "constant learning opportunities for people. It inherently creates a culture and morale for learning." Today, hundreds of organizations around the world are utilizing action learning as the key driver in bringing in the culture and the principles necessary to become a learning organization (Cho & Egan, 2010; Marquardt, 2011b). For example, Fraser and Neave, a global company headquartered in Singapore, has made action learning the cornerstone in building continuous "innovation Through Action Learning" (iTAL), in which complex problems will be solved innovatively with the tool of action learning. Other organizations, such as Humana, Intelsat, Goodrich, Microsoft, and Samsung, have discovered that the most effective way of dramatically increasing system-wide learning is to establish numerous action learning projects throughout the organization.

# The Action Learning Group: A Mini-model of the Learning Organization

Peter Senge, recognized as Mr. Learning Organization by many people around the world for his classic *The Fifth Discipline*, indicated that, in order for a company to become a learning organization, it needed to be able to integrate work with learning on a daily basis, to have a culture of continuously reflecting and learning. Action learning provides precisely that experience and creates the mind-set that learning and action are interchangeable, that one can learn from every action, and that learning only becomes real learning when it results in improved actions. The action learning group is a miniature learning organization in which all five subsystems of the learning organization are incorporated and integrated. Action learning groups develop the mind-set and the skills that enable members to become continuous learners and generate continuous learning throughout the organization.

## What Is Action Learning?

Action learning is a process that involves a small group of people working on critical, real organizational problems, while at the same time learning how to better solve the problems. In addition, they are learning how to work better as a group and exploring how their learnings can benefit each group member and the organization as a whole (Marquardt et al., 2009).

Action learning derives its power and benefits from these six interactive and interdependent components:

1. Problem
2. Group or team
3. Reflective questioning
4. Action
5. Individual, group, and organizational learning
6. Coaching/facilitation

The strength and success of action learning depends on how well these elements are used and reinforced. Each component is necessary to create the optimum capacity and potency of action learning. Employed properly, action learning programs can catapult individuals, teams, and organizations to much higher levels of learning and success. Let's examine each of these elements in more detail.

## PROBLEM

Action learning is built around a problem, project, challenge, issue, or task, the resolution of which is of great importance to an individual, a team, and/or an organization. The problem should be significant, fall within the responsibility of the group, and provide opportunity for learning. Why is the selection of the problem so important? Because it is one of the fundamental beliefs of action learning that we learn best when we undertake an action, reflect on it, and learn from it—especially when the action involves something real and valuable on which to focus, a subject that is relevant and meaningful. It also creates an opportunity to test our accumulated knowledge.

Examples of problems tackled by action learning groups include the following:

- Reducing turnover in the workforce
- Reorganizing a department
- Closing down a production line
- Improving information systems and reducing paperwork
- Increasing sales
- Retaining a dissatisfied customer
- Developing a learning program

## GROUP OR TEAM

The core entity in action learning is the action learning group, which is composed of four to eight individuals. Research has shown that this number is ideal because groups of less than four members do not display enough diversity, creativity, and challenging dynamics, whereas groups of more than eight are too complex and do not allow each individual enough airtime, an important element in action learning. Ideally, the group's makeup should be diverse so as to maximize various perspectives and obtain fresh viewpoints. Depending on the type of problem, groups may contain individuals from across functions or departments. In some situations, groups may be composed of individuals from other organizations or professions, such as the company's suppliers, or even customers.

The group should include people who have the power to carry out the group's recommendations, care about the problem, and know something about it—in other words, those "who can, who care and who know" (Sofo, Yeo, & Villafane, 2010).

## REFLECTIVE QUESTIONING

By concentrating on the right questions rather than the right answers, action learning focuses on what we do not know as well as what we do know. Action learning works through a process that begins with asking questions to clarify the nature of the problem, reflecting on and identifying possible solutions, and then taking action.

The procedure of asking questions rather than immediately providing solutions unfreezes the group and defuses defensiveness. Asking the right questions when everything is uncertain and nobody knows what to do next encourages outside-the-box creativity. The insightful questions of action learning may lead to a wide array of benefits, such as shaking up our underlying assumptions, opening us up to greater learning, developing listening skills and thus more caring and trust among group members, enhancing creativity, empowering each team member, developing new mental models, and attaining an elevated level of discernment and understanding that will lead to better reflection and more effective action (Yeo & Nation, 2010).

Action learning programs provide the time and space we need to stand back and reflect, unfreeze our thoughts, rise above everyday problems, and develop a common perspective. Reflection generates mutual support within the group as each member listens intently and draws out the others' experiences and practical judgments. This process of questioning and reflecting also encourages team members to view one another as learning resources.

## ACTION

For advocates of action learning, there is no real learning without action, for the effectiveness of ideas or plans can be determined only after implementation. Applying the strategies and ideas provides an opportunity to reveal whether they are effective and practical, whether any issues have been overlooked, what problems might occur as a result, what to do differently in the future, and how to apply these ideas to other parts of the organization. Therefore, members of the action learning group must either have the power to take action themselves or be assured that any appropriate and reasonable recommended actions will be implemented. If the group only makes recommendations, it will lose its energy, creativity, and commitment.

Action enhances learning by providing a basis for reflection, and, indeed, the most valuable learning in action learning occurs when participants reflect on their actions, not just on their planning. By analogy, a beginning tennis player cannot truly learn how to serve by developing a serving plan but must actually hit the ball and learn from experience. The "action in action learning is not about developing a recommendation; it is about taking action" (Dixon, 1998, p. 46). Action enhances learning because it provides a basis and anchor for the critical dimension of reflection. The action of action learning begins with taking steps to reframe the problem and determining the goal, and only then determining strategies and taking action.

## INDIVIDUAL, GROUP, AND ORGANIZATIONAL LEARNING

The solving of organizational problems can result in immediate, short-term benefits to the company. The more significant and longer-term benefit, however, is the learning gained by each group member and the application of the group's new knowledge throughout the organization. As stated in Dilworth (1998), the gains of action learning are of greater strategic value to the organization than are the tactical advantages of solving the immediate problem.

Thus, action learning places equal emphasis on accomplishing the task and on the learning and development of individuals and organizations. The action learning process results in powerful, transformative learning due to a number of key learning principles:

- Greater learning occurs when we are allowed ample time and space, when a sense of urgency exists, when we can see results, when we are allowed to take risks, and when we are encouraged and supported in our deliberations.
- Critical learning occurs when we are able to question the assumptions that underlie actions.
- Learning intensifies when we receive accurate feedback from others, observe the results of our problem-solving actions, and reflect on our actions.
- Action learning is most effective when learners examine the organizational system as a whole.

- By working cooperatively on real issues, the group can move to higher levels of learning relative to application, synthesis, and evaluation.
- Action learning is built on the entire learning cycle: learning and creating knowledge through concrete experience, observing and reflecting on this experience, forming generalizations from experiences, testing the implications of those generalizations through new experiences, and beginning the process again.

Participants also gain key organizational learning skills through the action learning process. These include new ways of thinking about the organization derived from the act of addressing unfamiliar problems, improved self-understanding gained from feedback from others in the group, the ability to reflect critically on their assumptions and reframe to initiate innovative and more effective action, and teamwork skills derived from examining their behavior and working toward resolution of problems.

## COACHING/FACILITATION

Coaching is necessary for the group to focus on the important (i.e., the learning) as well as the urgent (resolving the problem). The action learning coach helps the team members reflect both on what they are learning and how they are solving problems. Through a series of questions, the coach enables group members to reflect on how they listen, how they may have reframed the problem, how they give each other feedback, how they are planning and working, and what assumptions may be shaping their beliefs and actions. The learning coach also helps the team focus on what they are achieving, what they are finding difficult, what processes they are employing, and the implications of these processes. The coaching role may be rotated among members of the group or may be limited to a person assigned to that role throughout the duration of the group's existence.

Action learning is most powerful when all six of these components are in place. Some organizations employ variations of action learning that utilize fewer than these six components, but to the extent that they do, they lose much of the potential of action learning, not only in the problem solving but also in the individual, team, and organization development aspects. The difference in using five components, for example, would be like 5 squared (or 25) versus 6 squared (36) if all six elements were employed, or a 30 percent decrease in the power of the action learning process. Optimizing the power and ensuring the success of action learning requires all six of these elements, which interweave and reinforce each other.

## How Action Learning Contributes to Building a Learning Organization

Each of the six components contribute to the building of a learning organization. Each or all of them:

- Are designed to systematically transfer knowledge throughout the organization
- Enable people to learn by doing
- Help develop learning-how-to-learn skills
- Encourage continual learning
- Create a learning culture where learning becomes a way of life
- Use an active rather than a passive approach
- Are applied on the job rather than off the job
- Allow for mistakes and experimentation
- Develop skills of critical reflection and reframing
- Serve as a mechanism for developing learning skills and behavior
- Demonstrate the benefits of organizational learning
- Model working and learning simultaneously
- Are problem-focused rather than hierarchically bound
- Provide networks for sharing, supporting, giving feedback, and challenging assumptions
- Develop the ability to generate information
- Break down barriers between people and across traditional organizational boundaries
- Help the organization move from a culture of training (in which someone else determines and provides your development) to a culture of learning (in which everyone is responsible for their own continuous learning)
- Are systems-based
- Apply learnings to other parts of the organization as appropriate

Let's now explore how action learning builds each of the five learning subsystems.

## How Action Learning Builds the Learning Subsystem

As noted in chapter 3, learning is the core subsystem of the learning organization. The learning subsystem refers to levels and types of learning that are crucial for organizational learning and the relevant organizational skills. Learning occurs at the individual, group, and organizational levels, and there are anticipatory and adaptive types of learning. The learning skills of systems thinking, mental models, personal mastery, self-directed learning, and dialogue are also a part of this subsystem.

Action learning programs encourage and enable significant learning at all three levels of learning: individual, group, and organizational. As noted, action learning programs also strive for and develop the other two types of learning, adaptive and anticipatory (see chapter 3). Adaptive learning occurs when, in reflecting on past actions, the group attempts to develop a new action that represents a better response to the environment. Through its analysis of a variety of possible future scenarios or probable effects of different actions, the group acquires anticipatory learning skills. Action learning sets generate innovative, creative knowledge, and the time allowed for deep and frequent reflection provides the avenue for single-loop, double-loop, and even deutero learning. Action learning gives people in the organization the opportunity to build each of these learning disciplines.

Action learning also encourages and develops dialogue. Dilworth (1998) notes that action learning promotes a depth and intensity of dialogue that is uncommon in the normal life experience. Inherent in this approach is the ability to acknowledge that we frequently act in ways that may be incongruent with the values and opinions we espouse. Revans (1982) observed that it is the "social dimension of action learning that provides the challenge to misconceptions and ingrained mental schemata which predispose a person to overlook the ways in which he/she needs to change." In action learning, real problems are explored in non-defensive ways with colleagues who support, question, and advise.

Alan Mumford (2008) has identified ten valuable learning behaviors, all of which can be developed within action learning programs:

1. Asking questions
2. Offering suggestions
3. Exploring options
4. Taking risks and experimenting
5. Being open and up front

6. Converting mistakes into learning
7. Reflecting and reviewing
8. Talking about learning
9. Taking responsibility for our own learning and development
10. Admitting to inadequacies and mistakes

Perhaps there may be no greater demonstration of true team learning than an action learning session during which the team develops common basic assumptions, a common understanding of the problem, and common growth in creating new knowledge. At the end of each action learning session, the group, with the help of the action learning coach, seeks to identify ways in which its learning can be applied to the organization and thereby create organization-wide learning.

## Action Learning for Problem Solving and Culture Change at Constellation Energy

Constellation Energy (originally Baltimore Gas and Light Company), one of the oldest power companies in the United States, is among the largest providers of wholesale, commercial, and retail electric energy in the country. The electric-generating fleet is diverse and currently consists of 12,000 megawatts of generating capacity powered by nuclear, coal, oil, gas, wood, waste coal, hydro, solar, and wind electric-generating units in the U.S. and Canada. Constellation is actively expanding in the renewable (solar) market for retail and commercial customers. With annual revenues approaching $15 billion, Constellation has over 7,000 employees nationwide.

Constellation's use of action learning for problem solving for organizational restructuring began in the early 2000s, when it was introduced to Frank Andracchi, Vice President of Power Generation. One Constellation action learning group explored the problem of "how to retain employees until the last day of operation for projects which were currently highly profitable, but would shut down in four years, due to new legal regulations and laws." The group's task was to create a retention program that was fair to both the employees and company. The membership of the action learning team included both affected and unaffected employees, and business leaders from unaffected business units. In two four-hour sessions, the action learning team created a retention program that included a $500 per month "bonus-set-aside" for every month the employee worked as well as an additional two weeks of pay for every year of service as severance. It should be noted that most of these employees had only five years of service at this point in time. Four years later, Andracchi reported that "all four of these projects met all of their production goals until the last day of operation, with both the owners and operating company exceeding all of their financial projections for this investment. If the projects had not had the solution developed by the action learning team, the financial loss to the investors would have been $100 million, with another $7 million in losses to the operating company. Maintaining the staff until the very last day of operation was critical to the success of this investment."

Another action learning success was a major reorganization effort in which Constellation combined three business units into one involving more than 300 employees, leaders, professionals, and craft personnel. According to Andracchi, "The questioning approach of action learning was the key in accomplishing this reorganization in a very short period of time with relatively few meetings. Our questions efficiently helped us to determine goals, the resources required to achieve the goal, and the most effective way to structure those resources to result in a highly effective and efficient organization. This reorganization and elimination of reluctances will result in a minimum of a $1 million savings per year going forward."

Over the past few years, Constellation has had a number of other successes with action learning. Since introducing action learning into Constellation Energy, Andracchi observes, "This problem solving approach has been widely successful in solving both simple and complex problems. And the real benefit is that as your leadership team becomes knowledgeable with the action learning process, they begin to use it everywhere to solve day-to-day business problems effectively and efficiently. Action Learning has resulted in clearly definable cost savings and breakthrough thinking at Constellation, and has helped us become a better learning organization."

## How Action Learning Builds the Organization Subsystem

The second subsystem of a learning organization is the organization itself, the setting and body in which the learning occurs. The four key dimensions or components of this subsystem are culture, vision, strategy, and structure.

The culture created in action learning programs is one where learning is the most important and valuable objective. Throughout the action learning process, there is an emphasis on how the group can continue to expand upon and speed up their knowledge and learning capacities. Members are encouraged and expected to take risks and try new ways. They recognize that much of the greatest leaps in learning have come from learning from mistakes made. The culture in an action learning group is one in which learning is expected, rewarded, encouraged, and continuous, and one in which the learning is valued as much as action.

Action learning is particularly valuable in helping organizations develop a vision committed to continuous learning. Schein (1993), a pioneer in understanding organizational culture and organizational change, notes that "for change (learning) to occur, the organization must unlearn previous beliefs, be open to new inputs and relearn new assumptions and behaviors." Action learning is a powerful tool in helping to change these values and create these new visions.

Action learning organizations have a natural and powerful bias for reflection-in-action. The capacity to quickly take action and to generate information is critical to organizations. Senge (2006) observes that "learning cannot exist apart from action. Action provides a basis for the critical dimension of reflection." It is the expressed strategy of an action learning program to build in time, space, and opportunities for learning. And no strategy is more powerful for producing organization-wide learning than getting large numbers of employees involved in action learning programs.

The structure of an action learning set is very fluid and flexible. Hierarchy and protocol is minimized. Allowing the flow of questions and interactions to be concise and clear is critical in processes such as reframing the problem, identifying possible actions, and providing frank feedback to one another. Needless protocol, bureaucracy, and administrivia are discouraged, and leadership is distributed throughout the group.

## Using Action Learning to Build the Learning Culture at Deutsche Bank

Deutsche Bank, an international bank with its headquarters in Frankfurt, Germany, employs more than 80,000 people in 72 countries, with a large presence in Europe, the Americas, Asia Pacific, and the emerging markets of Africa. Revenues in 2009 exceeded $30 billion. Deutsche Bank received 2010 Bank of the Year Award, the financial industry's most coveted award from the prestigious *International Financial Review* (IFR) magazine, an award it also won in 2003 and 2005.

A few years ago, Deutsche Bank faced tremendous changes in its business and staff structure, with critical implications for corporate culture. Organizational change was critical, and action learning was employed to work on the following problems:

- Reconfiguration along divisional product lines
- Shift form regional to global operational structure
- Shift from multinational to global leadership structure
- Acquisition of several U.S. entities and their leadership model
- Change in corporate language from German to English

In order to solve these problems, Deutsche Bank recognized that it needed to develop its leadership and its problem-solving capabilities. Existing leadership development programs were focused on individual—not organizational—development. As a result, little knowledge got transferred to workplace or application of new skills to business challenges. In addition, the cost of off-the-job training and development was high and climbing. In searching for a tool that would develop leaders while simultaneously resolving these challenges, Deutsche chose action learning because of its just-in-time learning and self-managed learning efficiency.

Key business challenges were identified, and a six-month action learning program was begun. The CEO, program director, and/or program manager selected the problems best suited for Deutsche Bank and for the action learning participants. Four criteria needed to be met:

- Of strategic importance to bank
- Potential source of significant organizational change
- Strategic—not tactical—in nature, to "stretch" participants
- Broad in scope, offering rich learning opportunities

Twenty participants were selected. Following a two-day introduction to action learning, the four groups met over a period of six to eight weeks on a part-time basis to work on their problem. The final two days of the program included presenting actions taken as well as capturing the learning that could be applied throughout Deutsche Bank. The program was considered a great success, having attained innovative and cost-effective actions for each of the company's problems.

## Building the Learning Organization Culture with Action Learning at Panasonic

Founded in 1918, Panasonic has grown to become the largest Japanese electronics producer. In addition to electronics, Panasonic offers non-electronic products and services such as home renovation services. With nearly 400,000 employees worldwide, Panasonic was ranked the 89th-largest company in the world in 2009, with over $80 billion in revenues.

Although Panasonic, like other organizations, has used action learning for leadership development and problem solving, its primary purpose for introducing action learning into the company was to build a culture imbued with high ethical standards, a commitment of continuing learning, and deep respect for others. Accordingly, all new employees are now introduced to action learning and participate in action learning problem-solving, since these values are inherent within the principles and practice of action learning itself. Panasonic was eager to make action learning a part of every employee's experience because top management discovered how well it matches with the four components of the Basic Business Philosophy (BBP) of Panasonic's Founder, Konosuke Matsushita. Jasmine Liew, HR Manager at the Panasonic Regional Training Center in Singapore, describes how and why action learning and the Panasonic BBP intertwine so well (Marquardt et al., 2009):

## 1. COURTESY AND HUMILITY

Matsushita practiced and encouraged the skill of listening to one another with respect. To strengthen cordial work relationships, he advocated that there should be modesty and respect for the rights and needs of others. These virtues of courtesy and humility correspond closely to two key norms of action learning: (a) respect for the ideas and differences of each member of the group, and (b) setting aside time for learning as well as action. Everyone in the Panasonic action learning team is therefore treated with equal respect as they have equal opportunity to share by asking or responding to questions.

## 2. CO-OPERATION AND TEAM SPIRIT AND COLLECTIVE WISDOM

Matsushita had a penchant for asking questions and learning from others to create better alternatives for effective problem solving and decision making. He believed that wise leaders could not solve problems based on their own personal experiences and perspectives. Instead, "a wise person knows that those who ask questions are more valuable than those who simply spout knowledge."

In the action learning programs at Panasonic, by asking questions, leaders can gain more respect from others because this will reflect their desire to understand what their members know or think. Individuals feel appreciated, motivated, and gratified when they are given the opportunity to share their ideas and experiences with interested parties. Moreover, questions provide a fountain of collective information as a leader listens and taps on the wealth of the "collective wisdom" and experiences that lies within the team.

Action learning encourages "collective wisdom." It fosters a climate of understanding, an openness to different ideas, and the humility and willingness to interact and learn within a diverse team, seeking solutions to a common issue. The BBP encourages "co-operation and team spirit." With this in mind, Panasonic teams can expect to develop better solutions and to elevate their learning as individuals and as a team. This also enhances the team dynamics and builds effective and cohesive problem-solving teams.

## SUNAO MIND

The "sunao mind" is a Japanese phrase that means understanding the truth without bias or self-interest. One is willing to hear different perspectives and have an open mind. Panasonic employees are to practice "sunao mind" when they engage in conversations.

With an "open-mind," they are able to listen and empathize with the other person's point of view, look at things as they are from an objective and unbiased perspective, and thus have a concrete paradigm of the actual situation or issue under discussion.

In Panasonic's action learning teams, there is framing and reframing of the problem, and every team member must be objective, have an open mind, and remain unbiased. Through questions, the problem can be framed and reframed as the group practices "sunao mind" in accepting each other's interpretation of the perceived problem. With greater clarity of the real problem, a more effective action or decision thus emerges from the team to help in solving the problem.

## ADAPTABILITY AND UNTIRING EFFORT FOR IMPROVEMENT

Panasonic employees are to adapt their thinking and behavior to meet the ever-changing conditions of the business environment. Continuous learning, relearning, and unlearning are the foundations of action learning. The impact of learning through questions unfolds as members share their views when responding to the questions raised by team members. Members have to adapt to changes quickly due to the dynamic forces of questions, leading members to frame and reframe the contents, when the need arises.

Action learning truly serves as an effective learning technique for the manifestation of BBP and assists employees to further appreciate and apply the BBP in their day-to-day work and decision-making processes. The birth of "BBP and Action Learning" as a key HRD activity in PRTC took place in January, 2008. Since then, a series of training programs incorporating action learning have been successfully launched, including action learning application as a component of all of Panasonic's programs for high potential leaders.

# How Action Learning Builds the People Subsystem

The people subsystem of the learning organization involves learning by the employees, managers/leaders, customers, and business partners (suppliers, vendors, and subcontractors) of the organization, as well as by the communities in which the organization operates. Each of these groups is a part of the learning chain, and all need to be empowered and enabled to learn.

Action learning recognizes the importance of involving people from throughout the business chain in the problem-solving process. Action learning groups can become very effective if they are diverse, and if they not only incorporate different hierarchical levels of the organization but also bring in customers, suppliers, and interested community members to ask fresh questions and share fresh perspectives. Building learning alliances help organizations to achieve continuous improvement and develop the capacity to cope with discontinuous change. Learning from fresh faces is critical for success in action learning as it is in organizations. New partners and perspectives can:

- Enlarge the range of the continuous environmental scanning ability of those in the alliance
- Bring a wide analytical range—and a wider range of assumptions—to the learning process, so that discontinuities are more likely to be recognized
- Help members recognize and overcome defensive routines so that they can be more transcendent
- Take place at multiple levels within the alliance and improve the learning of all members
- Open up the boundaries of the organization and make possible completely new organizational forms, constantly open to importing chaos and evolving new forms of order

Empowering people to take responsibility for themselves rather than waiting for outside expertise is a key value of action learning. An essential part of all action learning programs is the development of leadership skills of the group members, particularly the skill of encouraging and enabling people around them to learn (Marquardt et al., 2009).

In learning organizations, a primary task of managers is to facilitate the staff's learning from experience. Through their experiences in action learning programs, managers recognize the importance of making time for seeking feedback, for obtaining data from a variety of perspectives, for encouraging new actions for old and new problems. They will also perceive the value in questioning their own ideas, basic assumptions, attitudes, and actions.

## Action Learning for Leadership Development at Microsoft

Founded in 1975 and headquartered in Redmond, Washington, Microsoft Corporation has nearly 90,000 employees worldwide. At Microsoft, as at other organizations, the business climate is constantly evolving, and the organization needs to continuously learn. And as the way of doing business changes, the requirements and skills of its leadership also must change.

One of Microsoft's key leadership programs is called "Leadership in Action," which uses the drivers of accelerated development and the action learning approach to advance leaders' skills and capabilities while, at the same time, making a direct business impact. In preparation for the Leadership in Action program, leaders attend a global Launch Event that explores the value of differentiation. At this event, Microsoft leaders consider how they can differentiate themselves as leaders by focusing on and delivering what matters most. The session helps these members to identify the "breakthrough problem or opportunity" within their role where they can create the visibility and momentum needed to propel their careers forward.

All selected action learning projects align with Microsoft's core capabilities and interests, as outlined in best practice guidance around strategic corporate social responsibility. The participants all have real, urgent business challenges that will benefit from the diverse perspectives being brought by the Microsoft leaders. The planning team ensures that both the high-potential participants and the partners benefit from the experience. For the partners, benefits include receiving consulting on critical business challenges, exposure to the action learning methodology, a best practice leadership development experience for a key staff member, and a strengthened relationship with Microsoft.

Microsoft has seen great value from action learning because it allows members to practice and develop leadership competencies, work together as high-potential teams, and learn to ask great questions as leaders, all while working on real, urgent business problems. In addition, leaders worked with each other on their own challenges and problems in what were identified as "action learning circles." According to Shannon Banks, Director of Worldwide Leadership Development, the selection of great problems and the diversity of the teams were the keys to the success of the problem-solving projects as well as the development of great leadership within Microsoft. Based upon the design and successes of Microsoft's action learning projects, the company was awarded the 2010 Organization of the Year Award by the World Institute for Action Learning.

## How Action Learning Builds the Knowledge Subsystem

The knowledge subsystem of a learning organization refers to the management of acquired and generated knowledge of the organization. It includes the (1) acquisition, (2) creation, (3) storage, (4) analysis and data mining, (5) transfer and dissemination, and (6) application and validation of knowledge. The implementation of action learning programs within organizations contains effective mechanisms for incorporating all six aspects of the knowledge subsystem.

*Acquiring knowledge:* In action learning programs, group members are advised not only of the importance of acquiring knowledge from external resources but also of the value of tapping the tacit, internal wisdom and experience of others within the group as well as within other parts of the organization. The internal networks developed in action learning groups heighten the awareness of organizational resources, facilitate exchanging and sharing of ideas, and generate tremendous amounts of valuable knowledge.

*Creating knowledge:* Participants in action learning programs realize the importance of constantly creating new knowledge, of being innovative so that they can discover new and breakthrough ways of solving the problems of the organization. Current or existing knowledge is rarely sufficient to solve complex challenges. Thus, members are constantly striving to create new knowledge and to encourage innovation within the set. Nonaka (2008) suggests that information creation is a fundamental requirement for the self-renewing (i.e., learning) organization. Creativity and innovation is natural in problem-solving groups that are diverse and whose members are continuously questioning each other for new knowledge and ideas.

*Storing knowledge:* Knowing what knowledge to store and how to store it is based upon the organization's ability to make sense of the data encompassing and surrounding it. The company must then develop sense-making categories for coding and retaining value-added knowledge. Through the ongoing reflection on learning and the knowledge acquired, action learning programs lend themselves well to the Kantian school of thinking, which "positions sense-making above mere sensing" (Botham and Vick, 1998). By reflecting on action, the action learning group develops the ability to "make meaning" of the data collected and stored.

*Analysis and data mining:* During the action learning sessions, group members regularly analyze the knowledge that has been acquired and created, synthesize it, and determine if it can be utilized in solving the problem given to them. Between sessions, the information that has been stored may be examined to seek ways it can be of benefit to the action learning project.

*Transferring and dissemination:* At the conclusion of each action learning session, group members are asked to identify what knowledge that has been gained during that session would be of value to the organization. Members determine who should receive this information and/or what knowledge management system should receive this knowledge. Of course, group members capture and store for themselves the knowledge and wisdom that will help them become better in both their professional and personal lives.

*Application and validation:* Between action learning sessions, action learning members are testing out the strategies that they have developed to test whether their ideas are valid and applicable. Action learning, as noted earlier, is built on the belief that only learning that is applicable is truly learning, and that all true learning can and should lead to powerful actions. At the final session of the action learning program, a number of strategies and actions are proposed to the organization, and are applied by the group members and/or other members of the organization. During and following the implementation of the strategies, the action learning group reflects on what has worked and what has not, and why.

## General Electric and Action Learning

General Electric (GE) has declared action learning a vital strategy in transforming itself into a global-thinking, fast-changing organization. GE's action learning teams are built around real and relevant problems that require decisive action. Formats may vary, but typically, two teams of five to seven people from diverse divisions and functions within GE work together on the project. GE has designed the projects so that participants receive feedback on strategies as well as on their leadership and teamwork skills. They also have the opportunity to reflect on the total learning experience.

Along with team building, the organization's action learning teams give participants a context for dealing with multicultural and global issues. Global action learning teams usually focus on potential GE markets. In a recent executive development course for global business leaders in Heidelberg, Germany, the action set spent the first week building team and leadership effectiveness as well as meeting with key European business leaders, opinion makers, and government officials from France, Germany, and Sweden.

During the second week, the focus shifted to projects from GE's plastic, lighting, and electrical distribution and control businesses. One team looked at the lighting strategy for Europe, reflecting the sharp rise—from 2 percent to 18 percent in 18 months—in GE's share of the Western European consumer lighting market, mostly resulting from GE's acquisition of Tungsram in Hungary and Thorn Lighting in the United Kingdom. The teams were encouraged to be creative and think of serious ways in which GE could change the market and create excitement among retailers and customers by adding value in new ways. The participants traveled across Europe to conduct interviews and gain firsthand experience of other cultures, languages, currencies, legislation, tax laws, and consumer preferences. Between interviews, the participants debriefed one another and prepared their final reports for GE leadership, including former CEO Jack Welch.

James Noel, manager of executive education at GE at the time of these projects, has stated that action learning was pivotal in building GE into a learning organization.

Action learning has made "participants active partners in the learning process. Because the team projects provide value to GE's businesses, it has an immediate return on investment. Action learning also provides a viable vehicle for dealing with issues of leadership and teamwork."

## How Action Learning Builds the Technology Subsystem

Action learning has the power to energize and augment both components of the technology subsystem: enhancing learning and managing knowledge. Technology alone will not enable an organization to take advantage of the new strategic opportunities to increase its learning and utilize its knowledge. Individuals and especially teams are needed to optimize the development and application of technology. Developing the best e-learning hardware and software requires a keen understanding of how individuals and groups learn; how they can access, transfer, and apply knowledge; and how their learning and knowledge can lead to corporate success.

Action learning groups, when appropriate, examine the possible technologies that might be used in the project and how technology can manage the knowledge and learning of the group and of the organization. If the solution involves learning and/or knowledge management, the group examines how learning or management technologies might increase the power and speed of the strategy implementation.

Technology and action learning also interact in other ways. Action learning teams can examine how and why knowledge is or is not flowing throughout the organization. Electronic Performance Support Systems can be designed and applied more fruitfully when developed by action learning groups. And technology plays an important role when action learning groups must meet virtually, a situation that is occurring with increasing frequency and proving to be very successful (Marquardt & Yeo, 2011).

## The Power of Action Learning in Building a Learning Organization

As described by theories and demonstrated by case examples, action learning can quickly and successfully contribute to the building of a learning organization. Since it is both action oriented and learning focused, it serves as a perfect model and practice arena for organizational learning. By its very nature, action learning enables people to learn by doing, mostly on the job, thereby modeling simultaneous working and learning. It promotes a culture of continual learning that encourages experimentation and allows for mistakes within networks where people feel free to share knowledge, offer support and feedback, and challenge assumptions.

Two significant events occur within action learning groups that help to create learning organizations. First, team members resolve problems, transfer the ideas and strategies throughout the organization, and constantly acquire relevant information and knowledge that will be valuable for future problem-solving episodes. Second, the body of institutional knowledge increases and the pace of institutional learning accelerates as more and more action learning groups proliferate in the organization.

Its systems-based design facilitates the transfer and application of knowledge throughout the organization, breaking down barriers between people and across traditional organizational boundaries. All these qualities help move an organization away from a culture of training, in which someone else determines and provides for our development, and toward a culture of learning, in which we are responsible for our own learning.

With this approach, action learning members spend time reflecting on actions planned and then identifying their learning, whether it is derived from successes or failures, whether it is technical or procedural in nature. An action learning program might begin in one area or department and later filter throughout the company, thus serving as a catalyst for change and learning across the entire organization. Action learning programs are so effective in building learning organizations because they begin and end where innovative strategies are needed and significant learning is required.

# CHAPTER 9

# Becoming a Learning Organization

Becoming a learning organization demands an understanding of and a commitment to mobilizing all five subsystems of the Systems Learning Organization model featured in this book. Taking the specific steps to build a learning organization requires well-orchestrated planning on the part of many people in the organization.

It is also important to remember that being a learning organization is not a static condition. Change is constant, and the need for learning is never finished. Initiatives such as continuous process improvement are just part of a learning organization's overall goal: for everyone in the company to learn as much and as often as possible in order to increase productivity. Specifically, this means that learning organizations practice and improve learning skills and principles throughout the organization as well as up and down the business chain. Maintaining this new, higher level of learning power is, perhaps, as challenging as initiating the process of becoming a learning organization.

There is no single, guaranteed way to become a learning organization. Each company must develop a structure and style that is best suited to its own people, history, skill base, technology, mission, and culture and then develop an appropriate learning structure and style. Gill (2009) emphasizes the importance of developing a learning culture that incorporates the best potential of people, technology, and resources.

Given these caveats, there are some clear guidelines and directions that can be of help to companies seeking to begin this journey. Analysis of the steps implemented by companies that have become learning organizations reveals a number of common strategies and sequences of action that enabled them to climb the organizational learning ladder (see Table 8). Intentionality and commitment to becoming a learning organization, not luck or circumstances, made their journey successful. However, it is important to remember that these strategies are intended as possibilities, not prescriptions. It will be up to you to determine exactly which pathway and choices might work best in your organization. As you review each step, ask yourself the following questions:

- Does your organization do this? If not, could it?
- What are the barriers that might prevent your organization from taking this step?
- What is needed to enable your organization to complete this step?

---

## TABLE 8

### 16 Steps in Building a Learning Organization

1. Commit to becoming a learning organization.
2. Form a powerful coalition for change.
3. Connect learning with business operations.
4. Assess the organization's capabilities on each subsystem of the Systems Learning Organization model.
5. Communicate the vision of a learning organization.
6. Recognize the importance of systems thinking and action.
7. Demonstrate and model commitment to learning.
8. Transform the organizational culture to one of continuous learning and improvement.
9. Establish corporate-wide strategies for learning.
10. Reduce bureaucracy and streamline the structure.
11. Extend learning to the entire business chain.
12. Capture learning and release knowledge.
13. Acquire and apply the best technology to the best learning.
14. Create short-term wins.
15. Measure learning and demonstrate learning successes.
16. Adapt, improve, and learn continuously.

## 1. Commit to Becoming a Learning Organization

The first step is for leadership to commit themselves to transforming the company into a learning organization. Whether the impetus for change comes from a single charismatic leader or a critical mass of managers, the organization must understand that business success depends on learning success. The reason is simple: A learning organization can rapidly transform its new knowledge into new products, marketing strategies, and ways of doing business. As an added benefit, a learning organization can be an exciting, enjoyable, and fulfilling place to work. Such an organization attracts and retains top people, thus bringing even more learning, productivity, and success to the company.

Most successful change efforts begin when individuals or groups within the organization take a serious look at the company's competitive situation, market position, technological trends, and/or financial performance and realize that either a great crisis or a great opportunity looms. This first step is essential because establishing a strong sense of urgency does much to gain the active cooperation of many individuals.

More than 50 percent of companies never get their transformation efforts off the ground because they fail at this first phase. There are any number of reasons for this failure. For example, executives sometimes underestimate the difficulty involved in moving people out of their comfort zones and may discover that they lack the patience to handle the preliminaries. Or they may be afraid of the risks involved in creating a new system of operations. Possible downsides include defensiveness on the part of senior employees, a drop in morale, the change process spinning out of control, or negative impact on short-term business results.

A key strategy at this point is to portray the status quo as more dangerous than launching into the unknown. Unless people see the situation as critical, the transformation process will not succeed.

## 2. Form a Powerful Coalition for Change

Although the aspiration may begin with just one or two people, successful transformation into a learning organization requires at least a certain number of individuals who are truly committed to this goal.

John Kotter (1995, 2008), a Harvard professor with extensive experience in assisting organizations in major change efforts, notes that "in successful transformations, the chairman or president or division general manager, plus another five or fifteen or fifty people, come together and develop a shared commitment. ... In my experience, this group never includes all the company's most senior executives because some people just won't buy in, at least not at first. But in most successful cases, the coalition is always pretty powerful—in terms of titles, information, expertise, reputations, and relationships" (p. 62).

Where to begin transforming a company into a learning organization? Is there a starting point? It is generally preferable to begin by acquiring the commitment of top leadership. However, this is not always possible, particularly in the early stages. Some leaders need to be shown that the transformation works, even if only at the unit level. Senior managers always form the core of the coalition, but the guiding light may often be a board member, a representative from a key customer, or even a powerful union leader.

But if organizations are, in fact, organisms, then each small part—every department or site—has the capacity to affect the whole organization. Any area may foster experimentation, get people to work together on real problems that will release their ideas and energies, tackle flaws in the system, and learn collectively.

The degree of difficulty you experience in effecting organizational change often depends on your position in the company. If you feel that you are working in the middle or at the margins, take action through committees and other structures that provide avenues for exerting indirect influence over decision makers. Clarify your situation by answering the following questions:

- What is your company's level of organizational learning?
- What is your position in the organization?
- What avenues and resources could you use to transform your company into a global learning organization?

The sense of urgency helps assemble a guiding coalition, but making progress requires a person who can bring these people together, help them develop a shared sense of the critical nature of becoming a learning organization, and develop the necessary level of trust and communication. Offsite retreats are especially valuable at this stage.

Companies that fail in this first step have usually underestimated both the difficulties involved in producing change and the importance of a powerful guiding coalition. Or their coalition may be unable to work as a team: Without a strong guiding coalition, a company may make progress for a while, but, sooner or later, other significant issues will emerge and block the efforts for change.

## 3. Connect Learning with Business Operations

Leaders who decide to build a learning organization must clearly and explicitly link the process and products of learning to the organization's strategic goals. Companies that succeed at becoming learning organizations are those that realized they would not be able to convince others to share their commitment until they defined and achieved measurable benefits from being learning organizations. Connecting learning to improved business operations is persuasive proof of the importance of taking this new direction, in spite of the initial difficulties and challenges.

One way to link learning with organizational strategy is to establish an advisory learning team that reviews the overall direction of learning. This team ensures that learning fits and promotes the organization's strategic goals. Some of the following points may help convince doubters in the organization.

First, make clear that learning is an important job task. In fact, it is as much an organizational task as are the production and delivery of goods and services. Productivity and profits, of course, are still important, but company-wide learning is the only way to improve them.

Second, explain how learning can and must fit into daily operations. Organizations can learn as they produce, without sacrificing speed and quality while doing so. Every activity—from planning through execution to assessment—is an opportunity to learn. Production systems can also be learning systems.

Third, point out that learning and the resulting knowledge will be stored with the organization, even if key individuals leave. Learning organizations are equipped to develop comprehensive and systematic ways of maintaining and using this knowledge for short-term and long-term business success.

## 4. Assess the Organization's Capabilities to Become a Learning Organization

As in most change efforts, a critical early step is to identify existing strengths as well as weaknesses, resources as well as gaps. Many organizations have done this informally, but more and more companies are realizing the importance of a comprehensive, systematic examination of their organizations' learning competence.

The Learning Organization Profile (LOP), in Appendix A, is one tool for assessing your company's status. This instrument has undergone extensive field testing and has been used successfully by more than 100 organizations from every part of the world. The LOP consists of ten questions that address each of the five subsystems of the Systems Learning Organization model. Individuals or teams rate their organizations on a Likert scale from 4 (highest) to 1 (lowest) on each question. (For further information on the Learning Organization Profile, contact Learning Organization Associates at mike.marquardt@wial.org.)

## 5. Communicate the Vision

Once your company commits itself to becoming a learning organization, it must communicate this vision to all employees and stakeholders. When everyone has the same goal, the new organizational vision will enjoy unparalleled enthusiasm and support.

A vision gives employees and the entire organization an overarching goal that helps guide strategic thinking and planning. In addition, people are more inclined to accomplish tasks that serve a purpose they understand and embrace. Vision generates powerful, creative learning that leads to high-quality products and services. It also provides a focus that keeps learning processes and efforts on course in the face of stress, frustration, and impatience.

Jim Gannon, former senior vice president of human resource planning and development for Royal Bank of Canada, underscored the absolute importance of communicating the vision of corporate-wide learning by stating that "visions are what energize the organization; they are the dreams that pull us forward." The learning vision, like any vision, must be communicated effectively, since even "the most sophisticated vision is of no use unless it can be clearly understood by others" (Marquardt, 2002, p. 215).

Successful transformation requires a vision of the future that can be communicated readily and appeals to employees and other stakeholders. Without this vision, efforts may easily dissolve into confusing and incompatible projects that lead in the wrong direction, conflicting directions, or nowhere at all. Kotter (2008) cites a useful rule of thumb: If you can't communicate the vision in five minutes or less and get a reaction that signifies both understanding and interest, you are not yet done with this phase of the transformation process.

Executives who communicate well incorporate the vision into their hour-by-hour activities. For example, in routine discussions about business problems, they may talk about whether or not proposed solutions fit the goal of a learning organization, or, during regular performance appraisals, they may explain how certain kinds of behavior help or undermine the vision.

Corporate leaders use every available communication channel to broadcast the vision. Company newsletters that were once boring and probably unread can be enlivened with dynamic articles about the vision. Routine and tedious management meetings become exciting discussions of the company's transformation into a learning organization. Courses that focus on the new vision replace old-style management classes. And, most important, these leaders consciously attempt to become living symbols of the new corporate culture of a learning organization.

## 6. Recognize the Importance of Systems Thinking and Action

A company cannot become a learning organization unless people in the company recognize the value of a systems approach. In other words, they must refrain from focusing on just one subsystem or one part of the organization.

Systems thinking helps organization members clarify patterns and identify more effective approaches to changing them. Recognizing and understanding the links between actions enables them to explore the reasons behind successes, challenges, and failures. Systems action helps people focus on high-leverage changes that may not be obvious and create archetypes of successful actions for others in the organization to follow. Companies such as Alcoa, Boeing, Procter & Gamble, and Walmart have encouraged their workers to adopt the techniques of systems thinking and systems action.

Maintaining a learning organization requires a broad systems perspective that recognizes the interdependence of organizational units and activities. It enables people to see problems and solutions in terms of systemic relationships among processes and to understand the connection between the needs and goals of units and those of the organization as a whole.

Learning organizations realize that there is more than one way to accomplish business objectives and work goals. An organization that supports variation in strategy, policy, process, structure, and personnel will be much more prepared to adapt to unforeseen problems. This appreciation of diversity provides more options and, perhaps even more important, allows for greater stimulation and richer interpretation for all organizational members. A variety of methods, procedures, and approaches will enhance future learning in a way that a single approach cannot.

## 7. Demonstrate and Model Commitment to Being a Learning Organization

Learning organizations need the commitment, modeling, and involvement of all leaders. Especially in the early stages of becoming a learning organization, leaders should have one aim: pursuing improved overall performance by implementing long-term learning by, and continuous improvement of, all individuals and teams.

Creating vision is not enough. Organizational leaders must be able to articulate the learning vision and become engaged in its hands-on implementation. Active involvement includes eliminating barriers created by layers of management, remaining visible at every level of the organization, and participating in early learning efforts.

As top managers become convinced of the learning organization's value, they must become models, eager to learn for themselves and encourage others to learn as well. Managers should view themselves as coaches, facilitators, and advocates who promote, encourage, and reinforce learning.

Leaders can create a corporate learning culture in a number of ways. They should provide opportunities for training and practice in organizational learning. At the same time, company norms must encourage staff members to overcome their fear of making errors and support those who make mistakes in pursuit of progress. Employees at all organizational levels should be recognized for their efforts and rewarded for innovative thinking and experimentation. When many people promote a new idea, learning takes place more rapidly and far more extensively. Effective learning environments utilize both top-down and bottom-up initiatives for enhancing organizational awareness or developing new competencies.

## Nokia's Ollila Makes Commitment to Learning

John Ollila is Nokia's current Chairman of the Board and former CEO. At Nokia, he developed a learning organization strategy that calls for continuous learning at all levels, which he believes best prepares the company for anticipated expectations. Ollila observed that as the level of uncertainty in the environment grew, it was important to use learning and knowledge in a way that would empower Nokia employees to act with purpose and confidence. Thus, the commitment at Nokia to invest in continuous learning for all employees and to build a learning organization developed.

## 8. Transform the Organizational Culture

Companies on their way to becoming learning organizations understand that they must transform their cultures in many significant ways. Let's explore several effective approaches.

### ENCOURAGE CONTINUOUS LEARNING

When building a learning company, ongoing learning should become a habit, a joy, and a natural part of work for everyone. Learning should occur as an automatic and integral part of production, marketing, problem solving, finance, customer service, and every other company operation.

Pledge to provide numerous opportunities for learning, including formal educational programs, speakers, coffee klatches, panels, tours, videoconferences, and monthly programs. By focusing on continuous learning rather than on one-time training events, you will forge a new relationship with employees, one that demonstrates your belief in them and their learning. Ensure a supportive and interesting environment, in which continuous learning yields reflections, insights, and new ideas that can be translated into action throughout the organization.

Maintain the high level of power in a learning organization by demonstrating ongoing commitment to lifelong education at all levels of the organization and clear support for the growth and development of all members. Communicate a palpable sense that learning and practicing are never finished. This factor is another way of expressing what Peter Senge (2006) called "personal mastery."

## STRIVE FOR CONTINUOUS IMPROVEMENT

Commitment to continuous improvement is a driving force for all learning organizations that strive to "delight the customer." Learning organizations thrive in a culture of continuous improvement because one important question is constantly on every person's mind: "How can we do this better?" This is why companies that believe in and practice total quality management (TQM) are already on the path toward corporate-wide learning. Quality management requires a comprehensive learning approach that encourages everyone to improve performance. A culture of continuous improvement is clearly a learning one.

Motorola began its transformation into a learning organization when the company committed itself to the Six Sigma improvement process, a standard of quality that allows no more than 3.4 defects per 1 million parts in manufactured goods. Reaching that goal, which Motorola has currently exceeded, called for constant attention to improving every action and interaction in the organization. It forced the company to find ways of continuing to improve—and that made them better learners and a smarter organization.

## EMPOWER EMPLOYEES AND OTHERS IN THE BUSINESS CHAIN

Employees must be empowered with the necessary freedom, trust, influence, opportunity, recognition, and authority as well as enabled through the necessary skills, knowledge, values, and ability so that they can contribute to the organization at their optimal levels. Illeris (2011) notes that employee empowerment is critical for building a learning culture and hence a learning organization.

Leadership should place decision-making power and accountability at the level closest to the action point. This freedom to serve the customer includes the ability to spend significant sums and cross functional borders.

Learning organizations understand that empowered and enabled employees are essential for global success. They therefore make generous allocations of time, money, and people toward increasing skills not only for present jobs but for future, unforeseen challenges. Some companies spend more than 5 percent of payroll on learning programs. Employees are much more comfortable with carrying out the company's vision and hopes when they have a major role to play and the skills to do it.

## 9. Establish Corporate-Wide Strategies for Learning

Quantum leaps in learning require strategies and tactics for expanding individual, team, and organizational levels of learning across the corporation. Some of the following strategies may be helpful.

Encourage and provide time for experimentation. Since learning comes through experience, increased numbers of guided experiences at any stage of the value chain will lead to more learning. Managers in learning companies continue to act like applied research scientists even as they deliver goods and services. Sustained learning organizations support the practice of trying new things and being curious about how things work. Motorola University, for example, has been an experimental venture from the start and constantly tries out new learning approaches. At Walmart stores, about 250 experiments are being conducted on any given day in areas such as sales promotion, display, and customer service.

Develop company-wide systems that reward learners and learning. People who attempt new and different things, who try and fail but learn much, become the new organizational heroes, not those who never take risks.

Recognize the importance of accessibility of information. Companies that continue to grow as learning organizations constantly expand open communications within and throughout the organization. Problems, errors, and lessons are shared, not hidden. Debate and conflict remain acceptable ways of solving problems. Much informal learning takes place during daily, often unplanned interactions among people.

Schedule regular meetings to exchange information, mingle, hold informal gatherings, and share learning experiences. National Semiconductor, for example, holds annual events at which teams of employees present their best projects, experiments, and innovations. Other companies write case studies about their successes and failures and use these studies at meetings and training programs.

Gain real business leverage by applying new learning in hundreds of different places throughout your organization. Free up and motivate all workers to use internal and external learning, and reward those who can apply the insights of others as well as those who come up with new ideas of their own. (Elkeles & Phillips, 2006).

## ENCOURAGE LEARNING AT ALL LEVELS

A learning organization promotes learning at three levels: the individual worker, the group or team, and the organization itself. All three levels complement and invigorate one another, so none should be neglected when it comes to learning. Here are some ways to encourage, expect, and enhance learning at each level.

Make learning a part of the job for individuals. Learning organizations clearly state that every person in the organization has two jobs: his or her current job and learning how to do it better. Promote responsibility by expecting all departments and people to take the initiative when it comes to their own learning. Organizations should provide continuous learning packages that encourage everyone to view learning as an everyday experience and to use all available opportunities for learning and development.

Team learning is vital because teams, like families in a community, are the basic learning units in learning organizations. Use a variety of ways to develop team learning, such as new job assignments, team projects, in-house activities, and group assessment of learning efforts. Intentionally moving people in and out of the various functions and businesses of an organization so they can learn across boundaries and levels is an important key to developing a learning organization, thus becoming a means to as well as an end for corporate-wide learning (Yeo & Nation, 2010).

Organization-level learning is most conducive to systems thinking and learning. Leveraging of knowledge is greater at this level because the connections among learning, resources, and organizational power are clearer. Learning organizations realize that sound learning cannot continue unless they are aware of their environments, and they maintain their interest in external happenings and the nature of surrounding circumstances. They persevere in gathering information about conditions and practices outside their own industries or geographic areas.

## STUDY OTHER LEARNING ORGANIZATIONS

Understandably, gathering information about learning organizations will help companies focus on learning. There are many ways to approach this task.

Every year the American Society for Training and Development (ASTD) selects the top learning organizations around the world. A special T+D issue describes the stories of these organizations—how they developed one or more of the five learning subsystems described in this book.

Locate and read the growing literature about learning organizations. Attend conferences and workshops on the subject. Invite the leader of a learning organization or a consultant or researcher in organizational learning theory and practice to speak on the topic. Arrange in-house workshops and discussions with a panel of people who work in or are leaders of recognized learning organizations.

Create or become part of a consortium of firms that are seeking to become learning organizations. Identify successful learning organizations from your industry and geographic region as well as from other industries and other parts of the world. Talk to people in these organizations and listen to their ideas. Benchmark their learning skills and systems. Consider joining the ASTD Benchmarking Forum, which provides the opportunity to network and learn from some seventy to eighty of the top learning organizations in the world.

## 10. Reduce Bureaucracy and Streamline the Structure

Bureaucracy is the bane of any organization that hopes to develop the power of learning in the workplace. It kills energy, creativity, and the willingness to take risks—all qualities that nourish the learning process. Forms and regulations for every possible scenario choke off learning. Therefore, it is important to eliminate policies and procedures that create unnecessary layers and structures (Elkeles & Phillips, 2006).

Begin streamlining your organization with some of the following methods:

- **Reengineer:** Eliminate business processes that decrease learning, the flow of knowledge, or empowerment of employees. This includes hard bureaucratic structures, such as vertical and horizontal barriers, and unnecessary policies and restrictions.
- **Refocus:** Build structures around projects and customers rather than traditional functional silos.
- **Decentralize:** Move power to the point of action—and learning—as much as possible.
- **Introduce fluidity:** Build the organizational capacity to quickly recognize and serve the needs of the marketplace.

- **Bond:** Combine all former functional activities into a seamless whole that works in a highly integrated fashion.

Organizations might also consider following the lead of Royal Bank of Canada, which encourages people to eliminate the bureaucracy by challenging unnecessary forms and rules, exposing and eliminating systems and processes that discourage learning, and rewarding and recognizing only those actions that promote knowledge and improved quality and service.

## ELIMINATE OBSTACLES

Successful transformations inevitably require the removal of obstacles. The main obstacles to organizational learning are these:

- Bureaucracy, which values policies, regulations, forms, and busywork above change
- Competitiveness, which emphasizes individuals at the expense of teamwork and collaboration
- Control, which may provide a "high" for those who wield it but is always a "low" for organizational learning
- Poor communications resulting from filters such as conscious and unconscious biases, selective listening, and delays
- Poor leadership from managers who neither preach nor practice learning and are most concerned with protecting their turf
- Rigid hierarchies that force people and ideas to go up and down narrow silos

In the early stages of becoming a learning organization, few companies may have the momentum, power, or time to get rid of all obstacles. But as growing numbers of people become involved and change progresses, major barriers can be confronted and moved. Action is important, both to empower individuals and to maintain the credibility of the change effort throughout the organization.

## 11. Extend Learning to the Entire Business Chain

Learning organizations can truly tap into all potential sources for knowledge and ideas if they expand the benefits to all stakeholders, including customers, vendors, suppliers, and surrounding communities. These groups have a vested interest in the outcome of an organization's learning and can assist in validating relevant areas such as needs analysis, learning goals, design of learning packages, and the link between learning and business goals.

Learning organizations should schedule activities that fit the time frames and learning styles of these stakeholders. Companies can also help train customers on applying the new knowledge to their workplaces.

## 12. Capture Learning and Release Knowledge

People at every level of a learning organization will be challenged to develop new knowledge, take responsibility for their ideas, and pursue those ideas as far as they can. The organization's key challenge is to create an environment that allows workers to accomplish these goals.

Learning organizations provide an array of opportunities to capture learning. They create structures, systems, and time to capture and audit learning. Learning audits measure whether structures, time, and other resources are available to create, enhance, and capture knowledge to the greatest extent possible. They also explore methods of linking new learning to organizational productivity.

Everyone in a learning organization is encouraged to seek information, ideas, and insights from other successful companies as well as from leading researchers. Manville (2001) notes that greater line ownership and leadership of programs makes learning part of day-to-day business processes, which means integrating skills development and acquisition into recruiting and deployment plans, performance management, and succession planning. Learning thus "becomes part of the overall process of new product development, sales and efforts to increase customer satisfaction and retention" (p. 40).

Transferring knowledge between people or from databases to people infuses energy and vigor into the body of the organization. Knowledge transfer based on mechanical, electronic, and interpersonal movements of information diffuses knowledge quickly throughout the organization—before it becomes dated misinformation. Workers who are encouraged to use new knowledge will apply innovative ideas and new approaches to their work.

Learning organizations thrive on quality knowledge and communications. Therefore knowledge should be easily accessible whether received from people or through information technology. It should flow up as well as down throughout the organization. Encourage open discussion and conversation throughout the company. Consider adopting the type of "lessons learned" meetings that are held regularly at the Nuclear Regulatory Commission. There, managers share their experiences and any new ideas that emerged on their most recent trips. National Semiconductor holds "sharing rallies," where workers release their best knowledge to the rest of the company.

## 13. Acquire and Apply the Best Technology to the Best Learning

Organizations that lack information technology or the capability to use it are at a severe disadvantage in the acquisition, storage, and transfer of knowledge. If knowledge is the journey, then technology is the road. Without it, you will not go anywhere quickly enough.

Technology also affects the quantity and quality of learning. It speeds the flow of information and stores more data than non-electronic methods. It is easier to update, provides better access to more people, and makes organizational learning more exciting for workers. Learning centers with multimedia technology are stimulating and challenging for both individuals and groups. Not only will the caliber of learning processes be higher, the costs will be lower.

Electronic performance support systems (EPSS) are becoming increasingly popular with organizations. An EPSS enables people to learn whenever and wherever is best for them. Because the EPSS responds with explanations, definitions, descriptions, demonstrations, practices, activities, assessments, feedback, and other resources as needed, workers can truly learn at the same time they are producing or serving customers.

## 14. Create Short-Term Wins

Because it takes much time and effort to become a learning organization, momentum may be lost without short-term goals that provide successes to celebrate. The learning coalition must actively look for clear performance improvements and reward those involved with recognition, promotions, and financial compensation.

After a few months of hard work, when the first signs of transformation appear, learning organization advocates may be tempted to declare victory. Celebrating progress is fine, but "declaring the war won can be catastrophic," declares Kotter (1995, 2008). "Until changes sink deeply into a company's culture ... new [changes] are fragile and subject to regression" (p. 66).

So leaders of successful learning efforts use the credibility afforded by short-term gains to tackle longer-term goals. They go after systems and structures that are inconsistent with the new vision and have not been confronted yet, and they pay more attention to how people are being developed. Becoming a learning organization takes years, not months. Even then the process is never truly finished.

## 15. Measure Learning and Demonstrate Learning Successes

Learning organizations expend considerable effort on defining and measuring key factors when venturing into new areas. They strive for specific, quantifiable measures. Discourse on metrics is seen as a learning activity and includes such issues as whether measures are internally or externally focused, degree of specificity, and use of custom-built or standard measures. This preliminary discourse is itself a critical aspect of learning, almost as important as the learning gained from metrics feedback.

Use business rather than training metrics. Focus on specific measurable outcomes of business values, such as customer satisfaction, product rollout speed, and talent retention. Learning organizations see performance shortfalls as opportunities for learning. As learning organizations examine the gap between targeted outcomes and actual performance, they proceed to experimentation and the development of new insights and skills. Well-established organizations with a long history of success often are not good learning systems because the feedback they experience is almost exclusively positive. Ironically, the lack of disconfirming evidence is often a barrier to learning.

One or more members of the learning organization may visualize something that was not noted earlier. This often leads to an awareness of additional needs or of assumptions that are no longer functional.

## 16. Adapt, Improve, and Learn Continuously

As noted at the beginning of the chapter, companies that are on their way to becoming learning organizations realize that they will never reach a state of perfection that will allow them to stop learning. Learning organizations are, by definition, always learning, knowing that knowledge is not finite and is always changing.

These firms are aware of what happens to companies that do not continue to learn: they soon lose their competitive advantages, and customers go elsewhere for better products, services, and prices. Learning organizations realize that they must always keep learning, always be hungry for new knowledge. They know the vital importance of continually uncovering, analyzing, and adapting the best practices of other organizations as well as their own. These companies employ all resources and stakeholders in their business chain. They learn continuously and consistently.

In the final analysis, the reality of the learning organization sticks when it becomes institutionalized, when it is incorporated into the essence of the company's identity. Until new behaviors are rooted in social norms and shared values, the learning organization's subsystems will be vulnerable to retrogression as soon as the pressure for change is removed.

Two factors are particularly important in institutionalizing change in the corporate culture. Successful learning companies make a consistent effort to show people how the new approaches, behaviors, and attitudes have helped improve performance. And these organizations take the time to ensure that the next generation of management personifies the new approach.

## Caterpillars, Cocoons, and Butterflies: Transition to a Learning Organization

A company must pass through several stages on its journey to becoming a learning organization. The transformational journey of the caterpillar may serve as an enlightening metaphor.

A caterpillar is limited in movement and can crawl slowly in any direction, pulling back slightly in order to proceed forward. It is vulnerable to predators that are more agile and powerful. Giving it more legs or increasing its rate of speed (like reengineering or TQM for organizations) is a patchwork remedy and does not enable it to reach its full potential; it is still earthbound.

At some point, the caterpillar enters into a cocoon, where an amazing process takes place. The caterpillar quite literally dissolves and then re-forms to emerge as a butterfly, a completely different creature with the power to fly in any direction.

Some organizations never leave their caterpillar state, and remain slow, weak, and defenseless; they never transform themselves into butterfly-like learning organizations with immense powers and opportunities. In contrast, a true learning organization empowers its people, integrates quality initiatives with quality of work life, creates free space for learning, encourages collaboration and sharing of gains, promotes inquiry, and fosters continuous learning opportunities. This kind of learning changes perceptions, behaviors, beliefs, mental models, strategies, policies, and procedures in people and organizations. All five subsystems serve as the body and wings to carry the organization skyward!

The superstars of organizational learning explored in this book are companies that have gone from being reasonably competent caterpillars to beautiful, powerful butterflies. They have metamorphosed and adapted themselves to the changing environment and workplace, to a changing workforce and customers, and have become leaders in their respective industries, across the world.

Learning organizations are places where global success is more possible, where quality is more assured, and where energetic and talented people want to be. I wish you the best of success becoming great butterflies and building your learning organizations!

# Bibliography

ASTD. (2009). Of angels and tigers. *T+D, 63*(10), 58–59.

ASTD. (2008a). Bank on learning. *T+D, 63*(10), 31–32.

ASTD. (2008b). Igniting a passion for learning. *T+D, 63*(10), 43–44.

ASTD. (2007a). Sales training as dynamic as big pharma itself. *T+D 61*(10), 35–36.

ASTD. (2007b).Those who lead, teach. *T+D, 61*(10), 39–40.

Argyris, C. (1999). *On organizational learning*. Oxford, England: Blackwell.

Argyris, C., and Schön, D. A. (1995). *Organizational learning: A theory of action perspective*. Reading, MA: Addison-Wesley.

Awad, E., and Ghaziri, H. (2010). *Knowledge management*. Englewood Cliffs, NJ: Prentice-Hall.

Belasen, A. (2000). *Leading the learning organization*. Albany, NY: SUNY Press.

Botham, D., and Vick, D. (1998). Action learning and the program at the Revans Center. *Performance Improvement Quarterly, 11*(2), 5–16.

Brenneman, W., Keys, J., and Fulmer, R. (1998). Learning across a living company: The Shell Companies' experience. *Organizational Dynamics, 27*(2), 61–69.

Broad, M. J. (2005). *Beyond the transfer of training*. San Francisco: Pfeiffer.

Casestudyinc.com. (2011). Glocalization examples. Accessed 3 February 2011 from www.casestudyinc.com/glocalization-examples-think-globally-and-act-locally.

Castro, D., Atkinson, R., and Ezell, S. (2010). *Embracing the self-service economy*. Washington, DC: ITIF Publishing.

Cho, Y., and Egan, T. (2010). The state of the art of action learning research. *Advances in Developing Human Resources, 12*(2), 163–180.

Credit Suisse. (2011). Assessed 7 February 2011 from http://emagazine.credit-suisse.com.

Dilworth, L. (1998). Action learning in a nutshell. *Performance Improvement Quarterly, 11*(1), 28–43.

Dilworth, L. (1995). The DNA of the learning organization. In S. Chawla and J. Renesch (Eds.), *Learning organizations*. Portland, OR: Productivity Press.

Dixon, N. (2000). *Common knowledge: How companies thrive by sharing what they know*. Cambridge: Harvard Business School Press.

Dixon, N. (1998). Organizational learning: A review of the literature with implications for HRD professionals. *Human Resource Development Quarterly, 3*(1), 29–49.

Easterby-Smith, M. (1990). Creating a learning organization. *Personnel Review, 5,* 24–28.

E-learning. (2011). Wikipedia. Accessed 5 February 2011.

Elkeles, T. and Phillips, J. (2006). *The chief learning officer: Driving value within a changing organization through learning and development*. Burlington, MA: Butterworth-Heinemann.

Fayyad, U., Piatetsky-Shapiro, G., and Smyth, P. (1996). "From Data Mining to Knowledge Discovery in Databases." Accessed 11 January 2011 from www.kdnuggets.com/gpspubs/aimag-kdd-overview-1996-Fayyad.pdf.

Fornell, C. (2007). *The satisfied customer: winners and losers in the battle for buyer preference*. New York: Palgrave McMillan.

Frappaolo, F. (2006). *Knowledge management*. Mankanto, MN: Capstone Press.

Friedman, T. (2005). *The world is flat*. New York: Farrar, Straus and Giroux.

Garvin, D. (2009). Building a learning organization. *Harvard Business Review Digital, 71*(4), 78–91.

Garvin, D. (2003). *Learning in action*. Cambridge, MA: Harvard Business School Press.

Gill, S. (2009). *Developing a learning culture in non-profit organizations*. Thousand Oaks: Sage.

Harris, P. (2010). Where people power makes the difference. *T+D, 64*(10), 33–34.

Honey, P., and Mumford, A. (2010). *Learning styles questionnaire*. King of Prussia, PA: HRD Press.

Hughes, A., and Morton, M. (2006). The transforming power of complementary assets. *MIT Sloan Management Review, 47*(4), 50–58.

Illeris, K. (2011). *The fundamentals of workplace learning: Understanding how people learn in working life*. London: Routledge.

Isenhour, L. (2009). HR Administration and HRIS. In M. J. Kavanagh and M. Thite (Eds.), *Human resource information systems: Basics, applications, and future directions*. Thousand Oaks, CA: Sage Publications, Inc.

Jackson, J. (2010). U.S. direct investment abroad: Trends and current issues. *CRS Report for Congress*. Accessed 8 February 2011 from www.fas.org/sgp/crs/misc/RS21118.pdf.

Junkunc, M. (2009). *Toward a greater economic understanding of entrepreneurial activity: Examining the nature and importance of specialized knowledge*. Saarbrucken, DE: LAP Publishing.

Kline, P., and Saunders, B. (2010). *Ten steps to a learning organization* (2nd ed). Arlington, VA: Great Ocean.

Kotter, J. (2008). *A sense of urgency*. Cambridge, MA: Harvard Business School Press.

Kotter, J. (1995). Leading change: Why transformation efforts fail. *Harvard Business Review, 2*, 59–67.

Liebowitz, J., and Beckman, T. (1998). *Knowledge organizations: What every manager should know*. Boca Raton, FL: CRC Press.

Limerick, D., Passfield, R., and Cunningham, B. (1994). Transformational change: Toward an action learning organization. *The Learning Organization, 1*(2), 45–56.

Mansfield, R. (2007). *How to do everything with second life*. New York: McGraw-Hill Osborne Media.

Manville, B. (2001, Spring). Learning in the new economy. *Leader to leader, 20*, 36–45.

Marquardt, M. (2011a). *Optimizing the power of action learning* (2nd ed.). Boston: Nicholas Brealey Publishing.

Marquardt, M. (2011b). Action learning around the world. In M. Pedler (Ed.), *Action learning in Practice* (4th ed.). Aldershot, UK: Gower.

Marquardt, M. (2002). *Building the learning organization* (2nd ed.). Palo Alto, CA: Davies-Black Publishing.

Marquardt, M. (2001). Action learning: A powerful new tool for developing individuals, teams and organizations. *Transitions, 9*(2), 2–7.

Marquardt, M. (2000a). Action learning and leadership. *Learning Organization, 7*(5), 233–240.

Marquardt, M. (2000b). Becoming a learning organization—The key to surviving in the 21st century. *Fintra, 3*, 4–5.

Marquardt, M., and Berger, N. (2000). *Global leaders for the 21st Century*. Albany, NY: SUNY Press.

Marquardt, M., Leonard, S., Freedman, A., and Hill, C. (2009). *Action learning for developing leaders and organizations*. Washington, DC: APA Press.

Marquardt, M., and Yeo, R. (2011). *Break through problem solving with action learning*. Palo Alto: Stanford University Press.

Marsick, J., and Watkins, K. (1999). *Facilitating learning organizations*. Cambridge, UK: Gower.

Maruca, R. (1994). The right way to go global: An interview with Whirlpool CEO David Whitwam. *Harvard Business Review, 3*, 134–145.

Maxwell, R. (1997). *Distance learning and human development at Nortel: The shift from classrooms to communities of learning*. Unpublished manuscript.

Meiklejohn, I., and Duncan, S. (1997, Autumn). Mining the data mountain. *Fast Track*.

Mumford, A. (2008). *Management Development*. New Delhi: Jaico Publishing.

Nguyen, F., and Woll, C. (2006). A practitioner's guide for designing performance support systems. *Performance Improvement, 45*(9): 37–48.

Nonaka, I. (2008). *The knowledge-creating company.* Cambridge, MA: Harvard Business School Press.

OneTouch. (2011). Accessed 31 January 2011 from http://www.bzzagent.com/bzzscapes/scape/ford/ford-star-training-facilities/.

Owen, H. (1998). *Riding the tiger: Doing business in a transforming world.* Potomac, MD: Abbott.

Priest, S. (2010). A community first. *T+D, 64*(11), 42–46.

Redding, J. (2000). *The radical team handbook: Harnessing the power of team learning for breakthrough results.* San Francisco: Jossey-Bass.

Reich, R. (2010). *Aftershock: The next economy and America's future.* New York: Knopf.

Revans, R. (1983). *The ABCs of action learning.* Bromley, UK: Chartwell Brat.

Revans, R. (1982). *The origins and growth of action learning.* Bromley, UK: Chartwell Brat.

Rossett, A., and Schafer, L. (2007). *Job aids & performance support: Moving from knowledge in the classroom to knowledge everywhere.* San Francisco: Pfeiffer.

Salopek, J. (2010a). From learning department to learning partner. *T+D, 64*(10), 48–50.

Salopek, J. (2010b). Re-discovering knowledge. *T+D, 64*(10), 36–37.

Schein, E. (2010). *Organizational culture and leadership.* San Francisco: Jossey-Bass.

Schein, E. (1993, Autumn). On dialogue, culture, and organizational learning. *Organizational Dynamics,* 40–51.

Schwandt, D., and Marquardt, M. (2000). *Organizational learning: From worldclass theories to global best practices.* Boca Raton, FL: St. Lucie.

Senge, P. (2006). *The fifth discipline.* New York: Random House.

Serrat, O. (2009). *Building a learning organization.* Washington, DC: Asia Development Bank Press.

Sofo, F., Yeo, R., and Villafane, J. (2010). Optimizing the learning in action learning: Reflective questions, levels of learning and coaching. *Advances in developing human resources, 12*(2), 205–224.

Stewart, T. (1997). *Intellectual capital: The new wealth of organizations.* New York: Doubleday.

Thomson Reuters. (2011). The knowledge effect. *The Economist, 398*(8719), 12–13.

Thurman, L. (1996, February). Ford takes the fast lane to dealer communication and training. *ED Journal,* 7–9, 10–13.

Venter, J. C. (2007). *A life decoded.* New York: Viking.

Waddill, D., and Marquardt, M. (2011). *The e-HR advantage: The complete handbook for technology-enabled human resources.* Boston: Nicholas Brealey Publishing.

Watkins, K., and Marsick, V. (1993). *Sculpting the learning organization.* San Francisco: Jossey-Bass.

Weick, K. (2009). *Making sense of the organization.* San Francisco: Wiley.

Weisbord, M., and Janoff, S. (2000). *Future search*. San Francisco: Berrett-Koehler.

Wheatley, M. (2001). *Leadership and the new science*. San Francisco: Berrett-Koehler.

Wiig, K. (1997). Role of knowledge-based systems in support of knowledge management. In J. Liebowitz and T. Beckman (Eds.), *Knowledge management and its integrative elements*. Boca Raton, FL: CRC Press.

Williams, D., and Stahl, S. (1996, November/December). Ford's lessons in distance learning. *Technical & Skills Training, 7*(8).

Wilson, W. (1994). Video training and testing supports customer service goals. *Personnel Journal, 6*, 46–51.

Yeo, R., and Nation, U. (2010). Optimizing the action in action learning: Urgent problems, diversified group membership, and commitment to action. *Advances in Developing Human Resources 12*(2), 181–204.

Zuboff, S. (1988). *In the age of the smart machine: The future of work and power*. New York: Basic Books.

# Learning Organization Profile

Below is a list of various statements about your organization. Read each statement carefully and decide the *extent* to which it applies to your organization. Use the following scale:

4 = applies totally

3 = applies to a great extent

2 = applies to a moderate extent

1 = applies to little or no extent

## Learning Dynamics: Individual, Group or Team, and Organizational

*In this organization . . .*

_____ 1. We see continuous learning by all employees as a high business priority.

_____ 2. We are encouraged and expected to manage our own learning and development.

_____ 3. People avoid distorting information and blocking communication channels by actively listening to others and providing them with effective feedback.

_____ 4. Individuals are trained and coached in learning how to learn.

_____ 5. We use various accelerated learning methodologies (mindmapping, mnemonics, imagery, music).

_____ 6. People expand knowledge through adaptive, anticipatory, and creative learning approaches.

_____ 7. Teams and individuals use the action learning process—that is, they learn from careful reflection on the problem or situation and apply their new knowledge to future actions.

_____ 8. Teams are encouraged to learn from one another and share what they learn in a variety of ways (via communities of practice, social networks such as LinkedIn, and electronic bulletin boards such as Blackboard).

_____ 9. People are able to think and act with a comprehensive, systems approach.

_____ 10. Teams receive training in how to work and learn in groups.

☐ Learning Dynamics (maximum score: 40)

**TOTAL SCORE**

## II. Organization Transformation: Vision, Culture, Strategy, and Structure

*In this organization . . .*

_____ 1. The importance of being a learning organization is understood throughout the company.

_____ 2. Top-level management supports the vision of a learning organization.

_____ 3. There is a climate that supports and recognizes the importance of learning.

_____ 4. We are committed to continuous learning in pursuit of improvement.

_____ 5. We learn from failures as well as successes, which means that mistakes are tolerated.

_____ 6. We reward people and teams for learning and helping others learn.

_____ 7. Learning opportunities are incorporated into operations and programs.

_____ 8. We design ways to share knowledge and enhance learning throughout the organization (systematic job rotation across divisions, structured on-the-job learning systems).

_____ 9. The organization is streamlined, with few levels of management, to maximize the communication and learning across levels.

_____ 10. We coordinate our efforts across departments on the basis of common goals and learnings, rather than maintaining fixed departmental boundaries.

| |
|---|

Organization Transformation (maximum score: 40)

**TOTAL SCORE**

## III. People Empowerment: Manager, Employee, Customer, Partners, Suppliers, and Community

*In this organization . . .*

_____ 1. We strive to develop an empowered workforce that is able to learn and perform.

_____ 2. Authority is decentralized and delegated in proportion to responsibility and learning capability.

_____ 3. Managers and nonmanagers work in partnership to learn and solve problems together.

_____ 4. Managers take on the roles of coaches, mentors, and facilitators of learning.

_____ 5. Managers generate and enhance learning opportunities as well as encourage experimentation and reflection on new knowledge so that it can be used.

_____ 6. We actively share information with our customers and at the same time obtain their ideas and input in order to learn and improve services and products.

_____ 7. We give customers and suppliers opportunities to participate in learning and training products.

_____ 8. Learning from partners (subcontractors, teammates) is maximized through upfront planning of resources and strategies devoted to knowledge and skill acquisition.

_____ 9. We participate in learning events with suppliers, community groups, professional associations, and academic institutions.

_____ 10. We actively seek learning partners among customers, vendors, and suppliers.

| |
|---|

People Empowerment (maximum score: 40)

**TOTAL SCORE**

## IV. Knowledge Management: Acquisition, Creation, Storage, Retrieval, Transfer, and Utilization

*In this organization . . .*

_____ 1. We actively seek information that improves the work of the organization by incorporating products and/or processes that are outside our function.

_____ 2. We have accessible systems for collecting internal and external information.

_____ 3. We monitor trends outside our organization by looking at what others do; this includes benchmarking best practices, attending conferences, and examining published research.

_____ 4. People are trained in the skills of creative thinking, innovation, and experimentation.

_____ 5. We often create demonstration projects as a means of testing new ways of developing a product and/or delivering a service.

_____ 6. We have developed systems and structures to ensure that important knowledge is coded, stored, and made available to those who need and can use it.

_____ 7. People are aware of the need to retain important organizational learning and share such knowledge with others.

_____ 8. Cross-functional teams are used to transfer important learning across groups, departments, and divisions.

_____ 9. We continue to develop new strategies and mechanisms for sharing learning throughout the organization.

_____ 10. We support specific areas, units, and projects that generate knowledge by providing people with learning opportunities.

Knowledge management (maximum score: 40)

TOTAL SCORE

## V. Technology Application: Knowledge Information Systems, Technology-Based Learning, and Electronic Performance Support Systems

*In this organization . . .*

_____ 1. Learning is facilitated by effective and efficient computer-based information systems.

_____ 2. People have ready access to the information highway via, for example, local area networks, the Internet, and an intranet.

_____ 3. Learning facilities incorporate electronic multimedia support and an environment based on the powerful integration of art, color, music, and visuals.

_____ 4. Computer-assisted learning programs and electronic job aids (just-in-time and flowcharting software) are readily available.

_____ 5. We use groupware technology to manage group processes such as project, team, and meeting management.

_____ 6. We support just-in-time learning, a system that integrates high-tech learning systems, coaching, and actual work on the job into a single process.

_____ 7. Technology is maximized to allow the organization to capture, store, and transfer knowledge.

_____ 8. We design and tailor our electronic performance support systems to meet our learning requirements.

_____ 9. People have full access to the technology they need to learn and to do their jobs effectively.

_____ 10. We can adapt software systems to collect, code, store, create, and transfer information in ways best suited to meet our needs.

Technology Application (maximum score: 40)

**TOTAL SCORE**

Five subsystems (maximum score: 200)

**GRAND TOTAL**

# Glossary

Many special terms are used in defining and describing a learning organization. In addition, some terms have different connotations in reference to organizational learning.

**accelerated learning:** A learning system designed to improve rate of learning and overall retention by incorporating creative, sensory-rich techniques.

**action learning:** process in which individuals, groups, or organizations learn while in action and after action; tool used by organizations to solve complex problems, develop leaders, create teams, and build learning organizations.

**adaptive learning:** An individual's, team's, or organization's learning from experience and reflection.

**ADL (advanced distributed learning):** Developing interoperability across computer- and Internet-based learning courseware through a common technical framework that contains content in the form of reusable learning objects.

**anticipatory learning:** Knowledge acquired by individuals or organizations in order to meet potential needs. The sequence of anticipatory learning is vision, reflection, action.

**application software:** Programs such as word processing, spreadsheets, databases, and desktop publishing.

**assessment:** The process of systematically evaluating a learner's or team's skill or knowledge level.

**assistive technology:** Hardware or software designed to help individuals with special needs.

**asynchronous learning:** Interactions among instructor and learners occur intermittently with a time delay. Examples are self-paced courses taken via the Internet, Q & A mentoring, online discussion groups, and e-mail.

**ATM (asynchronous transfer mode):** A network technology for high-speed transfer of data.

**audioconference:** Voice-only connection of more than two sites using standard telephone lines.

**authoring tool:** A software application or program that allows people to create their own e-learning courseware.

**Avatars:** graphical representations of humans that appear three-dimensional; these can be used as part of e-learning.

**blended learning:** Learning events that combine aspects of online and face-to-face instruction.

**browsers:** Software that allows users to find and view information on the Internet (e.g., Internet Explorer).

**CAD/CAM (computer aided design/computer aided manufacturing):** Software tools for the design and production of parts or structures.

**CBT (computer-based training):** Using computers for instruction and management of teaching and learning processes. Also referred to as computer-assisted instruction, or CAI.

**CD-ROM:** A format and system for recording, storing, and retrieving electronic information on a compact disc that is read in an optical drive.

**cloud computing:** Internet-based computing that enables users to access software applications, hardware data, and computer-processing power over the web.

**COD (content on demand):** Delivery of an offering, packaged in a media format, anywhere, anytime, via a network.

**competency:** An area of capability that enables a person or an organization to perform tasks or fulfill responsibilities.

**competitiveness skills:** Skills that provide for future needs, such as systems thinking, team learning, visioning, and mental models.

**computer-based learning:** Umbrella term that includes all forms of computer use that support learning (see also *technology-based learning*).

**contiguous learning culture:** The milieu or environment in which people are encouraged and enabled to learn on an ongoing basis.

**convergence:** A result of the digital era in which various types of digital information (such as text, voice, and video) and the delivery mechanisms (television, telecommunications, and consumer electronics) are combined in new, more closely linked forms.

**core competencies:** Competencies based on what companies do best instead of according to product or market.

**CRT (cathode-ray tube):** The conventional display unit of televisions and desktop computers (compare to *LCD*).

**desktop videoconference:** Videoconferencing on a personal computer.

**deutero learning:** Individual or organizational learning that occurs through critical reflection on assumptions; an examination of how the learning is or is not occurring.

**dialogue:** Denotes a high level of listening and communication between people; involves the free and creative exploration of subtle issues, listening deeply to one another, and being willing to suspend one's own views.

**digital:** Transmitting information in discrete (binary) units. Digital signals are transmitted faster and more accurately than analog signals.

**distance learning:** Learning situation in which instructors and learners are separated by time, location, or both.

**double-loop learning:** In-depth organizational learning that looks at the norms and structures behind the company's methods of functioning. Double-loop learning questions the system itself and tries to determine why errors or successes occurred in the first place.

**DVD (digital videodisc):** A form of compact disc with the capacity to store substantial amounts of video.

**e-learning:** Delivery of content via Internet, intranet/extranet (LAN/ WAN), audiotape and videotape, satellite broadcast, interactive TV, and CD-ROM.

**electronic performance support system (EPSS):** A system that utilizes databases (text, visual, or audio) and knowledge bases to capture, store, and distribute information throughout the organization. The system consists of several components including, but not limited to, interactive training, productivity and application software, and expert and feedback systems.

**electronic text or publishing:** Dissemination of text via electronic means.

**explicit knowledge:** Formal, systematic, and easily shared knowledge.

**extranet:** A collaborative network that uses Internet technology to link organizations with their suppliers, customers, or other organizations that share common goals or information.

**FTP (file transfer program):** Software used to upload or download files between networks and PCs.

**generative organizational learning:** The learning that an organization generates or creates from its own reflections, analyses, or creativity.

**group or team learning:** The increase in knowledge, skills, and competency that is accomplished by and within groups.

**groupware:** collaborative software (also referred to as workgroup support systems or simply group support systems) designed to help people involved in a common task achieve their goals.

**HTML (hypertext markup language):** The coding language used to create hypertext documents for use on the web.

**hypermedia:** A program that contains dynamic links to other media, such as audio, video, or graphics files.

**hypertext:** A system for retrieving information from servers on the Internet using World Wide Web client software.

**individual learning:** The change of skills, insights, knowledge, attitudes, and values acquired by a person through self-study, technology-based instruction, and observation.

**informate:** Using computer-generated data collected during implementation for planning and decision making. For example, checkout data scans provide information—what foods were bought, who buys them, when they were bought—that enable the store owner to plan advertising, hiring, purchasing, and inventory control.

**information architecture:** A description or design specification for methods of handling and organizing information.

**intranet:** A network that links an affiliated set of clients behind a firewall or behind several firewalls connected by secure networks.

**ISDN (integrated services digital network):** Service that provides high-capacity digital transmission; allows communication channels to carry voice, video, and data simultaneously.

**know-how:** Value-added information.

**know-how company:** An organization that produces and sells information, ideas, and complex problem-solving services to others. Key features include nonstandardization, creativity, and high degree of reliance on the knowledge of individuals.

**knowledge acquisition:** The process by which existing knowledge is collected or obtained. Knowledge can be purchased, borrowed, or stolen.

**knowledge architecture:** The repository for shared knowledge and collective intelligence that is organized for easy access by any staff member, anytime, anywhere. For example, a database that collects key learning of individuals or an online newsletter that systematically gathers, organizes, and disseminates the collective knowledge of the organization's members.

**knowledge creation:** The development of new knowledge through innovation, problem solving, insights, or adaptation.

**knowledge management:** Capturing, organizing, storing, transferring, and utilizing knowledge and experience within and outside of the organization. This information is stored in a special database called a *knowledge base.*

**knowledge retrieval:** The acquisition of knowledge that is already in the organization and stored in various systems, such as human and computer, and in written documents.

**knowledge storage:** The coding and preservation of the organization's valued knowledge for easy access by any organizational member.

**knowledge transfer:** The process of moving and sharing information throughout the organization utilizing individuals and groups across various functions; accomplished by personal, mechanical, and electronic means.

**LAN (local area network):** A network of computers sharing the resources of a single processor or server within a relatively small geographic area.

**LCD (liquid crystal diode):** Flat display formats used with laptop computers and video projection devices (compare to *CRT*).

**learning management system:** Software that automates the administration of learning events.

**learning object:** A reusable, media-independent chunk of information used as a building block for e-learning content. Learning objects are most effective when organized by a metadata-classification system and stored in a data repository.

**learning organization:** A company that learns effectively and collectively and continually transforms itself for better management and use of knowledge; empowers people within and outside of the organization to learn as they work; utilizes technology to maximize learning and production.

**learning portal:** Any website that offers learners or organizations consolidated access to learning and training resources from multiple sources.

**mental model:** An image of reality. In organizational learning, refers to a person's values and beliefs regarding learning.

**mentofacturing:** Production of goods and services through the efforts of the mind. Mentofacturing (Latin, *mento:* mind) stands in contrast to manufacturing (Latin, *manus:* hand).

**metalogue:** A high level of dialogue in which a group thinks and creates together.

**mission statement:** The operational, ethical, and financial guiding direction of a company; not simply mottoes or slogans. The mission statement articulates a company's goals, dreams, behavior, culture, and strategies.

**mobile learning (also called *m-learning*):** Any sort of learning that happens when the learner is not at a fixed, predetermined location, or learning that happens when the learner takes advantage of the learning opportunities offered by mobile technologies.

**multimedia:** Encompasses interactive text, images, sound, and color.

**open space technology:** An innovative approach that enhances individual and group performance by bringing as many as 400 people together to organize and manage multiday meetings and conferences around complex issues.

**organizational architecture:** Structural form of organizations that evolves around autonomous work teams and strategic alliances.

**organizational learning:** The enhanced intellectual and productive capability gained through corporate-wide commitment to and opportunity for continuous improvement. It differs from individual and group learning in two basic respects. First, organizational learning occurs through the shared insights, knowledge, and mental models of members of the organization. Second, organizational learning builds on past knowledge and experience—that is, on organizational memory, which depends on institutional mechanisms such as policies, strategies, and explicit models used to retain knowledge (see also *group or team learning* and *individual learning*).

**organizational memory:** System established by the organization to store knowledge for future use. Memory is retrievable and can be lodged in individuals or in technology.

**organizational transformation:** Large-scale organizational change that affects mission, values, structure, and systems.

**patterns of organizational learning:** Four learning patterns based on tacit and explicit knowledge and their interaction: tacit to tacit, explicit to explicit, tacit to explicit, and explicit to tacit.

**personal mastery:** High level of proficiency in a subject or a skill area.

**quantum improvement:** Doing entirely different things better (versus gradual improvement, which is greater improvement along a continuum).

**RAM/ROM (random access memory/read only memory):** The two fundamental forms of computer memory that define the machine's capacity.

**reengineering:** Restructuring organizations around outcomes, not tasks or functions. It involves a fundamental rethinking and remaking of business systems that includes an overhaul of job designs, organizational structures, and management systems.

**satellite TV (also called *business TV*):** Transmission of television signals via satellites.

**scanner:** Device used to convert printed matter into digital form.

**server:** A computer with a special service function on a network, generally to receive and connect incoming information traffic.

**simulator:** A device or system that replicates or imitates a real device or system.

**single-loop learning:** Gaining information to stabilize and maintain existing operational systems.

**social architecture:** The cultural, symbolic orientation toward relationships that enhances learning by encouraging teams, self-management, empowerment, and sharing. Social architecture is the opposite of a closed, rigid, bureaucratic architecture.

**synchronous learning:** Interaction or transmission of information and knowledge in real-time (compare to *asynchronous learning*).

**synergy:** The sum is greater than the parts.

**systems learning:** Learning that emphasizes interrelationships.

**systems thinking:** A conceptual framework that includes a body of knowledge and the tools to make complex patterns clearer and identify effective ways of changing them.

**tacit knowledge:** Internal knowledge that is difficult to express (compare to *explicit knowledge*).

**TCP/IP (transmission control protocol/Internet protocol):** Protocol for information transmission over the Internet.

**technological architecture:** The supporting, integrated set of technical processes, systems, and structure for collaboration, coaching, coordination, and other knowledge skills. Technological architecture may include such electronic tools and advanced methods for learning as computer conferences, simulation software, and computer-supported collaboration, all of which work to create knowledge freeways.

**technology-based learning:** Video, audio, and computer-based multimedia training for off-site delivery and sharing of knowledge and skills.

**teleconference:** The instantaneous exchange of audio, video, or text between two or more individuals or groups at two or more locations.

**template:** A predefined set of tools or forms that establishes the structure and settings necessary to create content quickly.

**training:** Instructional experiences for learners, planned and delivered by trainers, generally in a formal setting (compare to *learning*, in which change is the responsibility of the learner).

**URL (uniform resource locator):** The standard way to give the address of any Internet resource that is also part of the World Wide Web.

**virtual reality:** A computer application that provides an interactive, immersive, and three-dimensional learning experience through fully functional, realistic models.

**vision statement:** The intended hope and long-term goal of an organization; for learning organizations, a picture of what they wish to achieve in terms of learning.

**Voice over Internet Protocol (VoIP):** a technology that allows you to make voice calls using a broadband Internet connection instead of using a regular (or analog) phone line.

**WAN (wide area network):** A network of computers sharing the resources of one or more processors or servers over a relatively large geographic area.

**WAP (wireless application protocol):** Specification that allows Internet content to be read by wireless devices.

**WBT (web-based training):** Delivery of learning content through a web browser over the Internet, an intranet, or an extranet.

# Index

## A

accelerated learning, 35–36

action learning: action necessary for, 194–195; benefits of, 192; coaching, 196–197; collective wisdom encouraged by, 203; company examples of, 199–200, 208–209; components of, 192–197; culture created by, 200–204, 210; definition of, 23, 191–192; description of, 42–43; dialogue development through, 198; foundations of, 204; group learning through, 195–196; individual learning through, 195–196; knowledge created using, 131; knowledge subsystem and, 206–209; leadership development through, 205–206; learning organization built through, 197, 209–210; learning subsystem and, 198–200; organizational learning through, 195–196; organization subsystem and, 200–201; people subsystem and, 204–206; power of, 209–210; problem, 193; reflective questioning, 194; technology subsystem and, 209

action learning coach, 196

action learning groups, 192–194, 200, 210

action learning programs, 198–199, 203, 210

activist, 171

adaptability, 204

adaptive learning, 23, 41, 198, 227–228

alliances: business-related, 26, 108, 118–119; learning, 204

American Society for Training and Development, 222–223

anticipatory learning, 23, 41–42, 58

association rule learning, 139

asynchronous e-learning, 164

automatic retrieval of knowledge, 141

automating of operations, 160–161

autonomy, 67

avatars, 169

## B

balance model, 106

benchmarking, 127–128, 223

boundaries, 77–78

brainpower, 12

bureaucracies, 80, 223–224

business functions, 159–160

business operations: automating of, 160–161; learning integrated into all areas of, 71–72, 215, 224–225; trust in, 38

business partnerships and alliances, 26, 108, 118–119

## C

capabilities: assessment of, 215–216; data mining, 151; description of, 123

career development plans, 56

centers for excellence, 90

MICHAEL J. MARQUARDT, EDD, is president of the World Institute for Action Learning and an international speaker and consultant whose worldwide clients include the World Bank, Nokia, Boeing, Alcoa, Caterpillar, Singapore Airlines, and the governments of Spain, Indonesia, and Jamaica. Professor of human and organizational learning and program director of Overseas Programs at George Washington University, he is the author of twenty-two books, including *Organizational Learning, Action Learning in Action,* and *The Global Learning Organization.*